CONCRETE DREAMS

·····································

CONCRETE DREAMS

Practice, Value, and Built Environments

in Post-Crisis Buenos Aires

NICHOLAS D'AVELLA

Duke University Press   Durham and London   2019

© 2019 Duke University Press
All rights reserved
Printed in the United States of America on acid-free paper ∞
Typeset in Arno Pro by Westchester Book Group
Cover design by Drew Sisk

Cataloging-in-Publication is available
from the Library of Congress.
ISBN 978-1-4780-0535-3 (hardcover : alk. paper)
ISBN 978-1-4780-0630-5 (pbk. : alk. paper)
ISBN 978-1-4780-0511-7 (ebook)

Cover art: The view from a terrace in Villa Pueyrredón.
Photo courtesy of Salvemos al Barrio.

An earlier version of chapter 1 appeared as "Ecologies of
Investment: Crisis Histories and Brick Futures in Argentina,"
Cultural Anthropology 29, no. 1 (2014): 173–99.
Unless otherwise noted, all English language translations are
by the author.

CONTENTS

....

ACKNOWLEDGMENTS

....

Like concrete, this book is the result of a long, slow process of growing together (*concrescere*); like dreams, neither it nor I would have endured without the people, places, and institutions that have helped nurture and sustain us over the years. Thoughtful and generous mentors formed an important part of the environment in which this project was conceived and developed. Marisol de la Cadena continues to offer a fierce set of commitments to ideas, ethnography, and forceful, careful writing that pushed this project beyond where it might otherwise have gone. Don Donham was a constant nurturing presence, always willing to read my work and pose direct, clarifying questions about my writing and thinking. Tim Choy continues to teach me to value subtlety and nuance, and through his presence as a careful reader he has helped me write in a way that feels true. Alan Klima, in addition to teaching me important habits of thought, taught me the rituals of a viable writerly life without which I would not have been able to finish this book.

Many people in Buenos Aires welcomed me into their lives, told me the stories this book is made from, and reflected with me upon the stories of others. Several people active in organizations dedicated to better urban life took me into their meetings and their homes in sometimes vulnerable circumstances in which they did not know whom to trust; I extend my gratitude to the members of Salvemos al Barrio, queremos buenos aires, sos Caballito, the Asociación Amigos del Lago de Palermo, and the Asociación Vecinal para la Reurbanización del Ex-Autopista 3. I especially thank Osvaldo Guerrica Echevarría, Osvaldo Saredi, Patricia Duró, Ariel Venneri, Abel and Nelly De Grande, Jorge Sardi, Jorge Bobbio, Beatriz Loria, Marta Yantorno, Magdalena Eggers, Edgardo Estrin, Marta Dodero, Mario Oybin, and Miguel Rosengana for guiding me through their barrios and the intricate details of their interactions with city government. Their tenacity and collective spirit continue to inspire me, and I hope I have done their stories justice.

Various friends put me in touch with family members so that they could share with me intimate details about their finances, including how much, in what forms, and where they kept their money; I am grateful to them for speaking openly with me about private matters. José Rozados, Mario Gomez, Miguel Pato, Damián Tabakman, and Juan Aramburu patiently answered my questions about the Argentine real estate market. Laura Leyt, Darío López, Mariana Yablon, Tristan Dieguez, Hugo Montorfano, Mariana Cardinali, and Pablo Suarez helped me understand the construction industry through their work as architects and builders.

It was a special privilege to spend a year with teachers and students at the Facultad de Arquitectura, Diseño y Urbanismo at the Universidad de Buenos Aires, where fate more than my own good judgment brought me to the Design 1 workshop of the *cátedra* Molina y Vedia–Sorín. Juan Molina y Vedia welcomed me with no questions asked, first into the workshop and years later into his home to listen to him recount, little by little and never in a linear fashion, stories of his life and work; I admire him as a scholar, teacher, and architect with a deep and subtle set of political commitments. The teachers in Design 1 also welcomed me with warmth, humor, and camaraderie. I thank Marta Algañaraz, César Dell'Angelica, Arturo Rovoira, Florencia Marasea, Gabriela Hermida, Deby Díaz Urrutia, Santiago Lanzillota, Juan Pablo Falczuk, Jorge Choque, María Luz Mango, Margarita Kwon, and Alejandro Elena for letting me learn from them and for opening up architectural worlds I hadn't yet dreamed of. Interviews several years later with Jaime Sorín and with the filmmakers of the documentary *70 y Pico*, Mariano Corbacho and Juan Pablo Diaz, helped me pull pieces together.

Close friends in Buenos Aires made fieldwork joyful, keeping my life full of music, literature, food, love, and endless collective reflection on Argentine economics, architecture, politics, and history. Adrián Landeira and Sergio García took me to neighborhoods no one else would take me to, welcomed me into their families and circles of friends, and shared food, songs, television, and political analysis. I was similarly nurtured by Ariel Escalante, Martín de Castro, Pablo Chico, and Pablo Nemec. Francisco Porras, Daniel Chong, Sergio Gorín, Javier Zavaleta, Armando Chanis, Ricky Alderete, and Nadia Quintana kept me laughing and dancing. Guilherme Morais gave me his love and affection. On my first night in Buenos Aires I met Florencia Fragasso, Julián Massaldi, Bárbara Panico, Esteban Magnani, and Sabrina Abran, and they all remain close friends and companions. I especially thank Flor for sharing poetry and literature with me on the many afternoons we shared in Buenos Aires' historic cafes, including a copy of Daniel Durand's *El cielo de Boedo*. Babette Wielenga, Brendan Martin, and Lauren Szczesny-Pumarada immersed themselves in Buenos Aires with me, and I was always grateful to be able to learn alongside them.

The scholarly endeavors surrounding the production of this book have been similarly touched by many colleagues and friends who offered their support, warmth, and feedback over the years. UC Davis was the place where this project was born and a first draft was written. Michelle Stewart, Chris Kortright, Timothy Murphy, Ingrid Lagos, Bascom Guffin, Diana Pardo Pedraza, Xan Chacko, Jorge Núñez, Camilo Sanz, Vandana Nagaraj, Bettina Ng'weno, Smriti Srinivas, Erin Paszko, Nick Sanchez, Ayesha Nibbe, Kristina Lyons, Lena Meari, Adrian Yen, and Simon Sadler were all present in important ways during these early years (and in many cases for years after). Joe Dumit created a nurturing environment for scholarship that touched many of us. Christiana Giordano offered helpful feedback and advice revising the introduction. Julia Morales Fontanilla opened her home to me on many occasions. Jake Culbertson has been a wonderful companion with whom to hold together architecture and anthropology; he and May Ee Wong offered helpful advice for the revision of chapter 5. I am grateful for all of their companionship and intellectual stimulation.

Cori Hayden has been a generous and supportive mentor since my first postdoc at UC Berkeley. I am grateful to have also enjoyed the company of those surrounding the Center for Science, Technology, Medicine, and Society, especially Harlan Weaver, Christoph Hanssmann, and Hélène Mialet. Leslie Salzinger, Mila Djordjevic, and William Stafford offered helpful comments on an early version of chapter 1. Mark Fleming, Michael D'Arcy, Milad Odabaei, and Johnathan Vaknin came into my life with friendship and adventure. I returned to New York through a postdoctoral position at The Cooper Union; I thank Bill Germano and my other colleagues for welcoming me there. My two years at Cooper were made especially meaningful by the students I had the privilege of teaching, many of whom touched this work through their curiosity, artistic engagement, and political acuity. My affiliation with the Hemispheric Institute of Performance and Politics at NYU has been another important scholarly home in New York. I thank Diana Taylor and Marcial Godoy for providing me with space and a scholarly environment grounded in the artistic and political concerns of the Américas. The incredible group of scholars clustered around the OIKOS working group at the Institute for Public Knowledge (also at NYU) has been a constant source of inspiring engagement. Lily Chumley,

Erica Robles-Anderson, and Caitlin Zaloom foster an environment of care and kinship that permeates and transcends our shared concerns for economic life; they, along with Sarah Muir, Ebony Coletu, Fabio Mattioli, Ainur Begim, and Elizabeth Deluca provided warm support and helpful feedback for various parts of this book. Bruce Grant deserves special thanks for his mentorship. Germán Garrido, Curt Gambetta, and Abou Farman Farmaian became close friends and intellectual companions.

Other colleagues I met along the way have nurtured the book with their insights and collegial warmth. I first met Daniel Fridman, Ariel Wilkis, and Mariana Luzzi through the Estudios de la Economía collective, organized by José Ossandón; I am grateful to have them as co-thinkers concerned with economic life in Argentina. Taylor Nelms offered feedback on an early version of chapter 1. Andrea Ballestero, Jenna Grant, Natasha Myers, Natalie Porter, and Ivan Small generously shared feedback on different parts of the book. Ignacio Farías, Anders Blok, and Yutaka Yoshinaka helped me think about the politics of voice in urban environments. Eli Elinoff, Smoki Musaraj, Sean Mallin, Georgia Hartman, and Bettina Stoetzer offered productive engagements on urban and built environments. Santiago Buraschi helped me think through the work of real estate market analysts, and Sebastián Malecki provided helpful feedback regarding the politics of architectural education in Argentina. Gary McDonogh was my teacher in the interdisciplinary program in the Growth and Structure of Cities as an undergraduate at Haverford College; I don't think this project would have come about without my exposure to the ideas I learned there. Marcos Mendoza, Sean Brotherton, Lilly Irani, Sarah Besky, Jerome Whittington, Fred Wherry, Pablo Ben, and Emily McDonald have offered support along the way. The community of writers at Academic Muse talked me through innumerable blockages and dilemmas over the years. I also thank those colleagues who engaged with my work through talks given at MIT and the University of Chicago's Anthropology departments; Princeton University's School of Architecture; the Institute for Sustainable Design at Cooper Union; and at NYU, St. Olaf College, Bryn Mawr College, and Haverford College.

Fieldwork for this book was funded by the Wenner-Gren Foundation, the National Science Foundation, and the Fulbright Program. An Andrew W. Mellon Foundation/American Council of Learned Societies dissertation completion grant allowed me time to write the book's first iteration. Balanced postdoctoral positions at UC Berkeley and The Cooper Union enabled me to make steady progress toward the book, and a Hunt Postdoctoral Fellowship from the Wenner-Gren Foundation allowed me to finish it. I am grateful to these institutions for their support.

Gisela Fosado, my editor at Duke University Press, supported the project with warmth and encouragement. Mark Healey and Cassie Fennell read the first version of the manuscript in its entirety and offered the kind of generous, deeply engaged feedback a writer dreams of. I thank them (and an anonymous reviewer who read a revised version) for guiding the book to its present form.

I also thank my mother, Laura, my sister Joanna, and my late father, John, as well as the rest of my family for their love, for encouraging me to follow the paths I felt were right for me, and for supporting me when those paths were difficult. Vernon Caldwell, Samuel Pinilla, Joshua Hiller, Shamus Khan, Diego Ellerman, Julio Ponce, Chris Cornell, Laura Goorin, John Welch, Jorge Piñero, and Garland Godfrey are a constant source of loving and supportive kinship.

I have written this book in the close presence of colleagues and friends who either sat literally across the table from me in cafés or, when work and life took us far from one another, in virtual proximities that allowed us to work together despite the distance. Along the way they read drafts, talked me out of tough spots, and helped me know when to hold tight to something and when to let it go; we laughed together, thought together, and grew together. Vivian Choi has been with me since our first day of graduate school and has been a constant source of shared thinking, laughter, and companionship. Rima Praspaliauskiene has reflected with me on various versions of most of this book. Mark Robinson has gotten deep into my head, often to help me get out of it. Jerry Zee helped me find my way deeper into some dense moments. Rossio Motta, Jonathan Echeverri Zuluaga, Stefanie Graeter, Aaron Norton, and Martine Lappé urged me on, both with ideas and with joyful copresence. I am humbled by how generous they have been with their thoughts and with their hearts.

Yo tengo tantos hermanos
Que no los puedo contar
En el valle, la montaña
En la pampa y en el mar

I have so many brothers
That I can't count them
In the valley, the mountain
On the plains and in the sea

Cada cual con sus trabajos
Con sus sueños, cada cual
Con la esperanza adelante
Con los recuerdos detrás

Each one with their work
With their dreams, each one
With hope before them
With memories behind

Yo tengo tantos hermanos
Que no los puedo contar

I have so many brothers
That I can't count them

—from the folksong "Los Hermanos" (1969), by ATAHUALPA YUPANQUI

Concrete Dreams

Mariela straps 50,000 dollars to her body and those of her brothers, who will accompany her from her bank to that of the seller. There, the U.S. banknotes will be meticulously inspected and counted and change hands. When it's done, Mariela will have converted her dollars into "bricks"—Argentine shorthand for real estate—and will own an apartment. Mariela is no stranger to conversion. Before her savings became dollars, they existed as dollar-equivalent pesos, trapped in her bank account by government edict in 2001 and later devalued. As soon as she could, she got her diminished stack of pesos out of the bank and converted them to dollars to shelter them from inflation. Now, she was converting them again: into an apartment worth dollars, but located in Buenos Aires. Mariela thinks back to an illustration she saw in a news article on real estate, in which hundred-dollar bills were stacked like bricks in the form of a house. She smiles despite her nerves and thinks that the cartoony image feels particularly real in this moment. Her plans for the future remain vague: she thinks that one day her son might use the apartment, and in the meantime it could provide some rental income for her family. She is nervous, but is also fairly certain this was the best decision she could have made in an economic environment that felt even more complicated than usual.

....

Bárbara leans forward in her stool, bringing her face close to the drawings of the cultural center she's been working on for weeks. She rubs her eyes. She knows that she's included all the required elements for her first major assignment in architecture school: the main multipurpose room, a small kitchen, two restrooms, and a storage space. She tries to project herself into the building she has drawn, like her teachers have taught her. In her mind, she looks out the window she's drawn and is pleased with the view of the park she imagines there—a result of how she oriented the building and where she had placed the main room relative to the others. She's less convinced by her placement of the bathrooms, which she's tried out in a dozen different places. She's pretty sure her teacher won't like her solution, but she couldn't find a better placement for them on her own. Only at the very edge of Bárbara's consciousness are the set of events that gripped both the nation and the architecture school almost forty years earlier, when leftist architects gained control of the university at a moment of sharp political upheaval in Argentina. Their struggles are part of the reason that she—a young woman from a family of modest means—is able to attend one of the country's most esteemed universities to study architecture. Nor is she focused on the ways that this particular assignment—to design a cultural center in a marginal neighborhood of the city, beyond the usual geographies of money and architectural engagement—is grounded in a set of pedagogic commitments bound up with those same political events. But still, this history is in some way present for her: every day she passes under a banner in the main atrium of the architecture school that bears the faces of students and faculty disappeared by a military dictatorship for whom the political commitments engrained in leftist architectural pedagogy embodied a vital threat to the order of things. Those dead were, in ways that were sometimes more apparent than others, somehow still with her.

....

On the other end of the city, Patricia ducks under her drying laundry to water the plants on her rooftop terrace—one of her daily rituals that brings her a little peace in the middle of a hectic life. She closes her eyes and feels the spring sun warm her face. The sound of traffic on the avenue is muted here. She breathes in a bit of the morning breeze. Then she opens her eyes and turns to face the new buildings that stretch up into the sky behind her. She feels as if she can reach out and touch them. The days are starting to get longer, and she reckons she'll have sun on the terrace for another few hours before it slips behind the new building and things become several shades darker and several degrees cooler. She looks at her plants. Some of them are doing fine, others seem to be wanting for the sun they used to have. The building is almost finished, its glass glimmering more sharply alongside the greening cement of her own aging apartment building. She looks up at the balconies of her future neighbors, rising above her terrace. What will they be like? Will they smile down on her and wave? Will they complain about the smoke from her barbecue drifting into their apartments? She lightly hums a tango about love and loss, set, as tangos often are, in the grimy streets of a humble urban world that feels at once distant and familiar to her. Back downstairs, she rifles through some of the papers she had promised to go over before her meeting that night with a small group of people from the neighborhood. It had been several months since she received the flier in her mailbox that called people together to figure out what to do about the new buildings going up all over the barrio. The group thought that her work as a secretary in a real estate broker's office might give her a leg up in understanding the world of requirements and regulations embodied in the Código de Planeamiento Urbano, or Urban Planning Code, which they had asked her to study, but the truth was she felt as lost as everyone else. Still, the meeting with one of the few legislators who had paid any attention to their complaints was coming up, and they needed to be ready.

res. let agency

....

This book is a sustained ethnographic reflection about a set of practices concerning buildings and the ways they operate as quotidian points of refraction for divergent politics of value in Argentina at the beginning of the twenty-first century. It is a book about the intricate, close registers in which buildings and their value are engaged, worked over, and remade—registers that are neither separate from, nor simple instantiations of, the wider fields of which they are a part. Each of the practices I describe are situated within worlds marked by variegated terrains of knowledge, history, and power—worlds that practitioners work to reformulate through quotidian, minor forms of action and intervention. They draw worlds into their practices and, in doing so, also remake them. Their practices are at once intimate, familiar, and small, but in their way, also eventful and expansive.

Value, as I use it in this book, is a concept that includes, but also exceeds, what is captured by the category of the economic. Think back to the three moments I offered earlier. Mariela is investing in a building to secure an economic future. She cares about what the apartment might be worth today and whether that might change in the future. Bound up with those concerns are questions about her own life and those of her children and what they might be like in the years to come. Bárbara, the architecture student, values buildings as well, in part as the means through which she will gain her livelihood, to be sure. But it is also part of the art she is learning, a refined sensibility about how to foster good human life in built environments. She is learning to care about the kind of light that enters a room, about the views one has through

follows practices which engage value of buildings

the widows, about how people practice quotidian tasks. Patricia, too, probably cares about how much her apartment is worth and certainly cares about the light and air. But she does so in a different way, through everyday practices of plant cultivation, cooking food, hanging out laundry, and spending time with those close to her, practices inflected through more widely shared cultural registers like the tango she hums. In this book, I am interested in the ways that different practices cultivate different kinds of value in buildings—forms of value that can include, but are not limited to, market value.[1]

Practice is a term I use to attend to the situated, historically constituted, material-semiotic environments in which buildings are engaged and worked on. From their inception and throughout their lives, buildings are distributed through the charts and graphs of market analysts, the drawings and models of architectural designers, the urban planning code of the city government, and the everyday life practices of neighborhood residents and the narrative forms they deploy to reflect upon them. None of these forms of engagement are simply at the disposal of practitioners who can take them up and put them down at will; rather, they are lively, integrated features of how practitioners know and engage their world.[2] Bárbara's care for buildings is not anterior to her ability to draw, for example; rather, she learns to value them in her particular way by drawing, just as Mariela does through the newspapers she reads and the dollars she straps to her and her brothers' bodies, or as Patricia does through the food she cooks on her terrace, the tango she hums, the plants she cares for. In this sense, practices are the domains of subjects who are unthinkable without the specific means through which they engage their world; these forms of engagement are an integral part of what makes an architect an architect and what makes architects different from investors, analysts, state planners, and neighborhood residents. They are central to the quotidian contexts and endeavors in which buildings are relevant to and valued by each group of practitioners. They reach into bodies and minds to help practitioners think, imagine, do, and feel in certain ways, but also impose certain obligations and requirements on them.[3]

Implicit in these distinct forms of engagement are particular ways of defining what a good building is or should be. These particular forms of value are woven through the historically developed, sociotechnical practices through which buildings are known and made. The set of practices through which Mariela engages her apartment—the physical dollars, the news article she thinks of—opens up a different set of questions and allows for the manifestation of different kinds of value than the drawings and models that Bárbara ponders over or the tango Patricia hums on her terrace. The tools of practice are not, therefore, value-neutral; instead, they help form the quotidian contexts in which buildings are valued and evaluated. This means that the kinds of value that different practitioners hold in buildings are not anterior to the practices through which they engage them, but rather are constructed through them. Far from abstract values operating in a realm of ideal immateriality, the values practitioners hold in buildings are bound up with material forms of engagement that extend far beyond brick and mortar. To speak of practices and value together, then, is to speak about differences that go beyond opinion, but are embedded in the particular means through which buildings are engaged.

Approaching value through practices also helps deepen and extend attention to the ways that values are made real in the world as part of broadly shared processes that sprawl across time and geography. Mariela's practice brings buildings into relation with a world of dollars, pesos, and bank accounts, and by extension with the particular historical dynamics of global currency exchange and transnational banking. Bárbara's pencil and paper, her floor plans and elevations, connect buildings with histories of cultivated architectural expertise and a way of thinking about and relating to the built environment developed over centuries in far-flung points across the globe. And Patricia's plants, the spaces of the building she lives in, the tango lyrics, and the urban planning code she pores over unite her own quotidian experience with realms of law, urban planning, state power, and metropolitan culture that extend far beyond her terrace. At the same time, none of these are simple exemplars of the wider sets of practices of which they are a part. Economic investment, architecture, and neighborhood life do not operate in the same way in Buenos Aires as they do in any other part of the world. Rather, they are situated in particular histories that may converge with related practices at some moments and diverge from them at others.[4] Mariela's purchase of an apartment may have something in common with real estate investors in other parts of the world, but it is also situated in an economic history replete with crises that sets her practice apart from others; Bárbara's architectural education was significantly impacted by the country's political history, including efforts to reform architectural education in line with the needs of a poor, peripheral country and violent purges of faculty and students under dictatorships; similarly, Patricia's relationship with her terrace and her neighborhood group's political advocacy unfold in the particular cultural history of neighborhood life, urban planning, and city politics in Buenos Aires.

There is a lesson to be drawn here from the peculiar materiality of concrete. While concrete is said to be the most widely used building material in the world, concrete is not just one material—not exactly. Concrete is a *material compuesto*, or compound material: a material composed of other materials, namely a combination of Portland cement, water, and stone aggregate. The purported oneness of concrete can be troubled still further when one considers that both the water and the rocky aggregate are typically drawn from sites close to construction, producing local specificities. For example, a special issue on concrete in the architectural supplement of a major Argentine newspaper explains that "the use of granitic sand in the center of the province of Buenos Aires produces concretes that are rougher and more difficult to work with compared to those that use riverine sands, whose particles are smoother," and that "concrete's elasticities differ depending on whether the rocks used are granitic, quartzose, silicose, basaltic, or lime" (Becker 2008). In other words, no concrete is exactly like any other—a difference tied closely to geographic forms of emplacement, the terrains from and on which it is built. Concrete both spans the globe and at the same time is deeply emplaced. As a compound material, concrete is thus both more than one thing and less than many things, to think along the lines used by Donna Haraway (1991) to describe the cyborg and Marilyn Strathern (2004) to describe Melanesian personhood: a non-unit composed of incommensurable entities, existing in a way difficult to think through the analytical dualism of singularity and multiplicity (see de la Cadena 2015, 31).[5]

Thinking from the particularities of concrete as a compound material suggests ways that anthropology might push concrete's aggregates beyond even those of water, rock, and cement to deepen attention to buildings' divergent manifestations across a range of practices. Consider again the forms in which buildings appeared in the vignettes I offered earlier: an illustration in a newspaper article, the drawing of an architecture student, a place for plants and barbecues and looking at the sky, the lines of an urban planning code, the lyrics of a tango. In this book I argue that these, too, are part of concrete's compound materiality. Working through practice displaces major-key materialisms predicated on global forms and, instead, fosters practices of attention that stay with the particular. When approached through practices, buildings' materiality becomes fractal and distributed. So, too, does their value.

"Concrete dreams" is the concept tool that this book develops to speak to the intertwined relationship between value and practice, between dreams about concrete (particular aspirations for buildings and what they could and should be) and the concrete forms in which those dreams are articulated. With my oxymoronic concept, I seek in part to unsettle the ways social theory has often simultaneously sanctified and relegated concrete to a place of the really real, in which it stands as the other to ideas, imagination, and dreams. William James offers an alternative to this formulation when he observes that "thoughts in the concrete are made of the same stuff as things are" (1996, 37; see Shaviro 2009, 21). Like thoughts, dreams have concrete forms, too. Drawings, graphs, stories, and codes embody both dreams for buildings' futures and the media in which those dreams are worked out in the world. Considering them part of concrete's compound materiality marks the extent to which dreams about buildings are permeated and sustained by material forms of engagement, nudging dreams out of a realm of ideal immateriality to instead ask how they are composed in the presence of things, the stuff of practice. At the same time, it works to trouble the apparently settled, unified realness often imputed to the concrete to instead hold close the ways that diverse forms of material practice are imbued with hopes, aspirations, and possibility.

Concrete dreams are not only representations that reflect already existing ideas or states of affairs. As the forms of engagement through which possibilities are produced and in which they live, they do things in the world. The dreams I speak of, then, are not the opposite of action, and much less of politics. Jacques Rancière, in *The Distribution of the Sensible*, has observed that "politics and art, like forms of knowledge, construct 'fictions,' that is to say *material* rearrangements of signs and images, relationships between what is seen and what is said, between what is done and what can be done. . . . They draft maps of the visible, trajectories between the visible and the sayable, relationships between modes of being, modes of saying, and modes of doing and making" (Rancière 2004, 39, emphasis in original; see also Rancière 2010). Just as Rancière finds in art and politics the material rearrangements of signs and images that construct relations between what is and what could be, so too are concrete dreams material practices through which modes of being, saying, and doing are reconfigured to craft possible worlds. Concrete dreams thus blur the lines between the actual and the possible and forge potential realities poised to recraft the contours of shared worlds.[6] They are political in the sense that they build out divergent forms of value in the world—values that exist in the presence of others, and often in tension with them. In working with models, graphs, stories, and codes, the practitioners in this ethnography are asking fundamental questions about what buildings are and might become. Not all of their dreams will be realized as buildings, but they remain present, poised to inflect those that do come into being. The book's central argument is that it is through these concrete dreams—dreams articulated in

Stakes of that tension?

paper and PowerPoints, cardboard and stories—that divergent visions about the value of buildings are held in tension across partially shared urban worlds.

....

The stories I tell in this book are grounded in a construction boom that un-folded over the course of ten years following a major economic and political crisis in Argentina in 2001 (I return to these events in more detail shortly). The boom took place in a post-crisis economic and political environment in which questions of value were an important axis of debate. Among the many things evoked by the crisis was a broad rethinking of the economic logics that underwrote the neoliberal reforms that were implemented throughout the 1990s, when widespread privatizations and the installation of free-market logics were a guiding principle of governance. The crisis provoked a popu-lar reexamination of these ideas, but not only in ways relevant to questions of state economic policy. In the post-crisis reexamination of and skepticism about markets, I see the development of a powerful political sensibility atten-tive to conflicting forms of value. In the years after the crisis, the importance of figuring out how to get and hold onto economic stability and well-being were lost on no one. At the same time, struggles to trouble market value's place as the hegemonic definition of what matters seemed ever more rele-vant: there was a sense that the country had lost its way in the 1990s, drunk on a cocktail of privatization and free markets, and people seemed ready to look for a different path to the construction of viable futures.

The events and sensibilities that came to the fore during and after the crisis had deep and expansive roots: they redounded upon earlier historical epochs in Argentina while resonating with contemporaneous experiments through-out the region to carve new, more inclusive paths beyond neoliberalism. The first decade of the twenty-first century was a time of great transformation in Latin America, one that witnessed a turn to the left in the political leadership of countries across the region that centered, among other things, on the re-jection of neoliberal policies and the search for other paths toward collective well-being. Post-crisis Argentina was part of this moment. This book and the political impetus that sustains it are inseparable from this time in Argentina, which some have called post-neoliberal and others have called the *decada ganada*—the decade gained or won, as in won back from a history heavy with dispossession—a decade in which important changes were afoot that had little truck with the promissory futures offered by neoliberalism and the Washington Consensus.

How the practices of people like Mariela, Bárbara, and Patricia—and the values produced by them—articulate with these major-key historical moments is part of my concern in this book. My method is to historically situate practices: in bodies, in tools, and in political and economic life. Throughout the book I track between close, intimate encounters with buildings and the more epochal events that have helped define these practices and to which practitioners seek to respond. Mariela, Bárbara, and Patricia make manifest in the world divergent, and often precarious, forms of value. I am interested in how buildings were made into new kinds of economic objects after the crisis and how sets of practice that produce and depend upon other forms of value—like those of architecture and neighborhood life in Buenos Aires— were made to endure in the face of buildings' increasingly central place in Argentine economic life. What could buildings become—of what transformations would they be capable and engender—in these post-crisis economic and political atmospheres?

The construction boom was a moment that pressed upon a set of disagreements about what buildings are for and therefore what they are. Ranciére has described disagreement as not just the conflict between one who says "white" and another who says "black," but as "the conflict between one who says white and another who also says white but does not understand the same thing by it" (Ranciére 1999, x). I think of buildings in a similar way, as embodying conflicts between one who says "building" and another who says "building" but does not understand the same thing by it. Buildings became for me the shared terrain on and through which divergent ways of living and knowing cohabit in tension—at times with the full weight of overt contrast, at times barely noticeable beneath apparent agreement. This book is about disagreements over what buildings are and what they could be—and the economic, social, and material means through which these disagreements were lived.

LA CRISIS: MAJOR-KEY HISTORIES

"Welcome to the biggest default in the history
of capitalism!"
From the ass of the world to the head of globalphobia.
In December of 2001, Argentine society went
crack and we all went into limbo.
—Fragment from ¡Crack!, by MARTÍN KOVENSKY, 2002

In the hot December summer of 2001, street protests erupted in Buenos Aires that overthrew five consecutive presidents in fourteen days. Clashes between protesters and the police and military claimed dozens of lives that summer, as Argentines faced tear gas, rubber bullets, and worse with chants, drums, rocks, and their bodily presence in the streets. This uprising is sometimes referred to as the *argentinazo*, an untranslatable term whose suffix communicates violent collision (a *codazo* is a blow with the elbow, a *cachetazo* a slap in the face). Others simply refer to it as *la crisis*, naming more directly the series of economic events that led to the uprising. Still others, keen to hold present that it was just one crisis in a long history of crises, specify it as *la crisis del 2001*.

The crisis in question followed a decade of neoliberal restructuring in the 1990s, which included a blend of privatization and austerity that drew on a profound faith in free markets as the solution to national economic ills. In Argentina, reforms also included pegging the Argentine peso to the U.S. dollar to mitigate the chronic instability of the inflation-prone peso—a move that brought stability to the national currency, but that battered national industries and depended on a near-constant influx of foreign capital, a key source of which was foreign debt.[7] Taking on this debt required implementing structural adjustment policies, a set of economic measures embodied in the neoliberal Washington Consensus: public companies were privatized and sold; protections to local industry were lifted; and social safety nets for the poor and unemployed were dismantled. By the late 1990s, this set of reforms began to see its limits. Growing numbers of poor and unemployed *piqueteros*, or picketers, began to blockade streets in protest. At the same time, the country's debt levels began to creep too high for its creditors' tastes, and the resulting decline in the influx of dollars made dollar-peso convertibility unsustainable. The IMF began to slow the pace of loans, which were the only thing keeping the country and its currency afloat. In the face of near-certain devaluation, money began to flee the banking system, and the government placed sharp restrictions on bank withdrawals. The restrictions drew a large cross section of Argentine society into the streets, where they joined poor piqueteros in protest. As liberal economists and politicians continued to call for increased austerity in the interest of servicing the escalating foreign debt, the street protests forced the elected president and several appointed replacements to resign. Weeks later, the peso was unpegged from the dollar and devalued, and Argentina announced the largest sovereign debt default in the history of the world.

Interpreters of capitalism, globalization, colonialism, and politics would come to read many histories and many futures through Argentina and the crisis of 2001. Like many crises, this one was a kind of overdetermined moment in which relations of all sorts would unravel and become questioned.[8] Martín Kovensky, in his visual and poetic diary of 2002, called this time a limbo, a liminal time in which a series of contradictions at the heart of Argentina's history and position in the world were brought into stark relief. Argentina's very name, he observes, comes from *argentum*, silver, or *plata*, a word for money. With irony, he notes that the country, founded on contraband trade in colonial times, later becoming one of the breadbaskets of the world, had been transformed into a place in which people were starving. In the book, a collage made from fragments of shredded pesos shows money dripping out like tears or blood from Argentina, falling off the edges of the earth (see figure 1.1).

The spectacular nature of the crisis placed Argentina at the center of a series of debates about neoliberalism that extended well beyond Argentina. In the 1990s, the country had been held aloft as one of the great success stories of what could happen when states submit to the tutelage of the institutions of the Washington Consensus to reorganize fiscal, monetary, and trade policy around free markets. If Argentina had been a poster child for neoliberalism before the crisis, the country's unraveling was held aloft by critics on the left as a defining moment through which to consider neoliberalism's failures and to reflect on the intertwined histories of colonialism and empire that underwrote neoliberal reforms. The crisis secured Argentina's place as a potent symbol of capitalism's disastrous expansion and as a key site for the analysis of financial extractivism masquerading as a development model by promising to leverage the power of free markets to improve people's lives. Intellectuals on the left were captivated by the popular revolt of the argentinazo and leveraged the rampant poverty and urban barter economies brought about by the crisis—shocking in one of the most developed countries of Latin America—as a cautionary tale about neoliberalism.[9]

With the argentinazo, Argentina became cast as something of a vanguard for the left, bearing promise for new directions in economic and political life as part of a Latin America lauded as "the first region of the world in which popular struggles, votes, and new policies manifested a refusal of the imperialist neoliberal order" (Duménil and Lévy 2011, 324). The popular revolt provided a beacon of hope for a world in which the hegemony of free markets seemed to have an iron-tight grip: events in Argentina carried the promise of a different future, embodied in a flourish of direct-democracy neighborhood assemblies, cooperative takeovers of factories by workers, and solidarity economies that

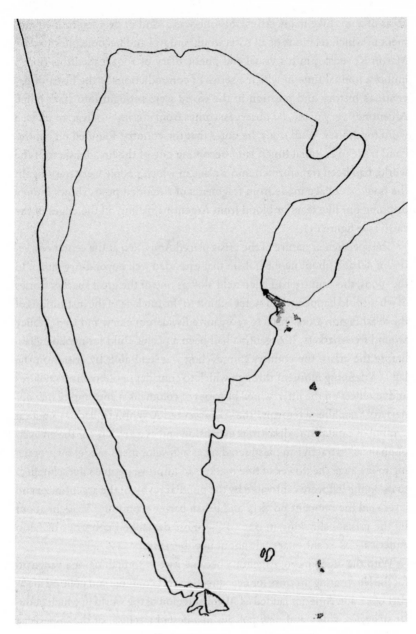

FIGURE I.1. *Map 1,* by Martín Kovensky. Drawing and shredded pesos.

unfolded in the wake of the crisis. Together, they offered signs of resilience and creativity in the face of global capitalism, experiments in new ways of living that were gritty and stark, but at the same time brimming with utopian potential.

In 2003, following two years of interim governments, elections were held and Nestor Kirchner began his term as president. His administration, together with the two-term presidency of his wife and political partner, Cristina Fernández de Kirchner, would seek to chart a path beyond neoliberalism. The crisis had served to strip markets of the patina of rationality and self-regulation that neoliberal policies had attributed to them; faith in *el modelo*—the model of the 1990s, in which markets provided rational and efficient solutions to the nation's ills—seemed shaken to the core.[10] The crisis was, in this sense, a moment in which taken-for-granted ideas were cast open and subject to collective interrogation, a moment inhabited with anxiety and irresolution, but also shared concern and the possibility of building a different world. In the decade that followed, the postal service, the national airline, the water company, and the former state oil company were all renationalized, social services were expanded, and protective trade policies that prioritized national production rather than ideals of global free markets were implemented.

In his inauguration speech, Kirchner reflected on the events leading up to the crisis through a series of epochal moments that are touchstones in Argentina's broadly shared historical lexicon (see text box). He prominently recalled the generation of leftist political activists disappeared by the country's last dictatorship in the mid-1970s and early 1980s—itself an early moment of neoliberal restructuring—and characterized the rest of the 1980s as a time focused on restoring democratic normalcy to a country marked by interruptions in democratic rule and the ongoing search for truth and justice for the disappeared. In the 1990s, he said, priorities turned to economic growth and stability, but they followed a neoliberal recipe that turned a blind eye to the inequality caused by economic restructuring. Reflecting on epochs of neoliberal dictatorship and neoliberal democracy, Kirchner sought with his presidency to bring democracy and economic development into a new kind of relationship: to "initiate a new time, one that finds us shoulder to shoulder in the struggle to achieve progress and social inclusion." His speech featured a now-famous refrain: *vengo a proponerles un sueño*—I come to propose to you a dream. "I come to propose to you a dream," he said, "to rebuild our own identity as a people and as a nation. I come to propose to you a dream, which is the construction of truth and justice. I come to propose to you a dream, of returning to an Argentina with all and for all. I come to propose that we

There were things Kirchner did not need to explain to those listening to his speech: defining moments in Argentina's broadly shared historical lexicon. They included key moments that continued to resonate with ongoing struggles over the intertwined relationship between political and economic life in the wake of the crisis. I offer a brief set of keywords for those unfamiliar with these histories.

Peronism

The rise of Peronism in the 1940s is a major historical touchstone in Argentine history. At the time, Argentina was one of the most heavily industrialized and prosperous countries in Latin America, but with a prosperity that was very unequally distributed. The ways this prosperity was accumulated and distributed underwent important changes through populist-inflected, import-substitution economic policies of Juan Domingo Perón, who had risen to prominence under a military government and was then elected president in 1946. Between 1946 and 1955, Perón, together with his wife Evita, implemented a host of programs favorable to the working classes, consolidating a place in the political imaginary of the country that is difficult to overstate. Alongside import-substitution, Perón nationalized the railways and public utilities, many of which were owned by foreign firms; inscribed worker's rights, including the right to work, to universal health care, and to retirement benefits, into the national constitution; and oversaw a sharp increase in real wages for the working classes.

Perón was overthrown by a military coup in 1955.[11] Between 1955 and 1973, the country was governed by a series of military governments, punctuated by brief periods of civilian rule. These years bore witness to an escalating struggle between competing factions of an increasingly polarized country. This included struggles over Perón's own legacy between leftist and conservative factions within Peronism. The former organized around worker's rights and was associated with efforts to move the country further along a path toward socialism, while the latter consolidated around a populist, anticommunist, Catholic nationalism linked with more conservative, authoritarian trade unionism. By the beginning of the 1970s, popular unrest, including escalating violence between military regimes and worker's movements, led to broad advocacy for free and unrestricted elections (Peronism had been prohibited from running candidates in the few elections held since 1955). Perón returned from exile and was once again elected president.[12] He died less than a year later, and his wife Isabel took over the presidency (his second and most famous wife, Evita, had died in 1952), only to be overthrown by another military regime.

Dictatorship

Between 1976 and 1983, the country was ruled by a famously brutal military government that assassinated and disappeared over 30,000 Argentines and ushered in a sweeping liberalization of the national economy. Wages were frozen, prices were deregulated, trade barriers protective of Argentine industry were dropped, and new financial laws were implemented that facilitated speculative foreign investment. These changes to economic policy would later be identified as some of the earliest global experiments with neoliberal economic policy, together with similar policies introduced by military regimes in Chile and Brazil under the tutelage of U.S. economists, most famously the Chicago Boys.

Neoliberalism

Argentina returned to democracy in 1983, but the president, Alfonsín, inherited from the dictatorship a battered national economy.[13] Amid an economic scenario of hyperinflation and general instability that seemed impossible to turn around, Alfonsín stepped down in 1989 to allow his successor to take office early. This president would institute sweeping neoliberal reforms throughout the 1990s under the tutelage of the IMF, reforms that were in many ways a deepening of the dictatorship-era economic policies of the late 1970s. After nearly ten years of apparent economic stability, things fell apart, and the events of the crisis unfolded. To this day, many consider even saying this president's name bad luck— the kind that causes major national economies to come crashing down. Instead, they call him Méndez (which is not his name, but sounds like it) or *el innombrable*, the Unnamable.

When Nestor Kirchner was elected president in 2003, the country seemed ready to reconsider the place of free markets and other neoliberal ideas in the construction of a more promising collective future. In placing equity and collective well-being at the front of policy agendas, both supporters and detractors found echoes of Perón's legacy decades earlier. Perón, dictatorship, neoliberalism, and what came after: these histories and the ways they fold over and reflect upon one another are parts of the wider frames of historical memory to which I will return throughout this book.

remember the dreams of our founding patriots, of our immigrant grandparents and pioneers, and of our own generation, which put everything on the line in order to build a country of equals."

Kirchner's dream was a big, epochal moment that focused on major, epochal transitions. It incorporated historical memory with a dream for the future articulated in the major key of politics, economics, and national progress. In this, it had something in common with the analyses of world-historical capitalist development captured in academic and left-political considerations of Argentina and what they tell us about intertwined histories and futures of capitalism, colonialism, and democratic politics. It was also bound up, in its own way, with reflections like those of Kovensky, who, in his visual and poetic diary of 2002, includes mass-media images of scenes shared with a nation during the crisis's long unfolding. But alongside these scenes, Kovensky's book also offers us others, including unremarkable subway scenes and close-up images of the plants on his balcony. Crisis, while an event that names an epochal moment, can also be made to intertwine itself across registers, binding the epochal to the everyday.

MAJOR AND MINOR KEYS: ECOLOGIES OF PRACTICE AND VALUE

What does it mean to think about everyday practices of economic investment, neighborhood life, or architectural pedagogy in the presence of the grand epochal moments of Argentine history that Kirchner laid out in his speech and that are a prime register of academic analysis regarding Argentina? How do the practices surrounding buildings matter alongside these more epochal concerns? Inspired by a set of the questions grounded in analyses of neoliberalism, capitalist expansion, and the violent suppression of alternative ways of organizing economic and political life, I nevertheless take a slightly different approach than one that grounds its analytic in these registers. I do so in the interest of opening up a series of questions about the politics of value. Let me explain.

Neoliberalism, capitalism, and imperialism are analytical frames typically deployed to characterize a set of global, epochal transformations in capitalist expansion and its relationship with forms of governance and with certain modes of subjectivity. The goal, when working in these registers, is to draw out and lay bare a set of general processes through which to understand a more particular series of events. These analytical frames are important. They allow us to find connections across what may be broadly shared processes and in their best moments open the possibility for alliance and resistance across a variety of apparently discrete situations. Such was Marx's (1990) goal in theorizing capital as a grounds through which workers of the world might unite in common struggle. More recently, Hardt and Negri (2000, 2004) have imagined a multitude that would come together in a global alliance against the forces of empire. Nestor Kirchner, in outlining the threats posed by dictatorship to democratic politics and by neoliberalism to broadly shared economic inclusion, was after something similar: to unite Argentines in the interest of building a more promising and just future. In these scholarly and political registers, finding alternative paths to capitalism and empire is approached through the critique of general processes on the one hand and the formation of an alternative, synthetic analytic on the other.

For others, this is not the only path. The attractive side of propositions in these registers is that they can be clearly read into epochal and globally resonant political struggles. But as with all analytical frames, working from this perspective can obscure other possible inroads into a problem and indeed other problems altogether. I worry that in such frames the minor forms of value produced through the practices of people like Mariela, Bárbara, and Patricia find little space to breathe alongside general processes that are taken to be both encompassing of them and more important than them. Their practices become either exemplars of, or footnoted exceptions to, processes that are presumed to be what really matters.

Here, I find it useful to think with a distinction drawn by Isabelle Stengers between what she calls major and minor keys. Intellectual work in what she calls a major key focuses on the production of general theoretical knowledge, drawing on but also abstracting from particular cases and contexts. As an example of working in the major key, she offers a line from Hardt and Negri's *Multitude*, in which they state that their aim is to "identify a theoretical schema that puts the subjectivity of the social movements at centre stage in the process of globalization and the constitution of global order" (2004). The value they place on the center stage and the production of an alternative world order situates Hardt and Negri in a major key, Stengers argues. Against more frightening major-key stories—like those that imagine capitalism as the natural progression of human history—this is certainly a more promising one. But it also gives pause to those of us interested in ongoing projects of difference that may enter less easily into major-key thinking or to those of us hesitant about the constitution of global orders.

Minor key — stays with ~ specifity

In contrast, Stengers describes thinking with practices as work in a minor key. In a minor key, "no theory gives you the power to disentangle something from its particular surroundings, that is, to go beyond the particular towards something we would be able to recognize and grasp in spite of particular appearances" (2005a). She calls this, following Deleuze, thinking *par le milieux*, or "with the surroundings."[14] Keeping the surroundings of a practice present means that rather than working from (or toward) a transcendent, overarching explanatory framework, one pays attention to the specific sets of requirements and obligations practitioners produce and confront in their work. Practitioners' milieus are social and political, but also technical, affective, and embodied, including diverse competencies, sensory forms, and material tools. Working in a minor key does not negate the relevance of broadly (but always partially) shared processes, but it does recast their relationship such that the latter do not become major or general in a way that is given the power to cancel the specific—not given the power, to use Stengers' words again, to be disentangled from, or to function in spite of, particular appearances.[15]

Working in a minor key raises a series of methodological and analytical entailments that I take up in this book. One challenge that I concern myself with is to find a place for the everyday that avoids falling into scalar dichotomies in which general phenomena are taken to encompass—either analytically or spatially—situated phenomena. To move beyond, in other words, the perception that an architectural student learning to draw is somehow contained within and explained by something like neoliberalism or capitalism or is best understood as a case (either exemplary or exceptional) in the analytical service of a more general category. In considering an architecture student hunched over a drawing in the university alongside epochal registers of political economy, which picture is the "big picture"? Or is this relationship between big and small, container and contained, general and particular, theory and empirical evidence not something itself that deserves rethinking—something that is perhaps an artifact of a certain analytical perspective? For me, asking how these practices can be relevant without being subordinated to master categories is a question as relevant to politics as it is to our ethnographic imagination.

These are not new problems in anthropology. While many anthropologists find in Western categories of critique the vital grounds through which to approach enduring challenges in global politics, others have expressed concern over the application of more general analytical frames, especially in light of post-structuralist developments in the field.[16]

My own stake in working in the minor key grew out of a growing dissatisfaction with the possibilities offered by intellectual and political work carried out in a major key. I spent the first several years of my graduate work heavily invested in Marxist analyses of global political economy, the commodity form, and the kinds of subjectivities and governmentalities that capitalism depends on and helps to produce. I remain invested in the desire for a better and more just world that underscores these analytical projects. But I found that major-key thinking often served to shut down as many possibilities for a better world as it opened up. On the one hand, major-key analytics seemed unable to give real, honest attention to minor projects of worldmaking that, alongside the ongoing march of capitalist expansion, can be made to feel precious at best or barely appear as a blip on the radar. Sweeping, radical breaks come to the fore and are a locus of hope, while practices that break less cleanly can be written off or overlooked. In keeping analysis focused on the "big picture" of major-key processes, minor-key practices can be devalued.[17] This is perhaps especially the case when practices fail to meet the test of a pure resistance from a radical outside. In certain conversations about Argentina, for example, the fires of the argentinazo had barely cooled when some observers were ready to declare attempts to carve a path out of neoliberalism a failure, written off as just another articulation of dominant modes of power carried out with a set of tweaks and dressed up as an alternative. The possibilities some scholars saw in Argentina immediately after the crisis seemed to vanish as quickly as they had appeared: Argentina, despite pretensions to the contrary, was still stuck in neoliberalism after all, and for some the conversation might end there.

My dissatisfaction grew stronger the more time I spent in the field, armed with the toolkit offered by the intellectual practice of critique. Critique is a tool that is very good at finding hegemonic ideas and dominant power structures within everyday frames of action but is less useful at finding the promise and political openings and possibilities that people put into practice, and into the world, every day.[18] What would an analytic look like that could attend to and analytically foster these minor interventions rather than dismiss them as just another part of systems of power that always seemed beyond them? I worried that the tools of critique were inadequate to the actors I was working with in the field, who bore little traces of the kinds of radical alterity and political purity that many critical scholars and political movements find worthy of admiration and attention. This was as true of the neighborhood groups (whose advocacy was, at least at first blush, grounded in private property and middle-class homeownership) as it was of the architects (bourgeois art!) and real estate investors (capital personified?). How, I asked myself, could we think of possibility in a way that promises something other than clean breaks from existing hegemonic structures of power?

Years later, in the classroom, I felt this dissatisfaction in a different register, as I engaged with politically savvy students primed to the nines with the deconstructive tools of critique. I was struck by how easy it was for them to dismantle texts, political movements, and each other by zooming in on a set of unmarked privileges or ideological failings hidden beneath apparently good intentions. Similarly, conversations about early versions of parts of this book chafed with some audiences, who wanted to hear a stronger critical voice with regard to my subjects: weren't struggles over neighborhood life grounded in a set of class privileges not afforded to, say, residents of shantytowns? Isn't the education of architecture students part of a class-based ideological system from which architects, try as they might, can't really escape? These are good questions. But I worried that there was also an extent to which the questions were coming from a certain critical reflex—a sense that our intellectual project is one of critique and, absent that, an uncertainty about what, if anything, could be said.

This book's focus on practice seeks to sit within the muddied waters of unclean breaks and to foster an analytical practice geared toward minor-key difference and possibility. It is written from the premise that politics takes place in many registers and that minor-key analytical practice is an important way to value and help construct more livable worlds. I am not unconcerned with the epochal ruptures of the crisis, but I am committed to holding this concern present in a way that makes analytical room for the minor-key endurances, quotidian forms of survival, and intimate practices of care that permeate such events. My methodological approach thus seeks in the field minor-key moments in which hegemonic forms of value are placed in tension and attends to the friction of those moments, drawing out some of their entailments as well as the structures through which hegemonic forms maintain their hold. Bracketing some of the pessimistic probabilities offered by critique—that capitalism, in the last instance, wins—for me offers an opportunity to let possibilities stand out in the presence of probabilities.

....

J. K. Gibson-Graham first taught me to think of capitalism not as a totality, but as a system shot through with other forms of value, and to find in those forms of value the promise for a different world.[19] Approaching capitalism in this way opens up attention to what they call the "proliferative and desultory wanderings of everyday politics," producing zones of cohabitation and contestation between multiple systems of value (Gibson-Graham 2006, xxi). Thinking about markets as zones of contestation between divergent forms of value means thinking about the tense forms of copresence that partially connect them and to ask how the forms of value they enact are made to endure in the presence of others.

I approach these tense forms of copresence by attending to the ways multiple forms of value sit alongside one another across striated, territorial sets of knowledge and practice.[20] Stengers has conceptualized the way practices unfold in the presence of others as an "ecology of practices."[21] "Approaching a practice," she writes, "means approaching it as it diverges, that is, feeling its borders" (Stengers 2005a, 184). Divergence, as de la Cadena explains, is a potent tool for holding both connection and difference in relation: "Different from contradiction, divergence does not presuppose homogeneous terms—instead, divergence refers to the coming together of heterogeneous practices that will become other than what they were, while continuing to be the same—they become self-different" (de la Cadena 2015, 280). One can find such divergence reflected in the nomenclature through which practitioners refer to their object. What I have been calling buildings also go by other names that reflect the particularity of their place in ecologies of practice: for market analysts and experienced investors, they are *inmuebles* (pieces of real estate); for architects, they are *proyectos* (projects of design); for the people who live in and around them, *casas* (homes) in *barrios* (neighborhoods). These different nomenclatures are not incidental, but refer to real differences between the objects that each group engages and produces. Buildings, in this sense, are parts that do not resolve into wholes, even while their different striations do not remain isolated, but stand in relation to one another. None of these buildings, in other words, are alone. Concrete dreams are partially connected to one another through the force of their shared objects—shared, but in a way that doesn't erase the divergent practices of those who engage them.

My dictionary tells me that the English word *concrete* comes from the past participle of *concrescere*: to grow together. In this vein, Alfred North Whitehead has described the concrete as a "concrescence of prehensions," which Haraway explains as "graspings," a "reaching into each other" through which "beings constitute each other and themselves" (2003, 6). Scientists call the process through which concrete grows together hydration. Many people think that concrete hardens as it dries, but the opposite is true: it hardens through a long, slow process of getting wet. After an initial dormancy in which it remains malleable, the cement grains begin to dissolve in water and release calcium silicate ions, which grow into needles and platelet-shaped crystals that hold the rocky aggregates in place. Hydration continues long after the concrete seems solid: typical cement cured in moist conditions will reach 80 percent hydration only after twenty-eight days and continue to slowly hydrate and strengthen over the course of months or even years. Practices, too, bear the trace of such long, slow processes of growing together in ongoing, divergent projects of value-in-relation—reaching into, though also at times working to reach across or around, one another.

This is slightly different than thinking with chains of production, which might imply an additive, linear process—investment, production, consumption—one link of the chain added to the next. The chain metaphor can be helpful, but risks overlooking more complex forms of relation, the kind of more-than-one-less-than-many copresence evoked by an ecology of practices. Thinking the question of value from the standpoint of an ecology of practices casts the question in a slightly different relief, attending to simultaneous rather than linear dimensions of difference while taking seriously the chains that threaten to shackle all creative acts to the service of a market.

Approaching value as part of an ecology of practices is a way of keeping minor, intimate, quotidian politics of value present in what could otherwise slide into major-key histories of capitalism, colonialism, and national political struggles. The increasing incorporation of ever more ways of living into hegemonic projects of economic value production—and the concomitant reduction of worlds to one dominant metric of value—has been a part of many world-changing projects, including imperialism, globalization, and capitalism. Even in a place like Buenos Aires—for centuries a peripheral metropolitan outlet of extractivism from Latin America—there are, it seems, always deeper ways for lifeworlds to be mined for economic value. But lived worlds also continue to defy the monopoly of these projects to create one hegemonic measure of value. In this ethnography, I am interested in keeping attention on the threats facing forms of particularity that resist totalizing incorporation into a common world of value. Practitioners, in working to maintain the divergent requirements and obligations of their own practices, also care for the forms of value dear to them; they do this at times by formulating counter-hegemonic projects, or at times by simply looking for ways to endure.[22]

This is a book about buildings, then, but it is also a book about markets, the politics inherent in struggles over value, and how they emerge in and articulate distinct domains of practice. Different versions of buildings are produced and relate to one another in markets, but *not markets where only market value thrives*. Markets are full of other, divergent forms of value and the histories and dreams from which they are built in practice. In a context of subtle but fundamental transformations in the lives of buildings that transpired around the crisis and the argentinazo, various forms of value were set against one another. This divergence over what good buildings are and could be is the politics inherent to the practices I study. I understand markets as the rigged, nonneutral arenas in which multiple, divergent forms of value vie for continued existence.

Threats to the endurance of many of these forms of value are constant and severe, but so are the possibilities that they offer. Time and again capitalism, imperialism, and colonialism have proven themselves inadequate to the task of global conquest. It's not that they have failed to produce results or in many ways to strengthen their hold. But they have failed at total incorporation without excess or remainder—a remainder that continues to haunt. For every moment of deterritorialization of established ways of being, new multiplicities have flourished that continue ongoing projects of constructing livable worlds.

This book is written from the conviction that attending to minor forms of value operative in the world can be a first step in thinking about how to cultivate them. Mariela's endurance in an economic life marked by her peripheral place in global and national economies of financial extraction; Bárbara's drawings and the concern for the life that will unfold within them; and Patricia's life on her terrace with the sky and her plants, family, and neighbors: staying with their efforts to make forms of value endure is a way to stay alive to possibilities for building better worlds. It also means sitting with contradictions and impurities and few, if any, promises of great transformation.

DIVERGENT VALUES, MINOR KEYS:

BUILDINGS AFTER THE CRISIS

I carry vivid images of the crisis in my head, transmitted to me through documentary films like *The Take*, by Avi Lewis and Naomi Klein (2004), and *Memoria del Saqueo* (Memory of the Sacking), by Pino Solanas (2004). They are aesthetically evocative images of popular revolt: drums, rocks, tear gas, the people against the police. I'm told that's also kind of how the whole thing felt: ten years of individualized, consumerist, risk-mitigating, rational subjectivity constructed during neoliberalism's heyday scuttled in the jouissance of collective uprising. In the heady days of the argentinazo, the poor sacked grocery stores while the rich sacked the money of the entire country with sophisticated financial techniques that secreted money to offshore havens.

Somewhere between the two, an image of a blonde woman dressed for the office loops in my head. She's hacking at the screen of an ATM with a pen, over and over, while tear gas rolls up the street outside. Her face is set, focused, intense, and she's eventually led away from the machine, but she keeps her eyes fixed on it and the pen clutched in her hand. Of course, the money that the woman wanted wasn't actually inside that particular ATM, and that was part of the problem: even if she could break it open, she wouldn't get her money back.

For a student steeped in the ethnography of finance, the scene remains evocative. Ethnographic work in major financial institutions, of traders on Wall Street and the designers of derivative contracts, had taught me to pay close attention to the materiality of financial instruments, even when they appeared at first blush not to have a materiality at all.[23] The apparently immaterial world of finance, this work taught me, was in fact underpinned by a chorus of voices and hand signals in open-outcry trading pits, numbers coursing across the screens of digital trading terminals, and the paper derivative contracts moving through the departments of global investment banks. In Argentina, these forms of capital movement had enabled rich individuals and multinational corporations to escape the bank embargo that trapped the money of the woman banging the ATM in her account and the subsequent devaluation that would wipe out a big chunk of its value.

My own fieldwork began a few years after the crisis, in the context of an economy and polity looking for a way forward. As an anthropologist, I was interested in thinking through these broad shifts in political economy through a concrete set of dilemmas that could be studied ethnographically. I began with an interest in economic practice, following a thread from the crisis. Ethnographic work on finance had brought the study of financial institutions into dialogue with long-standing anthropological concerns about value and the choreographies of persons and things that unfold in exchange across social and geographical topographies.[24] But how did all this look from the perspective of everyday people in a peripheral economy like Argentina's?

What if the everydayness
of attending to environmental cost?
minor key of a globally
determined legate

Chapter 1 takes up the story of small-scale real estate investors like Mariela, describing the emergence of real estate as a central form of savings for middle-class investors following the crisis of 2001. The construction boom that would unfold in the years after the crisis hinged on the bank embargo and subsequent devaluation of the peso, which shook people's faith in banks and finance to the core and rekindled historical anxieties around the instability of currency in Argentina. A few years later, as the economy began to recover, people began to seek out forms of saving that were disarticulated from banks. Since the crisis had wiped out mortgage lending, real estate in the post-crisis years provided just what they were looking for. Many people like Mariela—*pequeños ahorristas*, or small savers, they are called—bought apartments, finding in buildings a more solid way to save their savings. That Buenos Aires' post-crisis real estate market was said to be driven by a distrust of banks installed during the crisis—the kind of animus toward banking manifested by the woman banging the ATM—drew out for me the question of real estate's place in economic life. How does real estate work as a form of investment that exists alongside others, including dollars and pesos, cash and bank accounts? What is particular about real estate in Argentina, and how is it incorporated into the economic practices of small savers burned by a national economic meltdown? The chapter considers these questions through stories told about economic history—in informal settings as well as in newspaper stories, comics, memoir, and jokes. I find in these stories the tools through which Argentines develop sensibilities about the economy that guide buildings' incorporation into post-crisis investment practices in which different media of savings bear contrasting capacities for conserving value and for staying put. Within these stories, the valorization of buildings hinges on their contrast with the seemingly ephemeral, transnational capital flows prevalent in Argentina in the 1990s that did so much damage during the crisis.

Chapter 2 turns from lay investors like Mariela to ask after buildings' existence within the practices of an adjacent group, professional real estate analysts, whose voices I found frequently represented in the news media on real estate investment. These market experts approached questions that were in many ways similar to those of small investors concerning the place of real estate in post-crisis investment ecologies, but did so using a different set of tools, including charts, graphs, and forms of historical narrative articulated with them. I was interested in learning how the practices of these experts worked to both understand and help form a market in real estate, which I undertook by both reading industry publications and attending conferences and seminars. The chapter begins by considering the process of appraisal through which an apartment's market value is determined, a process that involves a series of minute comparisons that ultimately allow buildings to circulate with one another in a market through a number: price per square meter. While such numerical instantiations of buildings are at times sought after because of their ability to construct comparative economic frames for apartments that allow the market to function, numbers are never sufficient tools for market analysis, I learned. In the second analytical practice I examine, analysts reload these numbers with historical content, constructing narratives about the rise and fall of prices over decades and placing price into thick historical contexts in order to forecast potential futures. By juxtaposing these two stories of buildings' numerical lives, this chapter highlights the relationality of numbers within broader systems of their production and legibility.

The values people held in buildings extended far beyond economic spheres, however—a trouble I was interested in staying with. I found one set of frictions within various neighborhood movements to limit construction that began to make headlines in 2006, when an organized group of residents in the neighborhood of Caballito forced the city to freeze the issuance of construction permits in a sixteen-block area of the city through a deft series of legal and political actions. The boom was felt particularly strongly in neighborhoods like Caballito, Palermo, Villa Pueyrredón, and Villa Urquiza—parts of Buenos Aires that were historically less dense than upper-class neighborhoods like Belgrano or Recoleta, but that were respectable enough to attract investment when the boom took off. The buildings built during the boom were of many different sorts: some were refined works of architecture; others were luxurious high-rises with amenities like gyms and rooftop pools; the vast majority were unremarkable except for their size, often reaching ten stories tall in neighborhoods where all the other buildings were only one or two stories tall. As construction moved ahead, in some neighborhoods at a dizzying pace, neighborhood groups across the city (like Patricia's) organized against the spate of new construction, questioning the state planning structures that permitted them and drawing attention to the urban lifeworlds being lost at the hands of real estate development.

Chapter 3 focuses on the particular kinds of environments around which people like Patricia organized—the barrio (typically translated as neighborhood)—and the kinds of values produced through practices of barrio dwelling. One of the first articles I read about political efforts against tall buildings featured an interview with a retiree who spoke about the ten-story building that went up next to his house, cutting off the sun from his garden. The deep sadness in his description of the loss of his garden could easily be disregarded as geopolitically insignificant. But for me, it opened up a realm of humble quotidian practices that served to link up questions of the built environment and the habitus of neighborhood life with the apparently distant concerns of national political-economic transformation. Was it possible that practices like gardening offered a perspective from which to open up the politics of value in barrio life as irreducible to, but also connected with, broader post-crisis public sentiments that had cooled to the suggestion, much touted in the 1990s, that market-driven economic development would produce a better collective life for Argentines? Standing with Patricia and looking up at the ten-story buildings going up around her little rooftop terrace, neither of us could ignore the resonance with the rampant privatizations of the 1990s, when the post office, the national petroleum corporation, the national airline, electric and phone companies, pension funds, and more were privatized with the promise of improved service and benefits for all—promises that never materialized in the first place and definitively went up in smoke during the crisis. If the major political events that had defined Argentine political and economic struggle over the past several years seemed far afield, there was also a sense in which they were right here, literally in her backyard. From her small terrace in Villa Pueyrredón, it felt as if they were coming to take the sky itself.

In this chapter, I show how practices of care for plants and green space— in parks, gardens, patios, and terraces—helped foment a mode of attention to the built environment that led *vecinos* into political advocacy. The practices of barrio life are extended and valorized through concrete dreams such as poems, song lyrics, and literature about barrio life that help sustain barrios' value as particular, historically resonant sites of relationality between people and their environments. In this sense, barrios are important sites in which buildings' smooth incorporation into economic forms of investment did not always have easy tread—a topic I examine through some of the public political actions carried out by neighborhood groups that sought to make noneconomic forms of value endure in the face of persistent real estate development.

In chapter 4, I follow some of these neighborhood groups into the halls of city government, where their efforts to rewrite the city's urban planning code drew them into the legal and bureaucratic world of state institutions surrounding buildings. They became experts at reading and interpreting these codes, conducted audits of construction to detect code violations, and engaged the political and bureaucratic machinery of urban construction. The state that neighborhood groups took me into contact with was not a rational bureaucratic state engaged in top-down, expert-driven planning, nor did it conform to the participatory democratic projects that are often held up as a kind of gold standard in conversations surrounding the democratization of urban planning. Instead, authorship over the urban planning code—yet another concrete dream in which buildings were manifest—was understood to be linked to the machinations of a powerful but obscure set of monied interests working in collusion with state actors to resist any limits on the real estate and construction sector. For all the neighborhood groups I worked with, whatever hopes they initially held at approaching legal and bureaucratic bodies with a well-reasoned set of arguments about the impact of private development, in order to receive a rational and reasoned response, were quickly dashed in the face of a world of shady collusions between money and power. I knew that the history of planning was marked by both early modern efforts by states to intervene in construction in the interest of public hygiene and access to air and sunlight and by struggles against powerful state planners on the part of democratic movements who saw their neighborhoods threatened by state urban renewal projects. How did neighborhood groups' advocacy around planning recast historical relationships among capitalist development, urban planning expertise, and state politics? And in what ways did they refract ongoing tensions in Argentina between democratic politics and the power of money and development? I consider the structure of power and knowledge implied by bureaucratic codes and follow neighborhood groups in questioning the purported democratic nature of this bureaucratic instantiation of buildings. I do so by attending particularly to buildings' appearance in the intrigue-laden narratives of political storytelling circulated as gossip and tales of corruption—stories that situate buildings within dense networks of power and money.

Chapter 5 examines buildings within another terrain of value and practice, that of architectural pedagogy in the University of Buenos Aires. In the same year that the neighborhood residents of Caballito made their front-page headlines, a feature article in the Argentine architectural journal *Summa+* brought together a roundtable of small entrepreneurial architecture firms who were engaged in a new way of building buildings that had emerged in this changing economic landscape. During the course of the crisis, many mid-sized construction companies had folded when the bank credit and mortgage lending

on which they depended disappeared from the country's economic landscape. At first, this left only the largest and most well-financed developers,
who focused on construction in elite zones of the city. But as more and more
pequeños ahorristas sought out apartments, small groups of architects, many
of whom were out of work, began to find ways to build buildings. They cir-
cumnavigated bank lending by selling apartments (for cash) before they were
built, collecting enough capital through down payments to buy property, and
funding construction with later installments. The article in *Summa+* was a
conversation among architects who were reevaluating their place in the chain
of production, moving beyond their traditional roles as designers and beginning to insert themselves in *negocios*—the business side of construction. This
new place in the construction process required the development of a different
set of skills and a reformulation of the concerns and forms of engagement
that many architects had with buildings.

Such transformations were not without their detractors. While some saw
the opportunity to usher in a new era of design in which architecture could
come into its own without the interference of developers, others saw market
forces reaching more deeply than ever into the hearts and minds of architects.
These concerns unfolded in a post-crisis context, but also in relation to a history of sensitivity to architecture's place in commodity society, both within
the discipline and in Argentina in particular, through which architects sought
to foster the production of more inclusive, livable worlds beyond the limits
of market-based construction. I was convinced that these kinds of commitments and their endurance in architectural circles were not insignificant.

In my conversations with architects, they frequently cited the university—
where many continued to be involved as teachers or in postgraduate work—
as a key site through which their practice of architecture could find expression beyond the demands of market-based production. Their comments
brought me into the architecture school at the University of Buenos Aires,
where I observed professors teaching students like Bárbara to care for lived
experience in built environments in a way that exceeded—even if it did not
escape—those defined by real estate. I begin by describing how architectural students like Bárbara are taught to think through their own bodies and
through practices of drawing and model making, which I argue are generative
of a politics of care that offers the possibility of conserving human-building
relations in the face of alternative relational possibilities that threaten to
overtake them. Also present in the architecture school—though not always
in an explicit way—were inheritances of the violent political struggles that

gripped the university during two dictatorships, the first from 1966 to 1973, the second from 1976 to 1984. One of the two lead professors I worked with was subject to a political purge from the university during the first (while the other was a student), and both had to go into hiding during the second, in which many other students and colleagues were disappeared. In the brief interregnum between the two, both were involved in a leftist reformation of university pedagogy that sought to problematize architecture's place in commodity society and direct educational praxis toward addressing the needs of more popular sectors of society—projects that they continue to make endure in very different economic and political environments today. Like the neighborhood groups described in chapters 3 and 4, I see in the architecture school the maintenance of minor forms of value that operate in tension—at times implicit, at times explicit—with the hegemony of buildings' economic value.

In the epilogue, I reflect upon more recent economic and political shifts in Argentina and Latin America, leveraging them to describe the value I see in concrete dreams' minor-key articulations of possibility vis-à-vis major-key political projects. Thinking through minor-key values—and the politics, histories, and concrete forms of the practices that sustain them—can give substance to some possibilities worth holding onto in the work of producing livable futures.

....

"*Cada cual con sus trabajos / Con sus sueños, cada cual,*" wrote Atahaulpa Yupanqui in the song I used to open this book. Each one with their work, with their dreams, each one. A folk singer dedicated to articulating the everyday lives of the popular classes with big-stage political dreams, Yupanqui was inspirational for the *nuevo cancionero* singers of the 1960s, 1970s, and 1980s who used song as a tool to express the dreams, struggles, and hopes of a people working toward a better world in a context of growing political repression and marked by histories of deep inequality. Listening recently, the words struck me for the way they maintain a place for divergence in a song about shared histories and possible collective futures: each one with their work, with their dreams each one. The song continues: With hope before them / With memories behind. The word for hope—*esperanza*—contains within itself a sense of durative time (*esperar* is also *to wait*), evoking for me the way inherited histories and possible futures are bound up with the endurance of divergent practices and values.

"Getting on together" is one of the ways Helen Verran (2001) has put the task she sees before us, part of the generative practice of "doing difference together" (Verran and Christie 2011) in the interest of composing livable worlds.[25] The practice of getting on together does not hang on a totalizing revolutionary transformation, but rather sits within the cracks of an edifice that is anything but solid. Remaining sensitive to real threats of capture while fostering ways of getting on together is a sensibility that feminist scholars have taught me to cultivate.[26] It's a mode of attention that could only come from the margins, I think, where possibilities are articulated in minor keys.

The story I tell here, then, is one of possibility and endurance as I learned about them from people in Argentina who have taught me that all is not lost. Studying the divergent practices through which buildings are valued is a way into thinking about markets and politics and the forms of difference made to endure within them. Penelope Harvey has written that "concrete's promise to operate as a generic, homogeneous, and above all predictable material is constantly challenged by the instability and heterogeneity of the terrains to which it is applied" (2010, 28; see also Gambetta 2013). The minor-key ethnographic and historical terrains I speak of matter in this way as well. As part of concrete's extended compound materiality—alongside water, rock, and cement—they form the particular, shifting, and never-quite-solid worlds on which concrete dreams are built.

CHAPTER 1

....

Crisis Histories, Brick Futures

Economic Storytelling and Investments in Real Estate

In November 2001, Mariela called up her friend, grabbed a suitcase, and headed for the bank. The Argentine economic crisis that would become fully apparent in December loomed on the horizon, and although widespread fears about the solvency of the banking system were only just beginning to set in, Mariela decided to follow her gut and get all of her money out of the bank. Doing so wasn't easy, however. "We got to the branch and they told me: 'Fill out this form, and in seventy-two hours we'll give you the money,'" she told me, remembering the day. "So I filled out the form, and in seventy-two hours we went back, and they told me that I would have to wait another day. The next day I went back again, and again they told me, 'Your money isn't here.' So I started to make a scene. 'This is a fraud! I'm going to the Consumer Protection Agency, to the Public Advocate's Office! You're going to give me back my money!'" The scene brought the bank manager out from his office. "The manager came out and told me: 'Ma'am, your money isn't in this branch. The only way to get it is to go to the main office. You can take a bit from here, but you'll have to get the rest there.'" But Mariela had had enough of the runaround, of chasing her money: "I said to him: 'Absolutely not. I put the money in here, and you are going to give it all back to me tomorrow.' And the next day, I went back with my friend and the suitcase. They made me go into a reserved room, where the bank's accountant practically threw the money at me."

Mariela wasn't the only one trying to get her money out of the bank. Many others had begun to withdraw their money as well, and ten days later the government placed strict limits on withdrawals in an effort to stem a full-scale bank run. These limits were called the *corralito*—the "little corral," or "the crib"—and they were part of the dramatic unraveling of a decade-long relationship between the Argentine peso and the U.S. dollar, to which the peso had been pegged throughout the 1990s. As the rich moved their money offshore and powerful international investors began to speculate against Argentine debt, the ban on bank withdrawals cut people off from their savings at a time when they needed them the most: unemployment was on its way past 20 percent, and more than half of the population would soon be living beneath the poverty line. For a while, money trapped in the corralito sat in the banks, but a few weeks later deposits that had been dollars or dollar-equivalent pesos were forcibly converted to bonds denominated in unpegged (and devaluing) pesos. By getting her money out of the bank, Mariela had escaped devaluation by the skin of her teeth.

Ten years later, I asked Mariela if she had regained her faith in banks. She leaned back in her chair and let out a long laugh. She had not. In 2010, like many others I spoke with, Mariela was keeping her money in U.S. dollars in a safe-deposit box. And also like many others, she was looking to use those dollars to buy an apartment—colloquially called *ladrillos*, or bricks. Beginning in 2004, when the economy had begun to recover, people like Mariela faced the problem of what to do with their savings. In Argentina, people with a "capacity to save" (i.e., who are not so poor as to not have any savings), who are at the same time not wealthy enough to engage in more elaborate financial or offshore economic practices, are referred to as *pequeños ahorristas*, or small savers.[1] They include pensioners, small business owners, and professionals. Beginning in 2003 or 2004, many of them would turn to real estate as a means to save their savings, producing a boom in construction that would change the ways many pequeños ahorristas would relate to their money and the ways *porteños* (residents of the port city of Buenos Aires) from a variety of walks of life related to their built environment.

This chapter examines how buildings were incorporated into the investment practices of people like Mariela: investment practices situated in the turbulent history of a peripheral economy that has been no stranger to crisis. I think about investment in two distinct but related ways. The first is the perhaps more obvious way in which real estate investment refers to the dedication of economic resources to the purchase of an apartment, with some expectation about a future economic outcome based on the implications of having those resources in the form of a building or apartment. In this sense, real estate is one possibility among a set of other possible ways in which to invest one's money. In practice, it frequently means that real estate investment is part of a more elaborate economic choreography between diverse economic media, of which bricks are but one possibility. In Argentina, these other media principally include pesos and dollars (which themselves can exist in different material forms, such as numbers on a bank statement or in cash); still other possibilities, including precious metals (like gold) or financial products (like stocks), are present, but are more marginal to the investment practices of pequeños ahorristas. On one level, then, I think of investment in real estate (or bricks) as part of this choreography of instruments drawn together in economic practice.

But these investment practices are not abstract strategies; they are instead highly contingent, historically and geographically situated practices through which people work to cobble together a viable life on often shaky ground. In Argentina, like in many other peripheral economies, near-chronic macroeconomic instability can make economic decision making a particularly fraught practice. Indeed, the crisis of 2001 was but one moment in a much longer history of economic instability in Argentina. This instability has been particularly marked since the 1970s, but it stretches back to include important but more sporadic crises since the late nineteenth century. Some of these were widely shared across much of the world, while others have been felt particularly strongly in the economic periphery. Real estate investment in Argentina is situated in this particular context, on the geopolitical margins of world economic stability. Through decades of economic crises, currency devaluations, and capital flight, Argentines have honed quotidian practices that draw upon different media of savings to cobble together investments on a constantly shifting economic terrain. These histories of living in turbulent economies and the lessons they may carry for the present and the future are the focus of much attention in Argentina.

This is the second sense in which I understand pequeños ahorristas to be invested in real estate: the sense in which they dedicate time, effort, and energy to understanding the particular contours of the world through which their money moves. One of the ways that they have managed to cobble together their economic lives is by investing a considerable amount of time and passion in economic storytelling: the narration of past economic events in a way that holds them present in memory with the intention of building a more promising future. These economic stories—like the one Mariela told me and others I'll describe later—are sites of popular analytical practice through which porteños both understand and reshape the intricate terrains on which economic practice unfolds. The storytelling is part of the practice of investment itself, the means through which the present and future events are formed in dialogue with historical memory and negotiated through material practice.

Real estate booms frequently conjure images of speculative investment on behalf of powerful financial actors and institutions. Indeed, the first decade of the twenty-first century was marked by a series of financially driven real estate bubbles in the United States, Spain, and Ireland that inflated and then burst, with catastrophic national and global ramifications. In the case of the U.S., for example, real estate surged in response to demand by international investors for mortgage-backed securities, a new kind of financial product that promised a reliable stream of payments that could beat the low interest rates being paid on other instruments, like federal government bonds. Mortgage-backed securities were supposed to be incredibly stable, and they succeeded in luring large institutional investors, like pension funds, which more traditionally invested in bond markets. But things didn't turn out as planned. To simplify only slightly, high demand for mortgage-backed securities drove banks to offer more mortgages so they could sell more mortgage-based financial products. Eventually, most prospective homeowners with the capacity to pay a mortgage already had homes, and so lenders began extending loans to people who were unlikely to be able to repay them. When these mortgage holders began to default on their loans, mortgage-backed financial products that were supposed to be stable instead became "toxic," causing repercussions throughout the major financial institutions that produced them and that had invested in them.[2]

The real estate boom in Buenos Aires in the years after the crisis was markedly different from these headline-grabbing booms and busts driven by mortgage lending, because in post-crisis Argentina there was no mortgage market to speak of.[3] Instead, the kind of construction that was most ubiquitous was funded by people like Mariela moving their savings into real estate for a complex set of reasons I explore in this chapter. They often did so in cash, with as little mediation through the world of high finance as they could manage.

Alongside the apparent complexity of finance, buying something with cash may seem straightforward. There is a popular tendency to think of finance as a highly complex world, full of arcane forms of expertise, institutional relationships, technological change, and innovation. In boosterish accounts, this complexity is deployed to attribute to financial experts a kind of privileged knowledge that is beyond the capacity for comment by everyday people. In more critical accounts, finance's complexity can be used to depict it as abstract and divorced from the real world of actual economic life. In both of these narratives, buying something with cash feels low-tech, straightforward, and more real. But the intricacy of economic practices like Mariela's is worth paying attention to. Finance *is* a complex and arcane world, but there's nothing simple or straightforward about nonfinancialized forms of economic practice either—a fact that has long been the focus of anthropologists and sociologists studying the material, spiritual, social, and political dynamics that are in play in even apparently simple forms of exchange.

Think back to the story Mariela told me about her savings and the transformations she ushered them through just in this brief story. At the beginning of the story, her money was materially manifest most directly in a set of numbers printed on her bank statements. Ostensibly this money was held in the bank and available on demand. But when she went to retrieve it, she was told to fill out a set of forms and come back in seventy-two hours. When she did that, she was told that her money was "not in this branch." By the reckoning of the bank manager, the bank's money in this particular branch was not fungible with the bank's money in other branches: although the bank is one corporation with many branches, the money in this branch was not Mariela's, as if there were a bag of cash with her name on it somewhere. Then there is the bureaucracy of the form and its inefficacy and the way Mariela countered the form with an emotional outburst in the bank: a loud insistence that even according to the bank's odd reckoning of the geographic distribution of its cash (was it here or in the main branch?), she had put her money in at this branch, and she wanted it back in this branch. Mariela's scene threatened to set off a chain reaction, evoking the scene from *Mary Poppins* in which Jane and Michael Banks cry out for their tuppence and cause a run on the bank. The fact that Mariela's scene seemed to be efficacious means that money, even in purportedly staid financial institutions, flows along affectively greased paths—affects that were manifest again when the bank manager tossed her money at her the following day. All of this—the bureaucracy, the strange geographic distribution of institutional funds, the affect—was necessary to turn her money from a bank deposit into cash. What for many of us is a straightforward and smooth transformation between account balance and bills was, for Mariela in this moment, anything but that.

The complexity continues: Mariela was lucky not only that she got her money out, but that she was able to withdraw her money as dollars instead of pesos. If she had made her withdrawal several weeks later, not only would her withdrawals have been sharply limited in quantity, but her ability to access them as dollars would be far more complex (and disadvantageous). The fact that she held her money in cash dollars meant a lot once the peso was unpegged from the dollar, since the devaluation of the peso effectively tripled the value of her cash.[4] National macroeconomic and political events, the federal default on loans, and the matrix of world financial institutions that influence the value of the peso pressed in and became felt in Mariela's economic practice. And then, as soon as she got the money out of the bank, Mariela found herself holding tens of thousands of dollars in cash and had to figure out what to do with them. Mariela didn't like the risk associated with keeping them in her house, and so soon after, her dollars were back in the bank in a safe-deposit box instead of an account. I will return to this complex set of relations and histories, but for now notice the way that money—the relationship between dollars and pesos, bank accounts and cash—isn't as straightforward as it may seem, a fact made especially apparent in moments of economic crisis, when relationships that may be smooth in other moments stretch or break at the seams. Over many years of living in a turbulent economy, Argentines have developed a fine-tuned attention to these particularities of connection and relation among various forms of economic investment. Real estate's disarticulation from finance and mortgage lending does not mean that bricks have their own inherently stable autonomous value. Instead, it means that a different set of relationships, of articulations and disarticulations with other media of savings, comes into focus: in this case, with dollars and pesos, bank accounts and cash.

I call these sets of relationships among diverse media of savings an ecology of investments.[5] I use the word *ecology* (instead of its close etymological relative, *economy*) because of the conceptual friction it brings to a conversation about money. My principal intention is to leverage the set of dense interrelationships that have become part of how we think about ecologies as a conceptual push to think more relationally about economies. The two words also share an etymological link in the oikos, the home or household. *Logos* (the second part of ecology) is frequently used to indicate speech, reason, "the study of," while *nomos* (the second part of economy) refers to management, the distribution of things. Holding these roots together is a way to approach the ways forms of knowledge (logos) embedded in storytelling about money and property affect their distribution and management (nomos) and how both reconfigure real estate and the built environment (the city as oikos, the home or dwelling place).

Thinking ecologically about investment means several things. At the core is the way in which ecology calls upon us to attend to an "emergent web of relations among constitutive and constituting parts, such as when one shifts attention from a particular organism to the entire ecology," as Tim Choy has described one of the word's key meanings (2011, 11–12). For the specific purpose of this chapter, I am interested in tracing the ways that dollars and pesos, bank accounts and cash, and gold and bricks are not just treated as objects unto themselves by Argentine investors, but are understood as part of an ecology, related to each other and the world around them in complex ways. People like Mariela don't treat any one investment like any other, but attend to their particular capacities and to the relational webs of which they are a part. This kind of ecological attention to investments approaches them as more than a series of abstract values seamlessly convertible from one to the other; rather, it pays close attention to the particular forms of connections that define them and works to imagine those that may become relevant in the future.[6]

Thinking about investments ecologically concerns not only relations between diverse things, but also relations between people and things. Investment, in this sense, doesn't just refer to a series of investments understood as autonomous objects (real estate, dollars, stocks). Rather, it draws attention to investment as a form of connection between persons and the things in which they are invested. Mariela doesn't just relate to an ecology of investments; she herself is part of it. Marilyn Strathern (2012) has described something similar to what I am after here when she distinguishes between a "metaphysics of having" and a "metaphysics of being." She follows Eduardo Vargas's reading of Gabriel Tarde to elucidate the contrast between the two: while "the verb 'to be' concerns identity . . . in the mode of Having, relation is alter-a(c)tion" (Vargas 2010, 212). In other words, if a metaphysics of being treats objects as self-enclosed, as having identities unto themselves, then a metaphysics of having disrupts this in order to draw attention to their constitutive relationality: things are what they are because of the relations that constitute them. Having takes as its object this relation, which Being treats as secondary. This implies, in the words of Viveiros de Castro (2003, 17), an "intrinsic transitivity and an originary opening towards an exteriority." Dollars, bricks, and pesos, in other words, are not things in themselves, but things constituted through their relations, both with each other and with those who have them. As Bruno Latour put it, "To possess is also being possessed; to be attached is to hold and be held" (2005, 217). Like possession and attachment, investment speaks to both investing and being invested. Reciprocal relations through which people and things become together, investments are constitutive of both persons and things: when Mariela moves her investments from bank to cash, she is not only changing the stuff of her investments, but also the way she relates to and is entangled with her world.

Investments are not only a means of relating people with objects, but also of relating people to one another. Gift exchange, in which relations between giver and recipient are formed through gifts, is a canonical example in anthropology.[7] In the cases I consider here, investments draw into relation people from disparate and far-flung worlds. The banking crisis and devaluation that Mariela faced, for example, was not just a relation between Argentines and their bank deposits, but was tied up with the investments of hedge fund managers and currency traders on Wall Street that can make the value of the peso rise and fall. Similarly, the value of the dollar sitting in Mariela's safe-deposit box is related to the decisions of politicians and technocrats in the United States, although it is not determined only by them: if people like Mariela (and much larger institutional investors like China) weren't invested in the dollar through their purchase of U.S. Treasury bonds, the value of U.S. currency would not have the strength it does today. Through their shared investment in dollars, Mariela is caught up in the decisions of the Chinese government about their purchase of U.S. Treasury bonds. Investments, in this sense, draw actors into a shared relational space, even if these relations are not always obvious.

Thinking ecologically about investment is especially useful for placing in tension conceptual frameworks of the economy that imagine a smooth movement of money and goods within a global space. Many popular considerations of global economies, for example, figure global finance as a world of seamless flows coursing across the world. But in fact, these apparently effortless flows are the result of an array of professionals, equipment, and laws that allow such flows to happen. In this light, one way of reading the number of recent ethnographies of finance is as studies of the production of infrastructures—human, technical, and legal—that allow for the production of a global economy in which flows can seem effortless.[8] Thus while global finance may not always live up to the hype of smooth and seamless exchange that financiers attribute to it—and that often makes its way into critical analyses of globalization (Ho 2005)—it is nevertheless a fact in the making, albeit one whose trajectory is far from certain or linear. Like scholars who have highlighted the frictions, excesses, and infrastructural entailments of the global economy, Argentines are especially careful about treating different investments as equivalent forms of abstract value in which one is like any other. Mariela became acutely aware that even the dollars she keeps in her safe-deposit box are not equivalent to the dollars she used to have in her bank account: dollars are only equivalent to other dollars under certain infrastructural conditions.

As careful as they have learned to become about accepting received notions of equivalence, a deep history of historical experience has also helped Argentines see ecologies of investment as rich with potential, and at times dangerous, connection. Their recent economic history is full of events that have expanded their capacity to perceive the panoply of actors and materialities that may come into play at any moment. To give just one example: in 2012 the Argentine naval frigate *Libertad* was detained for nearly six months in Ghana at the behest of the Cayman Island–based hedge fund NML Capital, whose parent company's CEO, the American billionaire Paul Singer, was unsatisfied with the terms of Argentina's sovereign debt restructuring following their default in 2001. His hedge fund had pressured various governments all over the world and managed to get a Ghanaian judge to impound the nineteenth-century historic vessel during its visit. As a result, a frigate docked in Ghana made a curious appearance in the middle of legal battles in Manhattan district court over the payment of Argentine debts to Wall Street vulture funds. The global is rich with such diverse (and at times surprising) gatherings of people and things. Thinking ecologically about investment thus requires care before attributing equivalence, but promiscuity in seeing potential connections. It is a way to follow the troubled connections not just between dollars and dollars or dollars and pesos, but between frigates, bricks, and other materialities that can become caught up in and form part of these ecologies.

Bricks became especially important actors in Argentine investment ecologies following the events of the crisis of 2001, when real estate came to be seen as the safest vehicle for their savings vis-à-vis other possible investments, including pesos and dollars, bank accounts and cash. This crisis, together with those that came before it, condensed a lack of confidence in Argentine currency, in the banking sector, and in finance in general, driving people toward an investment that they understood to be more solid, more local, and less likely to evaporate the way many people's savings did during the crisis of 2001. It wasn't the first time bricks had been treated as investments, but their constitution as investments unfolded on historically unique terrain, and the kind of investments they were—because of the specific relational ecology of which they were a part—was different than it had been in other moments. As I have mentioned, real estate became especially valuable to pequeños ahorristas because of its disarticulation from the world of high finance and because of its particular historical relationship with the U.S. dollar. This disarticulation from banks does not mean that bricks have an authentic, autonomous value of their own. Investment in real estate was not a reflection of anything transhistorical or universally true about real estate as such. This would be thinking through a metaphysics of being, as if real estate were something other than the particular set of relations that constitute it. Instead, real estate investment after the crisis had everything to do with the particular set of relationships bricks had developed with other forms of investment and the ways these relationships were read, understood, and responded to on the part of pequeños ahorristas.

INVESTMENTS IN THE PAST: HISTORIES OF MONEY AND BANKING

In Argentina, there is a pointed awareness that the past can provide important clues about how to live in an ecology prone to abrupt and surprising changes. While poor in teleology (one never knows what the future may hold, what relations may become relevant), the ecology of investment is rich with history. Argentines are, in this sense, not only invested in pesos, dollars, gold, and real estate. They are also invested in the past. Because of this, the history of Argentine economic life is under a constant process of (re)narration as Argentines reflect upon their rocky economic past in films and documentaries, comic strips and comic monologues, in memoir, art, and stories told among family and friends.[9] These narrative forms are richly textured, ranging from dry to absurd to tragic to comic, and often blend a range of styles and emotions. Stories such as Mariela's are part of this popular economic historiography, in which Argentines engage in a praxis of memory not unlike those practiced with regard to the country's violent political history.[10] My own historical narrative draws on the media that Argentines use to *hacer memoria*—to "do memory"—and invest in their past. Entangling anthropology with these investments is one way to develop our sensibility about economic lives rife with risky relations.

Argentine narrative practices about economic pasts are a central means not only of understanding their ecology of investments, but also of guiding its future formation. Argentines engage these narrative forms to sharpen, hone, and distribute their own particular sort of lay economic expertise about investment. Through these storytelling practices and the practices of investment that they informed, buildings became a central feature of pequeños ahorristas' post-crisis economic life. The act of their telling is thus part of, not apart from, eventful time.[11] They contribute to the development of an ecological sensibility honed to troubled histories in the interest of building promising futures. Their investment in the past is one I share here as I narrate the ecology of investment through popular narrative forms in order to capture this entanglement of people, things, and the very present histories through which Argentines work to find ways to live in a world unsettled by the movements of finance capital.

Two narrative threads about Argentine economic history were particularly important for composing the post-crisis investment ecologies in which bricks would come to attain a privileged place. The first focuses on histories of Argentine currency fluctuations, which became particularly strong and frequent beginning in the 1970s. These stories hold present the chronic instability of Argentina's currencies, which make legible the inability to invest in the Argentine peso as a long-term investment. The second focuses on the more recent history of Argentines' troubled relationship with banks through the depiction of events that unfolded during the crisis of 2001.

Histories of Inflation: Argentine Currencies, 1975–2001

Histories of inflation are central to Argentine knowledge about the ecological relationality of investments. A fall in the purchasing power of money, inflation marks the slippery relationship between money, other currencies, and things. One day, it takes three pesos to buy a dollar and one peso to buy an empanada; some time later, it takes twenty-five pesos to buy a dollar and thirty to buy an empanada. Although inflationary episodes have a long history in Argentina, they became particularly frequent and severe in the mid-1970s amid the financial deregulation, fluctuating presence of foreign capital, and liberalization of state economic policy that have become hallmarks of neoliberalism. Punctuating this history of inflation were measures aimed to deal with it, which included both brusque and severe devaluations as well as scheduled devaluations designed to strike at inflation's underlying "psychological factors."[12] The reconfiguration of the relationship between the peso and the dollar in 2001 (of which Mariela's story is a part) is one moment in this longer history.

Today, Argentines reflect upon this history in many ways. For example, a recent newspaper retrospective noted that if someone were to have gone to sleep with one thousand dollars in local currency under their mattress in 1975 and slept through the series of hyperinflations and devaluations, they would wake up in 2009 to find their savings worth 0.0000027 dollars (Guariano 2009). For Argentine readers, the absurdity of sleeping for fifty years is negligible alongside the number of zeros after the decimal point. The graphic accompanying

FIGURE 1.1. Inflation money grinder. From a newspaper article on inflation, *La Nación*, 2010.

the article shows hundred-peso bills going into the top of a meat grinder and emerging as ten-cent coins (see figure 1.1). In shorter intervals of time, inflation is tracked in quotidian experience in several ways aside from government statistics, which can feel abstract and are not always trusted.[13] Whenever I returned to Argentina after a time away, my friends would tell me the price of an empanada and monitor my degree of surprise, which we jokingly referred to as the Empanada Index. (I have seen the price of pizza sold in the pizza chain Ugi's used in a similar fashion in the press, while the *Economist* prefers the price of a Big Mac at McDonald's because of its internationalized supply chain.)

Argentina's history of inflation was not evenly spread over time. Though it is chronically high, there are moments in which it is particularly so, and these are often the moments that stand out in stories. One particularly impactful moment of high inflation was a period in the late 1980s that became known as *La Híper* (short for hyperinflation). Inflation during La Híper had powerful impacts on daily life and helped to change the relationship between people and their money at the deepest of levels. During its worst moments, prices went up sharply even from hour to hour. Osvaldo Soriano, in his memoiric essay "Living with Inflation," remarks, "While I am writing this article, the cigarettes that I'm smoking in front of the typewriter have passed from 11 to 13 and then to 14 australs"[14] (1989, 42). He also recalls asking a waiter for his bill and the waiter throwing up his hands: "Give me ten thousand and we'll see if it's right tomorrow!" he tells him. During times like these, people developed quotidian practices to make their rapidly devaluing salaries stretch to provide the basic necessities of life: Mariela told me of rummaging through store shelves looking for items whose prices had not been updated and of her tactical efforts to avoid the attendant, who waited near the checkout counter poised with a sticker machine to raise the prices of the goods in her cart.

Alongside inflation was a series of changes in the national currency, in which one type of currency was replaced by another. A monologue from the early 1990s by the comedian Tato Bores (which still circulates online) dramatized the rapid series of currency shifts and the strange, otherworldly mathematics that characterized monetary relatedness in popular experience (Bores 1990). Rifling through bills from the panoply of currencies of the previous twenty years, Bores does some math:

> Let me tell you something, look here: this Peso Moneda Nacional, they dropped two zeroes from it when they introduced this other peso, the Peso Ley 18.188 [in 1970]; they dropped another four zeroes with this Peso Argentino [1983], and then, as if that weren't enough, they took off three more zeroes with this Austral [1985]. And so, since they took off nine zeroes from this little peso here in front, then this Austral is worth one billion of this little peso here, this Peso Moneda Nacional. [A grin spreads across his face as he continues, now slowly.] And since back then you could buy one dollar with 83 Pesos Moneda Nacional, that means this Austral is worth: 12 million dollars!

The crowd ooos in amazement as the logical magician grins with pride at his discovery. "Which would be a joke, if it weren't a fuck-over as big as a house!" he concludes, as the crowd erupts in laughter and applause.

These reflections on Argentina's economic past illustrate a world in which the value of currency slips in unpredictable ways, producing a sense of surreality surrounding money in Argentina that extends into the present. Argentines did not live such shifts passively, however. Instead, they developed complex linkages with other currencies or financial devices, producing and navigating a rich ecology of relations between diverse monetary forms. In contrast to classical depictions of modern money, then, Argentines do not live in a world dominated by a single, universal-exchange currency in which all things are rendered equivalent on one scale of value. Instead, they have incorporated complex calculi that mixed currencies, bonds, and international price indexes into their everyday economic lives.[15] As Soriano (1989, 42) explains regarding La Híper, "Nobody negotiated the price of contracted services in australs, but in dollars. Since the law obligated the use of the national currency, at least in appearances, whatever agreement to be realized within six months would include a clause that stated, for example: 'The sum will be paid in australs equivalent to x dollars in Bonex value [an Argentine bond that paid in dollars] according to its valuation on that day as reported in the Oriental Republic of Uruguay.'"

Australs, dollars, Bonex bonds, Uruguay: Argentine currency was a signifier floating particularly highly, and people sought to stabilize it by establishing relations with other scales of value.[16] In this case, the Bonex bonds were used to established the relationship between the dollar and the peso, doing so from Uruguay, taken to be more objective for its location beyond the reach of possible local tampering with exchange rates. But in addition to the contractual intricacies described by Soriano, Argentines also worked to stabilize their monetary lives less elaborately by converting their cash to a more stable currency. People began buying U.S. dollars and converting them back to pesos as the need arose, a practice that was not typically necessary for short-term economic life but that would install itself firmly in the longer-term investment practices of the middle classes.

In 1991, the rich monetary ecology of La Híper became both less diverse and more institutionalized when the Argentine state took the drastic measure of scrapping the austral and pegging a new peso to the U.S. dollar in order to end hyperinflation. This time is called *convertibilidad* (convertibility), or *uno a uno* (one-to-one): a peso was made equivalent to a dollar, an era that lasted from 1991 until the devaluation of 2002. Prices stabilized, and alongside that stability, Argentines became increasingly integrated into the banking sector, opening dollar-denominated accounts, buying dollar-denominated CDs, and taking advantage of stable interest rates to take out dollar-denominated loans. Those Argentines who held onto their jobs in this era of neoliberal restructuring, with an exchange rate highly unfavorable to national industry, enjoyed a decade of life with monetary stability.

By the mid-1990s, however, the social cost of monetary stability became increasingly clear. Convertibility had altered the weight of actors tied into the relational networks of Argentine currency. Pegging the peso to the dollar meant that Argentina had no control over monetary policy and could only cover fiscal expenditures by taking on foreign loans rather than by expanding the monetary base or increasing competitiveness in trade through a devaluation, both important tools normally at a state's disposal for encouraging economic growth.[17] At the same time, the structural adjustment policies demanded by international lenders in exchange for the loans that made convertibility possible began taking deeper and deeper tolls. By the end of the 1990s, it became increasingly difficult for the government to obtain sufficient foreign currency reserves to meet both its payment obligations to foreign lenders and its conversion obligations to local savers. Neoliberal economists both at home and abroad advocated further cuts and more privatizations, but these had become politically untenable with a large population out of work and state services increasingly tenuous.

As the International Monetary Fund (IMF) began to drag its feet on new loans, new currencies began to flourish as both provinces and the federal government began to issue *quasi-monedas*, official bonds in bill form, which were supposed to stand in for the national currency: Patacones in Buenos Aires, Lecors in Córdoba, Quebrachos in the Chaco, Huarpes in San Juan, and the federal government's own Lecop (see figure 1.2). Initially used to pay public employees and pensions, quasi-monedas were estimated to account for up to 40 percent of currency emissions between July 2001 and the end of 2003, when they were removed from circulation. Quasi-monedas circulated in ways similar to, but not quite the same as, the national peso. As Mariana Luzzi (2010) explains, quasi-monedas existed within a hierarchy defined by the credibility of the province issuing the bonds and various situational criteria of use. Córdoba, for instance, reached agreements with supermarkets to ensure they would be accepted at face value through a program to convert Córdoba's Lecors into federal Lecops, which could in turn be used by the supermarket chains to pay federal taxes. Alongside these officially sanctioned circulations, informal exchanges emerged in which Argentines could trade quasi-monedas for pesos at fluctuating exchange rates or buy them at a discount to be used for paying taxes or buying groceries. A diversity of monetary forms had returned to an ecology that for the previous ten years had been dominated by peso-dollar convertibility, and Argentines again began to navigate a complex ecology in which quasi-monedas and the official currency existed alongside one another, with situated values and divergent uses—and all in the shadow of the U.S. dollar.

FIGURE 1.2. The Patacón, a quasi-moneda issued by the province of Buenos Aires. Centro Numismático Buenos Aires.

Circulatory Asymmetries: Banks and the Crisis of 2001

By March of 2001, large amounts of capital had already left the banking system as people began to doubt the solvency of the Argentine state. Large companies and wealthy individuals were the most effective in getting their money out, on what a congressional panel would later call a "highway" of money leading out of Argentina (Comisión Especial de la Cámara de Diputados 2001 [2005]). A final bail-out package from the IMF in June would forestall the crisis, but by the end of the year default was deemed imminent, and the IMF refused further loans.[18]

On November 30, to prevent a full-scale run on banks, the government instituted strict limits on the withdrawal of bank deposits—the corralito from which Mariela made her narrow escape. People could take out 250 convertible peso/dollars per week, and the near impossibility of feeding a family on such a budget led to the proliferation of barter economies. Meanwhile, the rest of their money sat in the bank. What wasn't at all certain was for how long that would be the case. The unpegging of the peso from the dollar was by this time a very real threat, despite government promises to the contrary. The two currencies had shared a long road together, but that journey, everyone seemed to know, was coming to an end. The corralito was not without certain possibilities for maneuver: debit and credit card purchases were permitted, and I heard stories of people traveling across the river to Uruguay to go to the casino, buying chips with credit or debit cards, and then cashing in the chips as a way to convert their deposits to cash. These possibilities were marginal, however, and despite such efforts, most people couldn't get their money out and felt their life's savings hanging in the balance.

Those who had kept their savings in cash, on the other hand, were in a far better position. The difference between having money in the bank and having money in cash—these two different material manifestations of what was purportedly the same underlying value system, the dollar—was brought into stark relief. The two forms of saving were divided by a sharp circulatory asymmetry: people could move and change their cash, but their bank deposits were stuck in the bank. Banks thus formed part of a monetary ecology that posed particular problems for small savers who saw their money circulating in ways that were not at all favorable to most Argentines.

The corralito drove middle-class Argentines to the streets in large numbers, where they joined the unemployed *piqueteros*, who had been blockading highways since 1997 to protest unemployment and neoliberal austerity measures. The revolt was directed not only at the government, but also at the banks (see figure 1.3). In scenes from the documentary film *The Take* (2004), middle-aged men and women dressed for the office are shown hacking away at the screens of ATM with pens or screwdrivers until they shatter or kicking in the glass walls of banks as bank workers peer out from the second floor in fear.[19] The infrastructures that allowed for smooth conversion between digital and paper currency had ground to a halt for them, even as more powerful investors had their money whisked away to offshore safe havens. Smashing the ATM was a powerful, visceral testimony to the false equivalences and limited fungibility between cash and bank balance.

On December 20, the first major political casualty of the crisis gave in. The president fled the Casa Rosada in a helicopter as angry crowds maintained a vigil outside. A succession of interim leaders began that would make the succession of currencies of the previous forty years seem slow in comparison. In late December the government announced that the country would default on its loans—the largest sovereign debt default in the history of the world.

FIGURE 1.3. Protest against fortified bank branches during the crisis of 2001. © Barcex/CC-BY-SA 2.5.

In early January 2002, it was announced that convertibility was over, and all bank deposits would be converted to the unpegged peso.

During the rest of a tense year, in which depositors' money remained stuck in their accounts (in what was then called "the *corralón*" or the big corral), the terms of the exit from convertibility were worked out. Deposits were reprogrammed at a rate of 1.4 pesos per dollar, while debts were reprogrammed at a rate of one peso to the dollar. Debtors, in many cases corporations that had already transferred their capital to foreign accounts, made out better than depositors. Banks were compensated for this disparity by taxpayers through federal bonds, meaning that the federal government assumed a large portion of the debt of many failing corporations but did not take equal responsibility for depositors' losses. Depositors, in turn, could accept pesos at these rates (which would quickly become unfavorable: the peso fell to nearly 4 pesos to the dollar before settling around 3, as I mentioned earlier) or a series of bonds called BODEN, payable in dollars over the course of the next decade—a timeline unimaginable for those who needed their savings in a tumultuous economic environment. Many would eventually accept the bonds only to have to sell them at a steep discount to international investment funds.

As in previous moments, multiplicity and differential circulations were key features of the ecology of investments. Under one program, BODEN bonds were permitted to be used for the purchase of new cars, farm equipment, and real estate, like a form of currency with restricted uses. Businesses that accepted BODEN as payment for goods were able to access the bonds' value transferred to them by bondholders in the form of deposits to savings and checking accounts. Although they could still not be officially withdrawn as cash (the corralón was still in effect), they were able to be accessed as checks, and there was an illegal but operative exchange market for these checks, through which they might be converted, finally and at a steep premium, to cash.[20] Those who exchanged BODEN for goods, in turn, would get their money out of the corralón sooner (without waiting for access to their accounts to be liberated or for their bonds to pay out) by spending it on goods. The real estate part of the program was expected to be the most popular, tapping into a strong cultural sensibility about the importance and stability of property as an asset that I'll return to shortly. An editorial in the newspaper *Página/12* captured the bind facing potential participants: "If you were living in a normal country, these things would be your materialist dream. But in Argentina your dreams are less pleasant. At night you dream about being fired, or that they might cut your salary.... Because of this, what little security you might have would come from liquid assets to live on if your nightmares were to become reality. Yet if you don't take the opportunity to dress up as happiness the acquisition of a new home or a car, what you hold on to is a virtual bank deposit, tied with barbed wire to an uncertain timeline, in a currency whose value could drop, and in a bank attacked every day by angry hordes" (Nudler 2002). The program was only marginally successful and was discontinued two months later.

The corralón officially ended in December 2002, and the events of that year remain part of collective memory as, among other things, a great confiscation of wealth from anyone with money in the bank. In the long year of 2002, it became clear that the diversity of monetary forms in Argentina was characterized by sets of asymmetries not only with regard to the stability of their value (dollars vs. pesos) but with regard to their capacities for circulating or staying put (bank savings vs. cash). Previously subtle distinctions between digital and print—bank deposits and cash—had been brought into stark relief.

Protests against banks would continue until long after the political situation had settled, as small savers continued their struggle to recover their deposits in the courts (see figure 1.4). The signs of the protesters bore slogans

FIGURE 1.4. "Banks, robbers, return our savings!" Uncredited image circulated in a viral message of unknown authorship for the tenth anniversary of the corralito.

still prominent in historial memory: "*Bancos = estafadores, ladrones*"; "*Bancos, chorros, devuelvan los ahorros!*"; and "*Nunca más bancos!*" (Banks = fraudsters, thieves; Banks, robbers, return our savings!; and Banks: Never again!).

COLCHONISMO: SAVING SAVINGS AFTER 2001

By 2004 the economy began to recover, and once again people had to figure out what to do with their savings. The ecology of investments in the years following the crisis privileged a form of savings divorced from the banking sector and its unpredictable flows, known as *colchonismo*. A *colchón* is literally a mattress, and colchonismo translates as something like mattressism: people keep money under the mattress. Colchones are said to be "green" in Argentina, meaning that people save in U.S. dollars. While it's difficult to know exactly how much money or how many people keep money buried in their garden, hidden in their house behind false walls or in their freezer or safe-deposit box, estimates in 2011 placed the total quantity of U.S. currency in Argentina at 145 billion dollars, or about 35 percent of GDP (Sticco 2011). Although Argentines are not alone in using dollars to mitigate local currency instability, this makes them an extreme case. Compared to Brazil, where there were estimated to be 6 dollars per person in the country in 2012, in Argentina the estimate was 2,000 dollars per capita (Zaiat 2012). Argentina shares with the former Soviet Union the distinction of being the largest foreign destinations for U.S. currency in the world: currency sent to these two regions accounts for more than net shipments to all foreign commercial banks between 1995 and 2008 (Judson 2012). If buried money is dead capital, then Argentina is an economic graveyard.

"What do I do with my savings? I buy dollars, I buy dollars, I buy dollars," Juan, an entertainment planner, told me nearly a decade after the crisis of 2001. Business is going well for him now, and one of the challenges he faces is what to do with the money he earns. "I'm terrified of banks. I have a checking account, I put the money I need to cover expenses in there. But the rest of it I save in dollars. Where? In my house. I say to my wife, 'Ana, there's 2,000 dollars here, don't forget. And over here there's 2,000 more,'" he told me. Other people I spoke with engaged in similar practices: Mariela, like several others I spoke with, buys a mix of dollars, gold, and euros and keeps them in a safe-deposit box; Sabrina buys dollars and keeps them in a shoebox in her apartment, hidden behind a ceiling panel; Nadia's father keeps dollars literally buried in the backyard. "Saving in the long-term in Argentine banks is unthinkable," Daniel, a real estate investment expert, told me. "The fact is that the average Argentine with a capacity for savings today disbelieves in any vehicle of investment linked to finance, be it Argentine or foreign."

Colchonismo did not emerge solely as the result of the devaluation of 2001. It has, in popular language, "always" existed. But 2001 did mark a transition from the *bancarización* (the "bankization") of the 1990s, when Argentines were drawn into the banking sector in large numbers by the stability of dollar-peso convertibility. Colchonismo, then, was a revival of old savings repertoires (Guyer 2004) that had largely gone dormant during the bank-centered 1990s. Diego, the manager of his father's small meat-pickling business, told me his own story of the corralito. His family lives in a humble house in Lanús, a suburb of Buenos Aires, and like Juan's, their family business had been growing. They, too, were saving in cash dollars. When I asked Diego about banks, he emphasized to me the contrast between the 1990s and post-crisis Argentina with respect to bank saving: "There are stories like ours that half of Argentina could tell you. Before 2001, there were ten years in which people gained confidence and put money in the banks. And when the economy stalled, all the money from the banks was stolen. The majority of people only recovered a quarter of their money. Do you know what happened to the rest, Nico? I don't know either, but that's what happened. The government said it was these other people, these other guys said it was those other people. But what we all know is that three-quarters of what we had disappeared. And I have that experience saved here, inside me."

In the years after 2001, colchonismo was driven by these kinds of stories told among Argentines about the crisis, stories that revolve around the dynamics of this ecology in which the circulatory asymmetries between savings held in banks versus in the colchón were taken to epic proportions, and the dynamics between the dollar and the peso shifted abruptly out of sync. The stories cut both ways, marking the bare escapes of those who were wise enough to distrust banks and the tragedies of movements among different media of savings that went horribly awry. When Mariela got her money out of the bank, she put her cash dollars into a safe-deposit box. In so doing, she became one of many people about whom I would hear stories who made fabulous gains through their distrust of banks, since after the crisis dollars had a substantially increased buying power in the local economy. She bought her first apartment with the money she got out of the corralito. There were others who were not so lucky. Juan, the entertainment planner, told me about his aunt, a teacher, who had her savings invested in CDs that got caught in the corralito. After the devaluation, she got her devalued pesos out of the bank and immediately went to buy dollars—unfortunately doing so at exactly the wrong time, when the exchange rate was AR$4.20 to the dollar (it would later settle at around AR$3, as I have mentioned). So first, her savings were turned from dollars into devalued pesos, and then she lost again by rushing to buy dollars when they were "overvalued." The timing in her jump from digital bank account balance to cash peso, and then again from peso to dollar, had gone all wrong. But how could she have known the corralito was coming? Or that the dollar would later settle at AR$3 and not where she bought at AR$4.20, or that it wouldn't go to five or even seven pesos, as many analysts were predicting?

The crisis, then, was in part a taking to the extreme of this contrast in materialities between the numbers in people's bank accounts and the paper bills in their mattresses and the reemergence of a contrast between dollars and pesos that had for ten years been more subdued through convertibility. Of the many consequences that would unfold from the crisis and the considerations of Argentina's past that it helped to consolidate, one of the most central was the installment of a profound distrust in anything but the most solid, tangible assets people could acquire. Colchonismo, the saving of cash dollars, was one outcome of that contrast in materialities. Yet in the aftermath of the crisis and the unraveling of the decade-long relationship between dollars and pesos, between bank account and cash, there emerged in the post-2002 investment ecology another contender for the privileged media in which to invest one's savings, an investment that would compete with the dollar in the colchón and would in fact lure many of those dollars out of their mattresses to transfigure the face of Buenos Aires: buried money would find a new vehicle for life in real estate, which Argentines refer to in its full materiality, as ladrillos, or bricks. Bricks came to represent everything that money in banks did not: stability, security, and safety through their concrete materiality.

FROM BANKS TO BRICKS

Real estate prices, like everything else, fell sharply in 2002. But by 2004, the construction sector had recovered, and the boom in construction that began that year continued for nearly a decade in a context of post-crisis economic recovery. Much of this construction, as I've mentioned, was driven by the redirection of savings, old and new, out of bank accounts and colchones and into real estate. For pequeños ahorristas, bricks offered a solid alternative to saving in banks or in cash. Real estate is not an investment like any other; like the other media of savings I have described, bricks' value as a solid investment emerged through their particular situatedness in a historical and material ecology of investments.

The post-crisis emergence of real estate as a solid form of investment both relied upon and reconfigured a longer history of property dynamics in Buenos Aires. When the city's population began to swell in the early twentieth century, most people found housing in rental units. For the popular classes, this included overcrowded conventillos, in which multiple families often lived in one room, while the middle class rented more modern and comfortable apartments in casas de renta. Avenues for homeownership included loteos, the auctioning off of parcels of land in previously undeveloped parts of the city, often payable in installments over a relatively short period of time. But for the majority, including the working class, property ownership was difficult to achieve: although there were some institutions that worked to foment homeownership, like the Comisión Nacional de Casas Baratas (the National Commission of Affordable Houses), their impact on patterns of property ownership was limited (Ballent and Liernur 2014, 286).

The rise of Peronism in the 1940s (see the text box in the introduction) marked a material and symbolic break with these earlier patterns of urban living, carried out through a series of measures explicitly aimed to recuperate the "social functions" of property.[21] Peronist policies surrounding housing and homeownership carried long-term ramifications. In 1943, the military government responded to overcrowding and rising rents through a rent freeze and prohibition on evictions. Perón later extended state oversight of the rental market in accordance with laws passed against profiteering and speculation. In addition to these measures directed toward the rental market, others were directed at making homeownership easier for middle and working classes. The *Ley de Propiedad Horizontal* (the Law of Horizontal Property), passed in 1948, created a legal structure allowing for the ownership of individual apartments (prior to that it was not possible to own property without owning the land it was on, so ownership was limited in those who could own an entire building). Perón also greatly expanded the reach of state institutions like the Comisión Nacional de Casas Baratas and the Banco Hipotecario Nacional (the National Mortgage Bank), on the one hand deepening the state's involvement in housing construction and on the other expanding mortgage credit to middle and working classes on very favorable terms. Together, these measures brought homeownership into reach for many: between 1947 and 1960, homeownership in Buenos Aires rose from 17.6 percent to nearly 46 percent.[22] These years also witnessed the installation of homeownership as a central symbolic feature of middle- and working-class expectations of a decent, good life, through what Rosa Aboy has described as "the Peronist dream of a metropolis of small property owners" (2005, 66).

Perón's overthrow in 1955 resulted in modifications to these programs, but by no means a complete reversal; housing had become firmly installed as a critical issue of state concern. The rent freeze, for example, went through several modifications, but wasn't fully overturned until 1976. State support for mortgage lending was substantially curtailed, however, part of a broader restructuring of the economic and banking system that had been redirected to serve social ends under Peronism (Ballent and Liernur 2014, 291; Yujnovsky 1984). In the place of state-supported mortgages, savings and loan plans were introduced, through which financing was still possible, but only for a more limited segment of the population.[23] Despite reduced state support for mortgage lending and often tumultuous economic contexts, however, the construction and sale of *propiedad horizontal* continued to expand in the 1960s and '70s, and homeownership rates in Buenos Aires continued to rise, peaking in 1980 at 68 percent, where they remained more or less stable until 2001.

Seen from up close, this history was less smooth, and stories about it are infused with drama as savings, credit, and home purchases were woven through shifting political and economic events, including inflation. Some stories involved fortuitous acts of timing, the near-perfect alignment of micro- and macroeconomic stars. The father of Adolfo, a retiree I interviewed in 2009, for example, had gotten a mortgage in the early 1950s under one of Perón's plans. Adolfo took the old document out of a plastic sleeve in the cafe where we were meeting and leaned across the table to read it with me: "54,500 pesos moneda nacional, at 5 % for thirty years. So more or less 360 pesos moneda nacional per month."[24] Adolfo, who was in his twenties at the time, had been skeptical; he couldn't wrap his head around the fact that over the next thirty years the family would end up paying nearly 120,000 pesos in interest and principal, almost double the value of the house. But things didn't turn out exactly that way. With the passage of time, the country's growing problem with inflation, the same inflation that ate away at the family's wages, also ate away at their mortgage payments. While wages typically lag behind price increases, especially for workers like Adolfo and his family, they do get adjusted. But their mortgage was on fixed terms, and over time the payments became more and more insignificant. By the time they paid off the mortgage, their monthly payments couldn't buy a pack of cigarettes. Adolfo's luck didn't end there; he managed the same feat two decades later, getting a fixed-rate mortgage in the early 1970s (when they were more difficult to come by), which was also "eaten" by inflation: "At the beginning, making those payments was difficult, but just a year later it wasn't so hard, and after three years, we were paying practically nothing!" he told me.

Not everyone had Adolfo's luck, and dramatic stories of loss exist alongside stories like his. For example, in 1980, the central bank issued a now-infamous Circular 1050, which introduced loans indexed to market interest rates to prevent inflation from eating away at them; when the interest rate soared beyond both inflation and wages due to an unanticipated combination of macroeconomic events, however, many people were unable to pay their mortgages. To make matters worse, mortgage debts also outpaced the growth of property values, leaving many buyers with debts greater than the value of their homes (a situation that entered the U.S. economic lexicon in the late 2000s as an "underwater" mortgage).

The often trying circumstances and heroic efforts involved in securing real estate are vividly portrayed in the novel *A History of Money* (2015), by the Argentine writer Alan Pauls. One of the episodes in the book revolves around the main character's pursuit of an apartment, weaving it through the broader political and economic events of the late 1970s and early 1980s. After inheriting 10,000 dollars from a wealthy relative, he is convinced to hand the money over to his father, a habitual gambler who nevertheless always manages to stay one step ahead and who has promised him a healthy return on his investment. His father puts the money into a series of black-market investments, and after nearly losing it all, squeezes his network of underworld connections until he recuperates the money and the return on his investments, eventually returning nearly 30,000 dollars to his son. His son in turn uses the money to buy a ramshackle apartment, which he sets out to refurbish. But just as the work is beginning, a bout of severe inflation sets in. He changes his money from dollars to pesos every week on the day he pays the laborers, always changing extra because he knows the price of the work could go up before he gets home. Buying the materials also requires tremendous effort, as prices trip upward from hour to hour. "It's crazy," the narrator relates. "Some days he has to go to five separate building supply stores—each a long way from the last and usually in remote parts of the city, so that he wastes hours traveling between them—before ending up not at the best one, nor at the one that's been recommended to him, nor even at the cheapest one, but simply at one that can give him a price—a price that he is able to pay, which, by this stage, with the cost of living rising by 150 percent every month, means a price that's unacceptable within reason— and where they haven't followed the example of most building supply stores and decided to hoard all their goods and wait for prices to go up again" (Pauls 2015, 88). After an agonizing year of working the connections among dollars, pesos, labor, and materials, he finally manages to get the apartment finished just as his money runs out. It's not what he imagined, however: the neighbors are loud, the textile factory next door makes the walls vibrate, there are problems with the pipes, and the ceiling caves in during an episode of heavy rain. His marriage falls apart, and they sell the apartment at a steep loss.

While the intense affective and organizational labor required to transform cash into bricks depicted in *A History of Money* was widely shared, the fact that the main character lost money on the apartment was a fairly exceptional event, deployed in the novel to drive home his tragic economic luck. For most people, and throughout most of these decades, while the value of money slipped in fitful bursts of inflation and devaluation and bank lending came and went, real estate pricing remained relatively stable, at least keeping pace with inflation.[25] This stability was made possible in part because one's home is the last thing people want to sell in contexts of economic instability. Housing's stability as an economic object was thus bolstered by its centrality to a stable life in other senses: the stability of the home, both as a symbolic and material good for the reproduction of the family and a good working- and middle-class life. Herculean efforts involving the artful and fortuitous navigations of currencies, inflation, bank lending, and political regimes were central to achieving homeownership, and once it was achieved people were highly reluctant to let it go. But throughout most of this history, bricks' stability as economic objects was secondary to these other forms of stability.

....

In the years after the crisis, bricks' economic stability became central to the investment strategies of pequeños ahorristas. It's difficult to quantify how many people began buying real estate as an investment separate from the place in which they live, since there are no statistics regarding which properties are bought as investments and which are bought as homes to live in.[26] Nevertheless, several data points support the broad consensus among professionals that the post-crisis real estate market was driven by small investors. The 2010 census revealed that homeownership rates in Buenos Aires, historically rising since 1947 (with the exception of a small dip in 1991), had fallen from 67.1 percent in 2001 to 57.4 percent in 2010, while the proportion of renters had risen from 22.2 percent to 29.1 percent—numbers that have been taken to represent a concentration of property ownership in fewer hands (Giambartolomei 2015). Real estate prices also moved out of step with wages: between 1976 and 2001, a sixty-square-meter apartment cost a young white-collar worker on average 48 months of salary; between 2001 and 2016, the average was 75 months of salary (Manzoni 2016). That prices increased faster than wages indicates that substantial prior savings were driving the real estate market.

But to say that real estate's place as an economic investment has become more central after the crisis is not to say that it is an investment like any other. Real estate's value as an economic investment in Argentina is particular and retains its focus on stability rather than, for example, on the search for profit. In fact, there is ongoing debate among professionals about whether investment in real estate is the most profitable investment decision people could make. There are many indications that it is not: rental returns have been historically low in the decade after the crisis because of a combination of the high price of property and the fact that rents have not risen at the same rate as the cost of other goods (Manzoni 2016). This has led some analysts to conclude that it would be better to invest in U.S. Treasury bonds (also considered extremely stable), despite their historically low returns, than to invest in real estate.[27] But this kind of debate about which investment gives the highest return was of marginal concern for the people I spoke with about buying apartments in the post-crisis years. While property owners would of course prefer that the value of an apartment go up, what they typically seek are long-term investments that, even if they were to fall in value, would not disappear the way the value of their money might, either through devaluation or events like the crisis of 2001.

Thus while money and finance have taken on an ephemeral quality through years of inflation and economic crises, the stability of bricks stands out as a contrast. Their brute presence and physical materiality play an important role in this stability: "It's about the physical presence of the thing," Daniel, the real estate market analyst, told me. "They can see it, they can walk through it. *They know it's there.*" Juan (the entertainment planner), like Mariela, Diego (the meat pickler), and nearly everyone else I spoke to with a capacity for saving, was weighing the possibility of buying an apartment. Juan reinforced Daniel's point, telling me about his brother, who drove past the apartment he had bought several times a week to check on the progress of construction: "A house, maybe sometimes it's going to be worth more, maybe sometimes it's going to be worth less, but *it's yours,*" he told me. So even when people stand to make next to nothing renting out an apartment, apartments sell well, Daniel continued, because they are considered the best refuge for money available: "The average Argentine understands a fixed-term deposit in Citibank—whether it's the Argentine Citibank or a Citibank in the exterior—as more risky than buying an apartment. Buying an apartment, whether the profitability is a lot or a little, whatever—the apartment is still there."

There is nothing transhistorically solid about bricks, however. Rather, their solidity was due to their specific place in post-crisis ecologies of investment. One critical relational characteristic of bricks post-crisis was their disentanglement from banks. In the wake of the crisis, mortgage financing, which had been relatively available during the 1990s era of convertibility, had dried up for nearly everyone, and nearly all home purchases during the following decade were conducted in cash.[28] Mid-size developers, who typically depend on bank financing, went bust. In the years that followed, small entrepreneurial architecture studios began gathering together contacts who had savings they wanted to invest. They bought property, sold unbuilt apartments to other small investors, and then used their down payments to fund construction. In this way, the disappearance of bank financing that might have spelled doom for an industry instead became one of its primary selling points: unlike their U.S. counterparts, which were integrated into the global financial system's mortgage-backed securities and collateralized debt obligations (and thus not solid at all for many U.S. homeowners in the subprime

FIGURE 1.5. "Bricks, the safe refuge." 2009. Photo by author.

mortgage crisis), bricks in Argentina had become disentangled from banks, which was exactly what small savers were looking for.

Bricks' special place in the post-crisis ecology of investments—as disentangled from banks and therefore more stable—was both exploited and reinforced by developers in the years following the crisis. On a visit to Rosario, Argentina's third-largest city, I saw buildings in construction bedecked with enormous banners evoking the place of ladrillos in Argentine investment ecologies (see figure 1.5). Echoed on the web page was a cartoon (see figure 1.6). The image, featuring three little pigs huddled comfortably next to a fire, bore the caption "While the crisis blows outside, our investment in ladrillos is a safe refuge." Variations on this theme have become common in the phraseology associated with real estate in contemporary Argentina and are meant to amp up the contrast with banks: "*El ladrillo nunca traiciona*" (Bricks never betray you), "*El que apuesta al ladrillo no pierde*" (He who bets on bricks never loses), and "*El ladrillo no defrauda*" (The brick does not defraud). Hid-

FIGURE 1.6. "While the crisis blows outside, our investment in bricks is a safe refuge." refugiomasseguro.com.ar.

den within these catchphrases are subtle practices of memory from prior economic eras: "el que apuesta al ladrillo no pierde" is an inversion of a notorious statement by Lorenzo Sigaut, economic minister of the military government in 1981, who said that "he who bets on dollars will lose," right before a devaluation in which those who had bet on the dollar would win phenomenally. Not defrauding, not losing, not betraying, a safe refuge: bricks' economic value was not based on profit, but on the avoidance of catastrophic loss in the context of a long history of economic life defined by such loss, both through deeper histories of inflation and the recent events of the crisis.

It was not just their disentanglement from banks that made bricks good investments, but also their special entanglement with dollars. Ladrillos have held this peculiar place in Argentine investment ecologies since 1977, when, in the face of economic instability brought about by the early liberalization of the economy under the dictatorship-era economic policies of Martínez de Hoz, the price of real estate began to be denominated in dollars, especially in major cities like Buenos Aires. Unlike some marginal economies in which dollars circulate alongside national currencies, in Argentina dollars have never been used for everyday transactions, but are reserved for special uses. Aside from travel, they are exclusively used for savings and real estate.[29] This special relationship serves to shelter real estate from the fluctuations of the national currency. Equally important, the affiliation between bricks and dollars means that the movement from dollar to ladrillo becomes an easily identifiable form of conveyance from one medium to the other. Bricks are, like dollars, a medium of economic stability par excellence. And, like dollars, they have a special purpose as savings, holding value in a way that is more like the dollar and less like the peso. This conveyance of value is prominent in the image production surrounding real estate in news media, in which dollars stand alongside, stand in for, and become one with bricks (see figures 1.7, 1.8, and 1.9). This relationship between ladrillos and dollars is also elaborately staged in the purchase of a property. When Juan's brother bought his apartment, he and his brothers went to the bank, took 60,000 dollars in cash out of his safe-deposit box, strapped it to their bodies, and rode the subway across town to the seller's bank. There, they sat in a reserved room for hours, each party recording the serial numbers of every bill in the event that any should turn out to be counterfeit. The materiality of cash dollars is translated into bricks through these tensely embodied transferences.

The historical emergence of this place of bricks as that which is separate from banks and in tight relationship with dollars illustrates some of the ways that the ecological sensibilities Argentines have developed for tracing connection between investments can have impacts on economic life. Narratives about currency and banks are not separate from the ecology but are integral to its formation, producing not just knowledge about but also new ways of living in ecologies of investment. As masses of small savers bought apartments in the years following the crisis, the dip in real estate prices in the immediate aftermath of the crisis would rapidly turn around, making real estate and construction industries the first sectors to regain their footing. Although monetary value was not the main thing small savers were looking for in real estate, their collective conviction that bricks were good investments made their value increase, drawing money out from under mattresses to transform the streets of the city. In so doing, Argentines helped to make their knowledge about bricks into a reality. Stories about the economic past—and the sensibilities about connection that they produced in Argentine considerations of the ecology of investment—literally made good investments.[30]

The place of bricks in Argentine ecologies of investment, then, has a lot to do with their material solidity and what that means for their capacity to stay put (in contrast with money in banks, frequently devalued or whisked away by powerful international actors). But their value is not about their materiality alone. Rather, it is about the relations that those bricks have with other actors in the ecology of investments and how those relations get read and remade by Argentines in light of their economic pasts. It is not bricks in themselves that are valued, but bricks situated in an ecology of relatedness. Their insulation from banks, alongside their historical relation with dollars, made them special and even more solid than their materiality alone ever could.

(*clockwise from top*)
FIGURE 1.7. The conveyance of value from dollars to bricks. Image from a news report on real estate. 2011. elinmobiliario.com.
FIGURE 1.8. Bricks hold value in a way that is more like the dollar and less like the peso. Image from a news report on real estate. *La Nación*, 2007.
FIGURE 1.9. The dollar-ladrillo. Image from a report on the dollar's value in real estate. 2013. dolarhoy.net.

CONCLUSION: STORIES MAKE GOOD INVESTMENTS

During the past several decades, Argentine small savers have learned to navigate a complex investment ecology, cobbling together a diverse set of investments to try to save their savings. Their relationships with national currencies are permeated by inflation and the diverse monetary forms that emerged to deal with it. In the 1990s, the pegging of the peso to the dollar formally institutionalized convertibility and suspended the need for more complex relational maneuvers. But the peso's rigid relation to the dollar, alongside other neoliberal reforms, brought new problems to the national economy, and when convertibility began to fall apart a diversity of investments sprang back to the foreground in the form of quasi-monedas. The crisis added another layer of experience to this ecology of investments, drawing out the contrast between digital and print media, between bank account balances and cash. In the wake of the crisis, dollars in colchones and bricks in buildings were drawn together on emergent historical terrains.

During this time, Argentines have continued to invest in their history, telling stories, reading newspaper retrospectives, writing memoirs, and telling jokes about money. They turn over past events, analyzing steps mistaken, dispossessions perpetrated, or gains attained through luck and cunning. In the process, they themselves have been reconfigured, developing sharply tuned sensibilities about relatedness and connection. "Every Argentine is an economist," said Diego the meat-pickler, grinning as he waxed theoretical to me about Argentine economic history. He meant it as a joke, a self-effacing jab at what he saw as a peculiarly Argentine arrogance about their own economic expertise. But he was also serious, articulating the extent to which knowledge about economic pasts are objects of concern for so many Argentines. Turning over the past guides their investments in the present and helps to construct possible futures as knowledge becomes bound up with materialities to reconstitute ecologies of investment in new ways.

Argentines are acutely attuned to the divergent capacities and possibilities offered by distinct media of investment.[31] While global investment banks might hype up a series of seamless, sublimated flows in which all that is solid has melted into air, there are also depositions or desublimations (Maurer 2000) in which the atmospheres of global investment banks become less gaseous. Recall the elaborate choreography of materialities surrounding the frigate *Libertad*, impounded in Ghana at the behest of a Wall Street investment fund in retribution for disputes surrounding bond payments, suggesting that investment banks might share with Argentines an ecological sensibility of a world full of possible and opportunistic connection. If all that is solid has not quite melted into air, then thinking ecologically about investments allows Argentines to follow the troubled connections not just between dollars and dollars, or dollars and pesos, but between frigates, bricks, and other materialities that are caught up in and therefore part of these ecologies. If Argentines are right in maintaining that the stories we tell about the economy matter in the construction of possible futures, an ecological approach might help to tell other stories and open up new ways of imagining possible futures.

Taking the ecology of investments seriously means slowing down before attributing to investments (even currencies) a status as stable arbiter of value that circulates through a geography that is everywhere the same. Instead of stable entities that circulate through a common world, investments remake connections, making worlds and being remade as they go. The dollar in the United States both is and is not the same dollar that appears in Argentina, because the ecology in which it exists, and that constitutes it, is not the same. Dollars, bricks, and other investments are partially connected (Strathern 2004) to multiple worlds, and the specificity of their articulations makes all the difference in helping us slow down before calling them equivalent. One dollar is only equivalent to another in very defined circumstances with the right infrastructures—infrastructures that always bear the possibility of breaking down, a fact well known by Argentines and others in parts of the world where people have felt the earth move beneath their economic feet with a particular degree of frequency.

In such contexts of frequently shifting economic terrains, Argentines have learned to pay close attention to the ecology of investments with which their futures are intertwined. They look to dangerous and promising new connections and ponder past events to ask the questions that might help them build their emergent futures. Clara Han (2011) has argued that credit is a central feature of constructing possible futures in contemporary Chile, as it allows for a time of waiting in which possible (and more hopeful) futures may come to fruition for economically marginalized populations. Hirokazu Miyazaki (2013) has described the ways that Japanese traders tell stories about dreams (*yume*) as a way to transmit techniques and sensibilities about finance across generations. My own story about Argentine histories of turbulent economic life is part of this broader concern with possible futures and how they are dealt with in the present. In Argentina there is a strong sense that economic time is cyclical, that the future always holds an impending crisis (Visacovsky 2010). Unlike cases in which people have developed elaborately rationalized or highly calculative ethos surrounding the future, the people I spoke with in Argentina remained studiously agnostic about the particular contours of what a future crisis might be like. There is nothing eternal about ecologies of investment; if anything, it is an awareness of volatility and the possibility of change that defines the ecological sensibilities I have described.

Living in the ecology of investment is the art of not knowing, done well— of not knowing what connections might make themselves relevant, of which configurations and conversions will become possible, of what their dangers and promises will be. History serves as a guide, but not one that brightens a clear path into the future. It is, rather, a sustained openness to the possibility of relations yet to be made, not teaching what the future will be, but about the art of asking questions well. Stories are the investments that help Argentines ask those questions well. They are stories that make good investments.

In the practices of pequeños ahorristas, dreams of economically viable futures are brought into relationship with tumultuous pasts through concrete practices of storytelling and everyday monetary conversions—conversions that also build dreams through literal concrete, in the buildings in which peque-ños ahorristas continue to invest. As I discussed in the introduction, however, buildings are not only economic objects, and their multiple existences are par-tially connected to one another. Real estate investment patterns in the years following the crisis led to important changes in the built environment. In addi-tion to extending the construction of apartment buildings to areas of the city historically dominated by low-rise buildings, the kinds of units built and pat-terns of urban living also changed. The vast majority of new units are studios and one-bedrooms (nearly 80 percent in 2011, up from 40 percent ten years earlier), a fact that responds to the high price of real estate and pequeños ahor-ristas' restricted capacity for investment (few can afford two- or three-bedroom investment properties) (Castro 2012). These units are also easier to rent out to the growing number of single young professionals who can't afford to buy an apartment without credit, but are eager to begin living on their own. But this market does little for families looking for places to live and offers even fewer options to the working classes, let alone the very poor. Ecologies of investment thus made incursions into other ecologies and into worlds of practice that hold dear other kinds of value in the built environment. The later chapters in this book focus on the tensions generated through buildings' prominent place as economic objects in the decade after the crisis. But first, in chapter 2, I turn to other kinds of stories told about money, real estate, and Argentine history from within the world of professional real estate market analysts (some of whom, like Daniel, have already begun to appear in this chapter). Their stories about real estate interweave with the popular historical narratives that were the focus of this chapter and are developed largely through a set of practices grounded in the quantified interpretive space of charts and graphs.

CHAPTER 2

A Market in Square Meters

Numbers and Narrative in Real Estate Market Analysis

Two different images of buildings offer productive touchstones for thinking about the work of real estate market analysts and the ways buildings are materialized and worked on in their practice. The first is a grid from a spreadsheet. Ten columns extend down the sheet, naming different qualities of an apartment, including its location, size, construction quality, and illumination. Two more columns at the end list the price of the apartment and its price per square meter. The rows extend across the sheet, each of which is assigned to a different apartment. For each apartment, the qualities listed in the columns are scored on a scale from one to ten. Good illumination gets a seven, poor location a three. The last two columns, price and price per square meter, are all filled in except for one: the apartment being appraised. After scoring each apartment for all the variables, their prices can be weighted based on the scores to arrive at an average price per square meter for all the apartments that accounts for quality: knowing that an apartment with an average score of 5 is worth US$900 per square meter and one with an average score of 7 is worth US$1,000 per square meter allows for one approximation of the price of an apartment with an average score of 6.

The second image is a graph. The horizontal x-axis indicates each of the eight years since 2001, and the vertical y-axis shows numbers from zero to 500. Four lines in different colors extend across the graph. One shows the value of used apartments in Buenos Aires' Northern Corridor. The others show the Argentine Consumer Price Index, the value of the U.S. dollar relative to the Argentine peso, and a measure to account for average salary levels. All the lines coincide in 2001 at 100, taken as the base against which changes can be graphed over the following several years. For the rest of the years, the analyst can track the relative change in the price of apartments alongside these other economic factors.

These two images capture different aspects of the work done by real estate market professionals, including brokers, market analysts, and consultants (who typically work for developers or large investors). The spreadsheet focuses on the work of appraisal, a process through which individual buildings or apartments are translated into terms that allow for their comparison with others and that enable their existence as market goods that can be exchanged. If the chart's work is to bring an apartment into existence as an exchangeable good in a market economy, the graph is part of analysts' efforts to understand that market as it exists in Buenos Aires (or a certain part of it) at a particular moment in time. The graph is part of a set of practices that allow analysts to postulate the market's characteristics with regard to who is buying and where the money is coming from and to suggest what this might have to say about the future.

Thinking about buildings' existence in these charts and graphs, it's possible to imagine that their numbers, laid out in orderly grids and charts, collapse messier forms of difference and specificity that escape them: that they transform a rich urban world into the flat language of number. Quantification, particularly when involved in economic valuation, is often understood as a reductive act.[1] In part, this is true: it is an empirical fact that no piece of real estate is the same as any other. How to account for a certain breeze, a view to a beloved tree, a dear neighbor, or the way the afternoon sun shines through a window in spring to warm one's body as they read? There is something that rightly seems flat about the spreadsheet and the graph and the kinds of value they ascribe to a built environment that is worth so much more than money. Paying attention to forms of value that exist beyond the monetary or economic is an important project and one that this book as a whole takes on, especially in the chapters that follow this one.

My approach in this chapter is different than one that sees numbers as only flattening, however. Instead, I take a cue from the social theorist Gabriel Tarde, who focuses on the ways that quantifying complex, lived realities not only reduces the world to numbers, but also introduces something new into the world. Rather than taking away from reality, numbers are added to it, helping to forge new realities.[2] Charts and graphs, in this sense, can be thought of as yet another set of realities in which buildings exist, another set of concrete manifestations through which they take form in the world.[3] Charts and graphs are devices that have to be assembled and that can be followed through the world as they do work within it. In this sense, they function both as the products of processes of abstraction *and* as material signs circulating alongside other signs.[4] While the world of money and number can function to reduce complexities to their own terms, it is important to pay attention to how and with what effects they do so.[5] While numbers may be abstractions of things, their existence is not abstract; instead, they emerge from particular ecologies of practice and circulate through others.[6]

Seeing numbers as material things is a way to help understand how they work as technologies of connection and translation—what Helen Verran, in her study of Western and Yoruban number systems, has called "doing relations" with numbers (2001) or has elsewhere described as number's work as a "generative device" (2012). Like Tarde, Verran does not find in numbers abstract mental representations of the material world. Rather, she shows how numbers are situated in dynamic contexts, the products of routinized gestures and utterances through which they are deployed in daily practice. Numbers are thus the products of relations at the same time that they enable the production of new relational connections, making numbers themselves emergent rather than stable and productive rather than reductive.

Through what tools do market analysts engage buildings, and what does their work accomplish? I approach this question by describing two key practices used by real estate analysts in their work, embodied in the chart and graph I described earlier. Numbers play important, if distinct roles in each of these practices. The first practice is the appraisal of apartments, in which numbers, in the form of prices, are the end result of a process that enables unique pieces of real estate to be understood in relation to one another—to circulate with other apartments as goods in a market. In the second practice, the analysis of historical data, numbers aren't the outcome but the starting point of analysis. Rather than answering questions, here numbers pose them: why were the numbers what they were? While appraisal uses number to allow apartments to circulate in the real estate market through the comparative power of quantification, historical analysis allows the real estate market to be situated in relation to other parts of the economy and within the broader political and economic history of Argentina so that analysts can think through the present and forecast potential futures. Juxtaposing these two stories of quantification highlights the relationality of numbers within broader systems of their production and legibility.

These practices of market analysis are partially connected to others from which they also diverge. On the one hand are global forms of knowledge about markets that, far from being seamlessly incorporable into Argentina, require a substantial amount of work if they are to be applied to turbulent contexts like the post-crisis real estate market. The charts and graphs market professionals relied upon offered footholds into understanding the market, but also had to be substantially translated to do any work in an environment in which so many things were shifting so quickly. Analysts' practices also interface with other forms of narrative practice about the real estate market in Buenos Aires. The reader may recall Daniel, the market analyst I introduced in chapter 1, who described Argentines' reticence to save in banks and the importance of their investments for the real estate market. Daniel and others like him rely on popular narratives like those in chapter 1 to understand the market better, but they also contribute to them through their own narratives, which get taken up and retold in the popular press. While they engage the market differently from one another, both share an interest in the ecology of investments in which real estate lives: the ways that buildings circulate asymmetrically with other mediums of investment. Like the stories I examined in chapter 1, the charts and graphs of analysts like Daniel are technologies that help make the real estate market work—on the one hand by making buildings into market goods that can be bought and sold through their comparability and on the other by situating that market in particular economic and historical contexts.

MAKING BUILDINGS COMPARABLE: THE ART OF APPRAISAL

It was late June 2008 when I entered the Centro Argentino de Ingenieros for a conference sponsored by *Reporte Inmobiliario*, or Real Estate Report, one of the principal real estate industry publications in Argentina. *Reporte Inmobiliario* produced and published its own statistical data about the real estate market, but also functioned as an important nodal point for a range of industry professionals to process and exchange information and to share their opinions about developments in the market. These professionals—including real estate brokers, investment advisors, and developers—worked to understand the present and how that present articulates with the past in order to forecast possible futures.

Clad in business attire, the 150 people who filed into the lecture hall bore the markings of traditional middle-aged professionals who were more classical than chic; the audiences were predominantly male, though sometimes as many as a third were women. This event (and others like it) were open to the public for a fee, but the mainstay of audiences drew from within the real estate industry, including other consultants and smaller, neighborhood real estate brokers. Only occasionally did it seem that attendees knew one another: at coffee breaks, there were more people talking on their cell phones than there were conversations between colleagues who knew one another well. These practitioners were brought together less by interpersonal connection than by the market—a market that they simultaneously studied and helped to construct through their shared engagements with buildings.

This particular conference was a seminar in which participants would discuss different approaches to real estate appraisal: the art of translating an apartment or building into price. Appraisal is not a straightforward task. Imagine two apartments. One is fifty years old, the other twenty-five; one is three blocks from good public transit lines, the other seven; one is on the second floor, one on the fifth; one is 120 square meters, the other 160; one has northern exposures, the other western; one is on a bustling central avenue, the other in a quiet neighborhood; one is in a more marginal area, the other historically wealthy. To what extent are these two apartments comparable in any way, such that one could say that one is worth this much more than the other? Putting a price on an apartment is a complex act of assessment about which experts can often disagree.

The seminar that day was led by a staff member at *Reporte Inmobiliario* who talked through a slideshow presentation that outlined three formal techniques to estimate the value of an apartment. The one that received the most attention was called the "comparative method with direct referents." This method, the presenter explained, arrives at the price of a property by relating it to other apartments that had recently been sold, using their known price as a means of estimating the price of the apartment in question. The method is based on the economic principle of substitution, which states that the value of a piece of real estate is equivalent to that of another piece of real estate with similar characteristics to the property in question. The challenge in applying this principle is the question of similarity: even apartments with identical floor plans in the same building may differ in whether they are on an upper floor or a lower one, whether they face the street or not, or the kinds of views and sunlight each of them has. Because no two apartments are exactly alike, the work of appraisal under the comparative method is more one of *making* two indistinct goods comparable than it is a question of *discovering* comparable features.

How can two fundamentally different things be made comparable? The chart that I described briefly at the beginning of the chapter is a critical tool in allowing comparison to happen. The first step is to select several properties that are similar in gross terms to that of the property in question. Generally, this

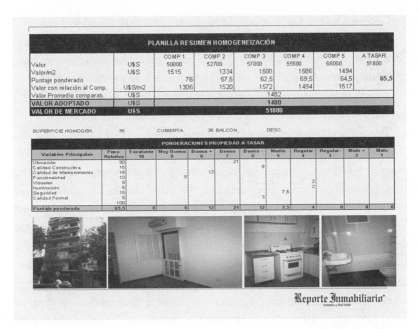

FIGURE 2.1. Weighted scores are given to various comparable apartments in order to homogenize their differences. Their weighted prices are the value in relation to the comparable apartment (*valor con relación al comparable*), and the average of those is the basis for calculating a standard price per square meter used to appraise the property in question. *Reporte Inmobiliario*.

means finding other apartments in the same neighborhood, size class (studio, one bedroom, etc.), and age class (new or used) that are either on the market now or (preferably) have been sold recently, so that their price is known. Once the appraiser settles upon a few properties with grossly similar attributes, they then engage in a more finely tuned process that was referred to in the seminar as the "homogenization of differences." Because none of the apartments selected as comparisons are exactly the same as the one being appraised, weighted lists of attributes are used in order to make price adjustments relative to the comparison properties based on variables such as location, age, and construction quality (see figure 2.1). For example, if one of the apartments used as a basis for appraisal is ten years older than the one being appraised, adjustments must be made to "homogenize" that difference in age, to account for the fact that the apartment being appraised should be worth more because it's newer.

The bottom chart in figure 2.1 shows how this kind of weighting was laid out in the example used that day in the seminar. The chart lays out a series of variables that describe different qualities of an apartment: its location, con-structive quality, maintenance quality, functionality, views, illumination, se-curity, and formal quality. Appraisers were instructed to weight the list based on the importance of each variable for the specific property in question, dis-tributing one hundred points across the variables. For instance, if the location was highly desirable (or undesirable) it could be weighted more, since con-siderations of light or formal quality might be considered less important than the quality of the location. In this case, location was given a weight of thirty points, while formal quality was less important, worth only a possible five points. Once the weights of different variables are established, the apartment can be ranked according to each of the variables, on a scale from one to ten. In the case in question, the location of the apartment being appraised is ranked "Good: 7" and thus earns the apartment twenty-one points out of a possible thirty. In the end, this apartment earns an overall score of 65.5. Notice here that the quantified chart nevertheless relies on the good judgment of the ap-praiser, who has to decide if the variables are good ones (maybe there should be others?), how much weight each should bear, and what the apartment's score in each category should be. The chart is a way of finely focusing the ap-praiser's attention and quantifying their judgment.

This process is then repeated for the apartments used as comparisons, ar-riving at a score for each of them. At the end of this process, the appraiser has five apartments scored with the same relative weights as the apartment being appraised. In the chart at the top of figure 2.1, the comparable properties are listed with their price and their price per square meter. That price per square meter is then weighted according to the score the appraiser has calculated for based on the variables in question. In the first example in the left column la-beled "COMP1," the apartment sold for US$50,000 and was thirty-three square meters (not shown), giving a price per square meter of US$1,515. This number is then weighted according to its score. Since the appraiser scored the apartment at 76, its value relative to the property in question is US$1,306 per square meter. This allows the appraiser to recognize first that COMP1 is nicer than the apart-ment in question (76 vs. 65.5 points), and then to weight the price accordingly: if COMP1 were to possess the qualities of the property being appraised, it would have sold for US$1,306 per square meter. This is the process through which the price is homogenized—made comparable across particular apartments.

The homogenized prices of the comparable apartments are then averaged to produce an average price per square meter—an average price that is specifi-cally attuned to the qualities of the property being appraised. In this example, the average of the five comparable properties, once passed through this process of homogenization, is US$1,480 per square meter. Multiplying that figure by the number of square meters in the apartment being appraised (thirty-five) thus provides one estimate of its value. The comparability between two apartments that is constructed, then, is the result of many micro-comparisons, and the final appraisal is the result of the aggregation of a series of other appraisals.

Two other methods of appraisal were described in the seminar. Each seeks to determine price through still other hypothetical situations (aside from the hypothetical situation set up in the comparative method, in which this apartment is equivalent to another apartment). One is called the "replacement cost" method, which appraises a building by asking how much it would cost if one were to build the same building again. This is done by adding the cost of a similar lot to the cost of construction. The cost of the lot is arrived at through the same process I described earlier, by working with comparables. Construction costs are complex to determine, requiring up-to-date information about labor and materials costs that can be especially difficult in a country like Argentina, where the rapid pace of economic change can cause abrupt shifts in the exchange rate that have strong impacts on import prices. In Buenos Aires, indices of the cost of construction for a typical square meter are published weekly in architectural and real estate supplements of mass-circulating newspapers to make cost projection easier. Nevertheless, the replacement cost method is not seen to give results that are as accurate as the comparative method, because the number of variables (fluctuating prices of a vast number of materials and labor) makes calculation difficult. It is therefore typically used only in unusual circumstances, such as the appraisal of a partially completed project or when, for whatever reason, there are insufficient comparable apartments. It could also be used alongside the other methods in order to provide a comparison for their comparisons.

The last method explained in the seminar on that day was based not on hypothetical construction (what would it cost to build the same building again?), but on hypothetical futures, and is called the "income capitalization model." It defines the current value of a piece of real estate as the sum of future rental income that the property can generate, taking into account capital outlays and inflation as well as rental income over an extended period of time. With a good estimate of net monthly rent over ten years and the costs one might have to lay out during that time, one can back-calculate what a reasonable price to pay for that apartment would be today. This is a basic economic method that can be difficult to apply to real estate, in which the life of a building is normally decades long and would require projecting costs and income over that lifetime—a challenge compounded in markets like Argentina's, where the future rental income is likely to be unstable. Like the replacement cost method, then, appraisers only utilize this method alongside the others or when the comparative method is for some reason impracticable. In its most general sense, then, appraisal is concerned with taking a piece of real estate and translating it into a number: the price of the apartment. This is perhaps the most classic example of the work that numbers can do in market situations—namely, making comparable otherwise unique goods through the quantification of their diverse attributes.[7]

In the practices of real estate market analysts, however, numbers only mitigate such differences temporarily. The work of numbers does not subdue specificity through comparison, but instead helps practitioners attend to specificities in the products they sell. The act of ranking and quantifying age between one apartment and another "comparable" one does not erase those differences. Instead, the differences are suspended so that the comparison can be made, but with the ultimate goal of highlighting the unique characteristics of a particular property. Commensurability, then, can be seen here in a somewhat different light. Here, number and measurement make possible new legibilities about specificity. In the process of appraisal, different apartments are brought into relation with one another as well as with imaginary constructions and imagined futures. Numbers are used as a means through which these relations of similarity and difference are enacted. Qualities specific to each apartment are folded into numbers, allowing apartments to move within broader networks of comparison, to circulate with other apartments in the market and be read alongside them, so that their value can be determined. Commensuration, then, does not reduce or ignore difference, but allows apartments to move within networks of comparison, to intermingle with other apartments in the market and be read alongside them, so that their value can be determined. The trouble of comparison—the difficulty of treating apartments as similar when they are not—paradoxically generates a kind of fine-tuned attention to difference.

CONVINCING MEASURES: THE VALUE OF
FORMALIZED KNOWLEDGE

The seminar on appraisal that day had a strange end, one that gestured toward other ways of knowing the market in real estate and the tensions between these forms of knowledge and the more formalized methodologies that were taught in the seminar. After working through a practical case of appraisal, the presenter arrived at a final price for an apartment. He asked the audience what they thought, and they reacted strongly and in unison: "It's too low!" They knew, despite the methodological nature and logic of the calculus, what the correct price should be.

Real estate analysis, in its quotidian work and day-to-day tasks, is not exclusively conducted by the kind of formalized methodology laid out in the presentation. This disagreement over price indicates the endurance of more informal ways of knowing and doing the work of measurement in the market, which Julia Elyachar (2012), following Karl Polanyi, has termed *tacit knowledge*. These forms of knowledge show little evidence of faltering in the face of more formalized methodologies.[8] The presenter himself knew this, mentioning at one point to the participants that "we of course don't always do these calculations on paper, but rather do them unconsciously. I have seen people who are able to walk into an apartment and give a price—and that price is not necessarily less accurate than we might arrive at with these methods." Indeed, as with this case, sometimes the prices arrived at through less formal means may be more accurate than those arrived at through methodological calculi. This exercise in appraisal, then, had turned into one that demonstrated the importance of a less formalized grasp on the market in the face of standardized methodologies.

This disagreement draws attention to some broader shifts in expertise and knowledge about the real estate market that had only recently begun to install themselves in Buenos Aires through the work of organizations like *Reporte Inmobiliario*. Informants referred to it as a process of professionalization in which more informal types of knowledge about pricing began to exist alongside knowledge work that was more focused on statistical analyses, charts, graphs, and economic models. José Rozados, one of the founders of *Reporte Inmobiliario*, explained to me that in the 1980s and most of the 1990s, the kinds of conferences *Reporte Inmobiliario* hosted did not exist. Some more formalized conversations may have happened in the closed, guild-type settings of different business and professional boards in the sector, but real estate was not typically discussed in the terms of knowledge drawn from the world of business. Things began to change in the mid-1990s with an uptick in the number of business-school programs in the country, several of which were particularly geared toward real estate, offering programs such as a masters degree in real estate development, often taught through Spanish polytechnical universities working in partnership with private Argentine universities. These programs had emerged during a decade of neoliberal exuberance in Argentina, when markets still carried the promise of rationality and efficiency that would be troubled after the crisis of 2001. As professionals began to pursue these degrees, the ways that they thought about real estate began to shift. A sector that had previously been dominated by less formalized practices of evaluation began to see its methods formalized as they incorporated the equations and standardized methodologies associated with a more scientific approach to market analysis.

"Before these programs existed, the business of real estate was more traditional," Rozados told me. Professionals didn't so much learn from school, but instead through experience—either their own or by learning from family. "Maybe someone had come from the family of an engineer who had built buildings and taught them something based on that experience, or their father was a real estate broker who had been working for years and had that experience. But there wasn't a lot of material to work with in terms of information," he told me. "It was all done in a way that was much more intuitive. I'm not going to say they didn't know what they were doing—but maybe they saw that they were covering their costs, they saw what the price was, and from their experience they knew what to do. But they didn't take measure of what kind of product was available on the market, or where. Also, there didn't exist more sophisticated tools that had to do with studies of the market . . . everything was done much more informally." Even today, local neighborhood brokers who gain their clients through dense personal connections in neighborhoods and have a deep knowledge of the particular area in which they work are important actors in the real estate market. Many of them continue working in family businesses while professionalizing through the information and events offered by *Reporte Inmobiliario*.

Reporte Inmobiliario was founded in 2003, soon after the Argentine economic crisis in 2001. On its website, the publication's origin story describes this as "a time of much confusion, when it was necessary to avail oneself of objective and clarifying diagnostics for the Argentine real estate market." The years following the crisis had been heady years for real estate in Argentina. In the two years immediately following the crisis, conditions in the market were not at all normal, even by Argentine standards, and the ability of professionals to conduct even routine tasks like appraisals had become particularly challenging. With the economy shifting so drastically and so many people in desperate situations, the task of understanding current prices took its place alongside the more typically difficult tasks of predicting mid- or long-term futures in an economy known for its brusque twists and turns. Immediately after the crisis, even the present was unknowable: how could analysts know how much an apartment was worth when the market itself was unlike one that they had ever known before? In this environment professionals began to turn to more formalized methods in an effort to try to understand the market.

By 2008, when I began fieldwork, the situation had become more stable. The market had begun to boom, and in a way that had become more understandable, even while it was different from previous booms in its particular historical configuration. The housing market had taken its place as the bedrock upon which personal savings would come to rest as money moved out of the banking and financial sector and into real estate, making the construction sector one of the leading sources of economic growth in a nation coming out of the crisis. *Reporte Inmobiliario*, meanwhile, had become a nodal point for a more professionalized approach to real estate and the statistics that undergird it. Like many other professionals in this emerging part of the field, Rozados had trained as an architect and then gone on to complete a masters in real estate business management during the crisis years. Founding *Reporte Inmobiliario* was a way of putting that knowledge to use and of bringing such forms of analysis to the broader real estate community in Buenos Aires. It was within this context—a booming market in post-crisis real estate, together with an emergent professionalized form of knowing the place of buildings within that market—that the seminar had proposed to reexamine the process of appraisal.

Rather than displacing tacit forms of knowledge, the formalized knowledge practices promoted by *Reporte Inmobiliario* existed alongside them. Presenters at these events often emphasized that the methodologies they were teaching were not strict or even universally applicable and that they wouldn't always arrive at the right number. Nor, however, did the presenters or participants seem particularly troubled by the imperfection of the equations. Rather, they were unhesitatingly practical heteroglots, emphasizing that a variety of methodologies should be used in concert with one another and that even after a variety of methodologies were employed, it was the good judgment of the professional that would be required to decide between them or to potentially contravene the numbers that could be arrived at through any calculus. Expertise, therefore, took on less the characteristics of a rigorously applied and universally valid methodology and instead blended such approaches with less formalized measures in which the expert was precisely the person who would be able to recognize when the formulae arrived at answers that were less than accurate. Formalized measurements, in other words, were more tools to think with than a step-by-step instruction manual through which to arrive at a correct answer.

What, then, was the value of focusing on these methodologies? The answer given in the seminar was that the formalization of knowledge provided a means through which to make explicit the kinds of work and requirements that appraisal is asked to do. Formulae, in this sense, are not just a means of arriving at the answer—an answer that, in many cases, at least for certain skilled individuals, might already be known. Rather, the formulae are also a way of formalizing otherwise informal ways of knowing. In making the variables explicit, they are useful for walking both experienced practitioners and novices through the complex set of circumstances in which the price of an apartment is asked to do work. Their work with charts and methods of calculation were therefore useful in part for explicating what might otherwise be taken as a given or natural fact.

Examining these calculative methodologies does more than just explicate already existing processes, however. Instead, it also serves to remake the qualities of the very processes that are examined.[9] In other words, the making explicit of implicit things that the calculative spirit engages is both a reading of relationships and a remaking of them, since reading is seldom a disinterested practice from which the text remains insulated. Consider that for analysts themselves, explaining something through formalized calculi and methodologies that they might already know otherwise was not understood as a futile task—a tedious exercise in making methodological something that could be known in simpler and more direct ways. Rather, as a participant in the seminar explained, such tedium was useful work in explaining to prospective clients why the numbers an appraiser arrived at were valid. If not always useful for arriving at the right quote for an appraisal, the methodology and the formalized explanatory power it had were seen as useful for communicating the validity of an appraiser's claims. This was important, because clients interested in selling would rarely call only one real estate agent for an appraisal. In such situations, the temptation for real estate agents is to quote a higher (and potentially unrealistic) price in the interest of capturing that client. But high early quotes often led to trouble in the relationship between the seller and their broker down the road. The seminar leader followed up on the participant's observation, arguing that the broker who was able to convince the client that the number that they had arrived at was the best one (not just the highest) would be the one who gained both their trust and their business.

Communication about calculability thus played at least as important a role in this process as the calculation itself, since even if an appraiser arrived at the right number, a failure to communicate the rationale behind that number could result in the loss of a client. In contrast, even clients who held an inflated idea about the market value of their property (as they were typically said to do) could be convinced to accept a lower estimate if the agent could do an effective job at communicating the rationale behind the quote they had given. Thus even while an appraiser might know the right answer before the equation did, the equation helped make right right by communicating it in a convincing fashion to the seller. The formalized system of knowledge, in addition to complementing tacit appraisal with methodological rigor, also influenced the market itself by attracting clients and shaping prices.

AGGREGATE MEASURES: THE NARRATION OF NUMBERS

Appraisal is one kind of work that real estate professionals engage in, and *Reporte Inmobiliario* has made some attempts to have a foot in that world through events like the seminar on appraisals and more steadily through their web portal, where they both publish a free weekly newsletter and provide a variety of material that is accessible behind a subscription-based paywall. Much of this material is geared to appeal to the daily tasks of brokers, offering, for example, statistical data about prices in certain hot neighborhoods or market segments. But there is also a substantial amount of content geared toward meta-analytical questions about the real estate market that go beyond the daily tasks of brokers and instead take a longer and wider view at what is happening in the real estate market. These analyses were the central focus of feature articles written by recognized industry experts that broached topics such as "Is there a housing bubble?," or "Dollar or brick?," which asked whether investing in dollars or real estate was better in the current market. Such meta-analytical questions were also the focus of semiannual conferences, which aimed to provide overviews that could take stock of the daily flow of statistics and opinions that circulated in blogs and industry reports throughout the year. These conferences featured panels of experts—usually investment consultants or the heads of major brokerage firms—who would address broad questions relevant to understanding the real estate market as a whole: Will the market rise or fall? Are apartments overvalued? With what other investment opportunities is real estate competing, and how does it measure up? Together, these meta-analyses were ways in which the industry came to understand itself and provided opportunities for collective reflection on movements and changes in the real estate market.

When approaching these questions, market analysts generally base their analyses on series of data, often laid out in historical graphs like the one I described at the beginning of the chapter (and that I'll return to shortly). These include data about changes in the total number of meters of construction permits granted or in the average price of an apartment over the course of years or decades. Numbers play a different role in these analytical practices than they do in the work of appraisal, however. In contrast to appraisal, in which analysts aim to *achieve* numbers (i.e., price), in market analysis, analysts *begin* with these numbers and seek to unearth the historical complexities that created them—to determine why the numbers were what they were. The numbers themselves don't answer questions, but require interpretation to be made meaningful.

Consider, for example, two graphs showing historical series of data. The first is a graph of construction permits granted between 1935 and 2008. In this graph, numbers are what is known; what isn't known is why they were what they were (see figure 2.2). Based on the statistics laid out here, one can reflect on the fact that the post-crisis construction boom is comparatively small in historical terms: it rises above historical averages and above any year since the late 1970s, but is dwarfed by peaks in 1958, 1970, and 1977. The graph begs the question: What makes this peak different from the others? Can it be compared to them, and if so, on what basis? Only other data and other forms of analysis can make an answer possible. There are many possible explanations for the 1977 peak; for example, an overturn in Peronist-era rent control laws in 1976 could have stimulated rental construction, alongside the liberalization of the economy and the dollarization of the real estate market (described in chapter 1). But as those with knowledge of these statistics told me, the peak in 1977 is most likely an artifact of measuring permits instead of actual construction. In 1978, a new and more restrictive building code was set to take effect, and so in 1977 every property owner who could submitted a plan to get it approved under the earlier norm, many of which did not end up getting built, at least not at that time. The strong dip afterward can be explained in part by the number of permits granted in 1977—everyone who needed permission to build had already gotten one. Whether and when these were actually built was another question entirely, but it certainly wasn't all in 1977. Such answers are not directly available from the data presented in this graph, however. The graph, instead, works to elicit the question. Similarly, a graph

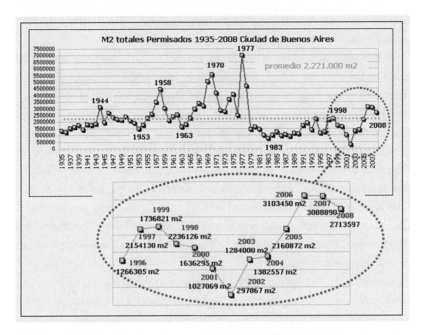

FIGURE 2.2. A graph of the total square meters of construction approved in Buenos Aires, 1935–2008. *Reporte Inmobiliario.*

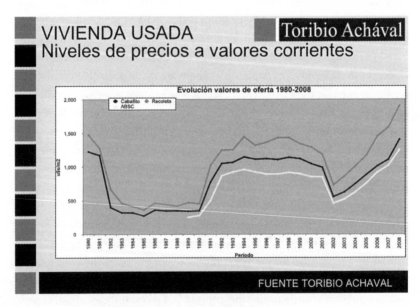

FIGURE 2.3. Used housing prices in real value, 1980–2008. Toribio Achával for *Reporte Inmobiliario.*

of the price per square meter of the average used apartment in Buenos Aires over the past thirty years in a way offers a striking paucity of information (see figure 2.3). Prices dipped in the 1980s, recovered in the 1990s, crashed in 2001–2, and recovered by 2005. What the graph doesn't tell us is why. Here, numbers, rather than providing explanations, are what need to be explained.

The practice of working with these aggregate statistics involves bringing these numbers into relation with still other numerical measures and with historical narrative. What is notable about the work that numbers do in these situations, then, is precisely the work that they cannot do—not alone. The questions brought to bear on these numbers—why prices moved the way they did, or why construction increased when it did—require a host of other information to enable the construction of a narrative about the market that forms the main goal of market analysts in these situations. In order to develop these narratives, real estate experts have to bring these numbers into relation with other data in order to make them meaningful.

Consider the graph I described at the beginning of the chapter, in which the average price of two-bedroom apartments in the Northern Corridor is graphed alongside the valuation of the U.S. dollar, average salary levels, and the Argentine consumer price index (see figure 2.4). Graphs like these begin to construct the broader economic ecology of which buildings are a part—to understand how their own variation tracks alongside other kinds of variation. In this particular case, the graph shows that changes in the value of apartments outpaced inflation, changes in the value of the dollar, and increases in salary. This means that real estate outperforms dollars as investments and is the beginning of an explanation of changes in the market that could attribute price increases to money being moved from savings into real estate. In a similar graph, the average reported salary level of Argentines in dollars is depicted alongside the price per square meter of an apartment (see figure 2.5). Here, what is thrown into relief is the breach between the two numbers that developed in the aftermath of the Argentine economic crisis of 2001. While salary levels in dollars fell sharply, the price of apartments rose, which is another way of saying that real estate became disarticulated from salary changes after 2001, while they had previously followed one another closely. Other studies have confirmed that while between 1976 and 2001 a young professional could purchase a sixty-square-meter apartment for an average of forty-eight salaries (i.e., forty-eight months of income), after the crisis they came to cost seventy-five (Manzoni 2016).

But determining that the price increase is driven by investment is possible only with other information: in the U.S., for example, a similar graph might

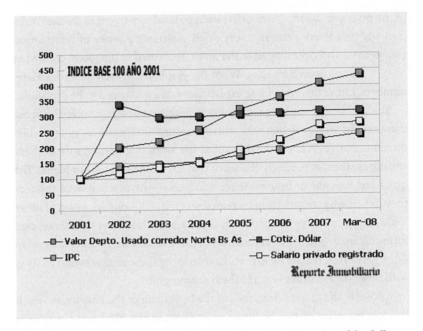

FIGURE 2.4. Value of a used apartment in the Northern Corridor, value of the dollar, registered private salary, and the consumer price index; changes relative to a base of 100 in 2001. *Reporte Inmobiliario.*

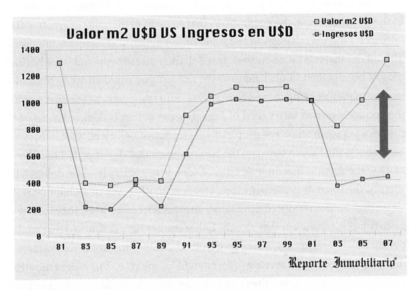

FIGURE 2.5. Value per square meter vs. salary in U.S. dollars, 1981–2007. Reproduction based on graphic by *Reporte Inmobiliario.*

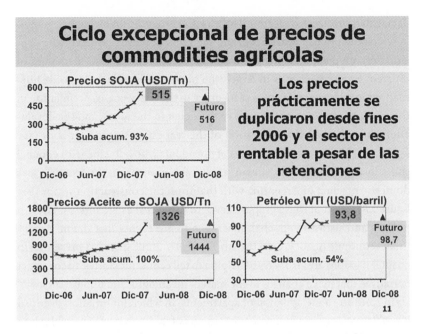

FIGURE 2.6. "Exceptional cycle of agricultural commodity prices." Graphs of soy, soy oil, and petroleum prices. Banco Francés for *Reporte Inmobiliario*.

represent price increases due to an expansion of the mortgage market, like the one driven by financial speculation in mortgage-backed securities in the lead-up to what became the global economic crisis of 2007–8. But in Argentina, where there was no mortgage lending to speak of, the price increase had to be coming from somewhere other than mortgages and somewhere other than salaries. Instead, most of the demand was likely to be coming from either a sector of the population with higher than average incomes or from those with prior savings. Perhaps unsurprisingly, the answer seemed to be both: in another presentation, an analyst examined changes in the global price of soy in a context of increases in construction and in the value of apartments (see figure 2.6). A mainstay of the agro-export sector in the 2000s, soy sold on international markets provides a large number of dollars to wealthy Argentine agricultural producers.[10] Alongside small savers with a need to save their savings, many of these soy dollars, too, are likely to have made their way into the dollar-denominated market in real estate.

Bringing these other forms of quantitative data into relationship with real estate data was one way to understand broad features of the real estate market in post-crisis Argentina. But graphs were also used to link up statistical data with more narrative forms of history. Consider the following two graphs, in which the price of apartments and the gross domestic product from construction are mapped alongside historical events. In the first, the names of different economic events in Argentine history are marked alongside fluctuations in apartment prices—plata dulce in the late 1970s, hyperinflation in the 1980s, the pegging of the peso to the dollar in the 1990s, and the devaluation and subsequent recuperation of the real estate sector after 2001 (see figure 2.7). In the second, the faces of presidents who coincide with epochal shifts in construction are shown on a graph comparing the overall gross domestic product of Argentina with that from the construction sector (see figure 2.8). Each of these graphs serves to bring real estate into touch with politics and with the epochal, macroeconomic events that define Argentina's economic history. Like the stories of economic history I presented in chapter 1, graphs are also ways of helping to tell economic stories, to construct narratives that make changes in the market meaningful and understandable.

In contrast to the appraisal of apartments, in which information overload is problematic and arriving at a price is a way of folding a host of variables into something that makes them manageable, here numbers require a great deal of interpretation to tell the stories they are asked to tell. This is not to say that numbers are "empty," because as much as numbers might require the faces of the presidents to nuzzle up against their peaks and dips in order to tell their story properly, they also provide much of the means through which the interpretation of the market is achieved: numeration allows apartments to cohabit the same graph as the price of the dollar or the value of soy—enabling real estate to circulate within these broader frames of reference. In this movement, numbers allow apartments to circulate within diverse spheres, and through their circulation, through this relationality with other economic goods and other histories, to become grounded and contextualized historically, so that the market's movements can be analyzed. Numbers in market analysis help make the market into a feature of national political and economic history, alongside fluctuations in the value of the dollar or the products of the agro-export sector.

These are, then, aggregate measures, not just in the sense that they aim to describe the market as a whole, but also in the way that they function as measures that aggregate, or combine, disparate elements, traveling alongside other numbers and other forms of narration, pulling them into their orbit. While in appraisal, the particularities of individual apartments are what appraisers are interested in discovering so as to be able to determine a unique

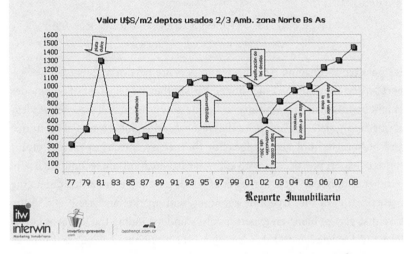

FIGURE 2.7. Annual variation in price per square meter of used two- and three-bedroom apartments, Zona Norte, Buenos Aires, 1977–2008. The arrows feature the names of economic epochs, narrating economic history alongside price fluctuations. *Reporte Inmobiliario*.

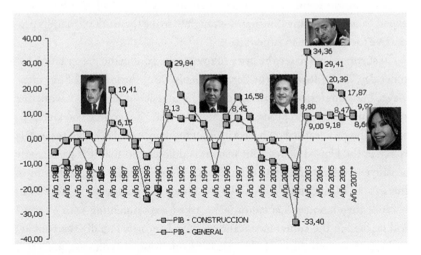

FIGURE 2.8. Argentine GDP vs. construction-sector GDP, with presidents' faces alongside price fluctuations. *Reporte Inmobiliario*.

price by constructing relationships with other apartments, here comparisons spiral out to pose the question of how real estate compares to other economic factors: to investments held in dollars, salaries, or the price of soy.

A MARKET UNLIKE OTHERS: ARGENTINE REAL ESTATE AND THE LAWS OF MARKETS

It's possible to imagine that these numbers are part of a global field of expertise, and they are. As I mentioned earlier, they rely on a set of techniques taught by international ventures in business education and on a set of ideas about supply, demand, and price that resonate with global forms of economic and business-school knowledge. But they aren't, strictly speaking, global forms of expert practice. As with appraisal, in which certain techniques useful in other contexts or for other types of goods have to be discarded due to the particularities of the Argentine economy, with market analysis it is also the case that part of being an expert involves understanding the limits of global forms of knowledge and developing a sensibility about when and how to apply which parts of that knowledge. Market analysts were practitioners who worked to understand Argentina's real estate market in the terms of abstract economic concepts, but also to specify them in order to make them useful not for a market in general, but for this particular market. Generic observations about, for example, supply and demand are both deployed by market experts and at the same time never enough to make the work of analysis productive for real estate in Argentina.

"It surprised me to see the price of soy graphed out in the presentation the other day," I told Rozados (of *Reporte Inmobiliario*) during one of our interviews. I was interested in hearing more from him about the kind of work that such graphs did in the process of market analysis. "Of course you were," he said, smiling, "because you have a form of thinking based on what real estate is like in the United States. Our market is different, in that it is particularly sensitive to the generation of economic surpluses," he explained, referring in this case to the income provided by soy for agro-export sectors. "You mean because there's no *colchón bancario*?" I asked, experimenting with a term I had learned in the conferences. The colchón bancario, literally the banking cushion, described the level of insulation from brusque economic shifts that mortgage lending would have provided to the construction sector, potentially offering stability to a market even if the economy were doing poorly. "Exactly," he said. "In the U.S., the key variable you look at is financing, the availability of credit. But here, it's necessary to look at where economic surpluses are coming from, what the volume of those surpluses is, and what interests those who have them hold when they think to invest. It's much more direct." In other words, whereas in the U.S. brusque changes in the balance of trade are cushioned by the financial sector, in Argentina they are felt more directly. There's no financial sector to cushion a fall in economic activity; if the money from soy or from people's savings were to disappear, the real estate market would dry up quickly. For this reason, analysts in Argentina have to track broad macroeconomic surpluses, such as the soy market, much more closely than they would in the U.S., where the primary source of money for real estate comes from mortgage lending.

Rozados had a similar answer when I asked him about whether there might be a bubble in the housing market. The answer, I knew, was not a simple one: as one analyst had explained to me, bubbles are only recognizable as such after they burst; before that, they're just rising prices. "That's exactly the kind of thing that we are always keeping an eye on," he told me. They do so not only by looking to increases in prices, but to understanding the particular forces behind them: "We try to understand the degree of speculation, which is about the *particular interests of the particular kind of buyer*. There are different classes of investor, among which there are those who are looking for a high and fast profit and those who want tranquility and a safe haven for their capital. The latter is precisely what is going on in real estate today. *Not real estate in general, but real estate in post-crisis Argentina*," he said. In other markets, housing prices increasing faster than wages might be indicative of a speculative bubble. But in post-crisis Argentina, he explained to me, this didn't seem to be the case. Instead, people seemed to be using apartments as a means of long-term savings, not as a means to make money in the short term. This was true, he said, both for pequeños ahorristas moving their money from banks and colchones into real estate and for those directing soy profits from the export sector into real estate. Because the market is based on cash and not on bank loans, default was not a concern; and because most of these buyers were looking for a long-term place to keep their money, it was unlikely they would be cashing out at the first sign of market trouble, thus decreasing the volatility associated with brusque movements of capital in and out of markets.

To reach these conclusions, market analysts could not rest on an unspecified understanding of buyers and their motivations, or what the analysts would call the composition of demand. The demand of their supply-and-demand thinking was at once abstract (it spoke for many people and no particular case) *and* particular (it could not be used to speak to contexts outside Argentina). In this case, it was distinguished from a demand whose goal was to increase profitability in the short term, such as the speculation in mortgage-backed securities that drove the collapse of the housing market in the U.S. Instead, the Argentine real estate market was characterized by investors looking to find a long-term resting place for cash, outside of the banking sector. This turn toward real estate was not strictly rational, Rozados told me. Textbook investment theory suggests that in situations of crisis, the best thing to do is to maintain liquid assets—cash dollars—and not to immobilize your money in bricks. But Argentines had a special affective and historical relationship with real estate, and that was something they had to take into account. "It's very difficult to extrapolate about the market in general, even the questions that should be the most rational from an economic perspective," he told me. "One has to look at the particular market, and the specific rules of the game at play in *that market.*"

Even the basic law of supply and demand, which suggests that higher demand and lower supply result in higher prices, has to be qualified for Argentine real estate. As Rozados explained to me, in Argentina "real estate prices never adjust because of the free play of supply and demand. Instead, if you look at the history, changes in prices have only happened following sharp adjustments in the exchange rate." More common than observing a shift in prices in these scenarios is to observe a shift in supply—people build less— in light of a shift in the price of inputs (e.g., imported steel) due to changes in the exchange rate. In Argentina, in other words, adjustments are made in volume, not in price, except under conditions when the exchange rate fluctuates sharply (like the crisis of 2001).

The real estate market that these analysts know, then, is not a real estate market in general, but rather one particular to Argentina. As much as their knowledge draws on the formalized methods of far-flung networks of expertise—including the business programs of Spanish polytechnical schools—they do not import these ideas without also translating them to be relevant to their context. This doesn't mean that all the rules are out the window: analysts are able to talk about many of the exceptional qualities of the Argentine market in the terms offered to them by these broader forms of expertise. Economic theory has a term for prices that don't shift with supply and demand, for example: they are said to be *sticky*. But this ability to describe the Argentine real estate market in the language of economic theory shouldn't be confused with a seamless application of global forms of knowledge. The market that they work to understand is hardly the "perfect market" of economic theory, and the demand they study (the people buying apartments) is something more situated than a generic *homo economicus*, economic theory's rational, utility-maximizing subject. Despite the best efforts of neoliberal reformers to make the Argentine economy and Argentine subjects conform to economic theory (Fridman 2010, 2016), this model of the economy and this economic subject are not hegemonic. Because of this, analysts of the Argentine real estate market must learn to work in a world of sticky prices and investors who turn to the solidity of bricks instead of liquid assets in situations of crisis. Their practice is one of remaining grounded in imperfect markets, and they have become experts at interpreting and navigating them. As they became equipped with new techniques of measurement and analysis through the formalized methods they learned in business programs, they adapted these tools to suit the market being analyzed. In the process of building such understandings, their charts and graphs became tools through which to understand this specific market.

CONCLUSION

As I mentioned earlier, it's possible to think of charts and graphs as flattening, reductive media, in which buildings are reduced, through a series of numbers and data points, to something cold and calculated, their value little more than the sum of dollars they can generate. The effects of money or valuation, like quantification, are also often talked about in this register. Although this is not entirely inaccurate, it is also not the only way to think about the practices of market analysts and the existences they enable for buildings through their practices. Their work produces a rich numerical environment in which buildings can live and through which market professionals both contemplate and remake buildings' economic lives. Far from a reduction of the world through abstraction, they introduce new abstractions into the world, making possible new relationalities and connections as part of grounded, situated practices.

In the work of appraisal, numbers laid out in charts provide a solution to problems of comparison. Price is one end point toward which appraisers work, but it is not the only outcome. Instead, measurement helps appraisers fine-tune their attention to difference, using numbers to bring different apartments into relation with one another so that they can be compared and their value relative to one another established. They don't work to erase specificity, but instead to attend to specificity in ways that allow apartments to circulate with others in a market. In market analysis, numbers displayed in graphs ask more questions than they answer, but they also enable analysts to understand real estate's relations with other sectors of the economy, like salary levels, the value of the dollar, or the price of soy, articulating buildings' economic value with other features of their economic environment and with key moments in Argentina's economic history. Through these practices, buildings are made into market objects, and that market is made legible historically and in broader economic contexts. The practices that enabled buildings to exist and be understood as goods in a market were forged in contexts of recent professionalization, built upon the expansion of business schools in Argentina over the prior decade; in relation to enduring types of knowledge that are "other than" what calculable methodological rationalities are able to account for on their own; of everyday business and the capture of clients; and in the wake of a turbulent period in the market, in which little was able to be known. Through the charts and graphs and the narratives they evoke, buildings are able to circulate with other buildings, within historical frames and with other goods in broader economic spheres.

The charts, graphs, and narratives of expert analysts gave concrete form to dreams of legible markets in which the real estate market's pasts and futures might be understood. As part of concrete's compound materialities, their practices stood alongside and occasionally interfaced with other ways of interacting with buildings. The small investors that I described in chapter 1 are one example: they incorporated buildings into their own ecology of investments, bringing them into divergent relation with other economic media—pesos and dollars, bank accounts and cash—as well as with their investments in narrating economic pasts to build more promising futures. In ways that are neither separate from nor reducible to one another, small investors and market analysts are both involved in the work of incorporating buildings into economic practices that inhabit a world rife with instability.

Another set of actors I worked with, somewhat more unexpected than small real estate investors, also made an occasional appearance in the conferences of market analysts: neighborhood residents, or *vecinos*. Vecinos appeared more than once in slideshow presentations in which analysts sketched out current market conditions by highlighting the strengths, weaknesses, opportunities, and threats facing the market.[11] Toward the end of the list of threats appeared *el tema de los vecinos*, the vecino issue. I and others in the room knew that this referred to several groups of neighborhood residents, working to limit the amount of construction permitted in their barrios, who managed to attract media attention and occasionally pass laws restricting construction. Their presence on the list was never expounded upon at length, but it did appear there, marking the way that their presence might impinge on the smooth functioning of the real estate market and the concrete futures imagined by market analysts.

Framing the value of buildings as primarily an economic question was thus not something that went uncontested in the years after the crisis. If anything, construction in those years brought into relief other forms of value that many actors saw threatened in the face of buildings' increasingly prominent place in post-crisis economic life. These include the neighborhood groups and architects that I describe in the rest of this book. In the following two chapters, I turn to examine the ways that buildings are valued in the everyday practices of barrio dwelling and then follow barrio residents into the city legislature, where they saw buildings worked on in still another ecology of practice, the legal and bureaucratic world of urban planning. Their dreams, too, provided aggregates to concrete's compound materiality, in ways that were often more frictional than the relationship between the forms of value held dear by pequeños ahorristas and market analysts.

CHAPTER 3

Barrio Ecologies

Parks, Patios, and the Politics of Articulation

Oscurece. nubarrones bruscos se han detenido en el sur, no tan alto, sobre la cúpula de la iglesia, sobre la luz roja de la torre más alta; hacia el oeste nubes incandescentes se retuercen exprimiendo el último gas del fulgor solar. El cielo bajo del oeste por donde se hunde la tarde es una franja celestísima de suavidad y esplendor. Un helicóptero recorre la línea costera, lleva una luz blanca fija y otra roja parpadeante; sobre la casa, un murciélago derrapa gira baja sube y obtiene los primeros datos de la noche fresca; los ventiletes de las escaleras de un edificio se encienden de golpe y a los dos minutos de pronto todos se vuelven a apagar.

It's getting dark. brusque storm clouds have come to a halt in the south, not so high, over the dome of the church, over the red light of the tallest tower; toward the west, incandescent clouds wring themselves, squeezing out the last gas of the solar glare. The low sky of the west, where the afternoon sinks, is the bluest border of softness and radiance. A helicopter travels along the coastline, bearing one white fixed light and another red and blinking; above the house, a bat skids turns dives climbs and obtains the first signals of the cool night; the small windows of the stairwell of a building light up suddenly and promptly two minutes later they all turn off again.

El esfuerzo unido de todas las luces de las avenidas del sur producen una rever-beración palidescente que se eleva desde el suelo, montañas amarillas detrás de las torres de la cárcel y de los pocos edificios altos que penetran el cielo.

The united force of all the lights of the avenues of the south produce a pallid reflection that rises up from the ground, yellow mountains behind the towers of the prison and the few tall buildings that penetrate the sky.

Aviones silenciosos se desplazan en dirección a Ezeiza y en el fondo comienzan a doblar, luego los tapa una nueva torre sin terminar, aún oscura por las noches; los más pequeños que van hacia aeroparque cruzan de sur a norte y pasan descendentes por encima de la casa: sus luces pestañean y segundos detrás del aparato pasa también el ruido.

Silent aircraft travel in the direction of Ezeiza and in the background begin to turn, later they are hidden by a new unfinished apartment tower, still dark at night; the smallest, which travel toward Aeroparque, cross from south to north and pass above the house in their descent: their lights blink, and seconds after the equipment, the noise passes as well.

Ahora el cielo se quedó sin nubes, las encendidas del oeste se licuaron en la oscuridad y las grises del sur han ido virando hasta que el poder de las estrellas las empujó fuera de la noche,

Now the sky is without clouds, those which were lit up in the west have blended into the darkness and the grays of the south have swerved about until the power of the stars pushed them out of the night,

eeaaa!!! una estrella fugaz casi invisible abre el pelaje negro de la oscuridad, pero nadie ha visto nada, no se escuchan comentarios.

eeaaa!!! an almost invisible shooting star opens up the black fur of darkness, but no one has seen anything, no comments are heard.

—Opening stanzas from *El cielo de Boedo,* by DANIEL DURAND, 2004

El cielo de Boedo (The Heavens of Boedo) is a book-length poetic meditation on celestial events during four seasons as observed from the rooftop terrace of a house in the southern Buenos Aires *barrio* of Boedo.[1] The poem offers a picturesque take on a more-than-natural urban ecology in which people, city lights, air traffic, and the absent sounds of neighbors cohabit a world with the sky and the clouds. By foregoing an easy dichotomy between city and capital-N Nature, the poem eschews a trope of urban alienation on the one hand and harmony with nature on the other that constructs cities as, in and of themselves, suffocating, overstimulating, and antihuman. Cities, of course, can be those things. But Durand's poem offers a glimpse of a different kind of relationship with the city that can take place within its borders, a relationship in which clouds and the sky intermingle with buildings, airplanes, and artificial light. It presents a relationship with the city that bears as an important characteristic a sort of dynamically manageable intensity between diverse features of the urban environment. In it, a sense of distance from dense urban social interactions does not require leaving the city behind, but rather being with it in certain ways: a certain kind of copresence.

The relationship with the sky that Durand puts into words in this poem has long conformed the dwelling practices of *porteños*, particularly in the more peripheral barrios of Buenos Aires, where, in contrast to more central areas of the city, the urban landscape is defined by low-rise buildings.[2] Here, terraces, like the one from which Durand writes his poem, are one of the prominent architectural features through which porteños cultivate ongoing relationships with the outdoors from within urban spaces. Together with balconies, patios, gardens, and parks, they comprise urban environments that offer zones of engagement with organic, celestial, and airy worlds. They form a patchy network of spaces that can mitigate the intensity of dense human and concrete environments through the ability to spend time with plants, animals, the sun, the sky, and the wind. Neighborhoods where everything is low and where the sky can dominate the view are, however, something that many people see as disappearing, as old buildings and empty spaces are demolished and new, tall apartment buildings are put in their place.

Durand's poem is part of a constellation of practices that cultivate attention and modulate attunement to urban environments. It is a tool for paying attention to the ordinary in an unordinary way, putting into words a broadly shared, quotidian porteño experience (that of looking at the sky), while sharpening and sustaining attention to that experience through the unique tools of poetry. The poem, like other "arts of noticing" (to borrow Anna Tsing's phrase), is more than a passive form of reflection; instead, it produces and sustains a particular way of relating to and engaging with the world.[3] Some arts of noticing are quotidian and widely shared (like looking at the sky), while others can be more episodic and exceptional (like the poem). The two feed into and play off each other, as the exceptional intertwines with the everyday.

During my fieldwork, I came to see a resonance between the practices of barrio residents and the work of poetry like Durand's. Like the poem, their practices help them cultivate attention to urban environments. Think back to Patricia, whom I introduced in the first pages of this book. The new, tall building that had been built behind her terrace cut off the sunlight from her plants, and the sense of reclusion she enjoyed there was replaced by consciousness of all the future neighbors who would be looking down upon her and who might be bothered by the smoke from her barbecue. Her daily life practices on her terrace made changes to the built environment noticeable and salient for her in a particular kind of way.

In this chapter, I am interested in the ways that jogging in parks, drying clothes, and tending plants helped produce attention to real estate and the politics of development, linking up urban environmental politics with broader concerns for markets in post-crisis Buenos Aires. I see such practices of attention as an important resource in creating an eventful presence that makes response possible. I am thinking here with Elizabeth Povinelli (2011), who has contrasted eventfulness with what she calls quasi-events—forms of presence whose chronic, endemic nature can, paradoxically, make them difficult to notice. Making a quasi-event into an event is about making it noticeable, eventful, and capable of standing out against its background. Like the practices of barrio dwelling through which people like Patricia develop a particular set of attunements toward changing urban environments, the political actions of barrio residents worked to make property and real estate eventful— to turn capitalism's chronic presence in the city into something able to be noticed and addressed.

For people like Patricia, barrio dwelling practices became part of a process of attunement to the commodification of space that was made to feel sharper and more salient in the years after the crisis. They also led to political action: Patricia formed part of one of the groups of vecinos I worked with who mobilized in response to changes in barrio environments brought about by real estate development (typically translated as *neighbor*, *vecino* also carries civic and political connotations loosely related to the word *citizen* in English;[4] as with barrio, I typically leave this word untranslated to preserve this specificity). The work of these groups of vecinos was in part about changing laws (which I examine in chapter 4). But it was also about cultivating an attention to life practices that had come to feel precarious in the context of the boom. As new tall buildings and more densified styles of living altered barrio environments, neighborhood groups worked to articulate a problem space that approached barrios as an ecology in which plants, the sun, wind, and the sky intermingled with built forms, legal codes, and money. Many of the vecinos I worked with considered themselves environmentalists. Among their number were bird and plant enthusiasts who cared for prominent urban outdoor spaces like the Parque 3 de Febrero or the city ecological reserve, where they participated in birdwatching and nocturnal moon-gazing outings; many others were simple gardeners or people who appreciated even the tiniest outdoor spaces in which they could spend time with family, raise plants, cook outside, and see the sky. All of these practices worked to hold present urban environments that exceed concrete and give space to sun, light, wind, and soil—environments they sought to make endure in the shadow of an intensified real estate market and the kind of construction it privileged.

The barrios that vecinos lived in, constructed as a political object, and worked to valorize did not just exist within their own practices of barrio living, however. Like other environments, barrios are more than a background on which human action unfolds, but are instead the emergent products of diverse practices of knowledge and intervention.[5] Barrios in particular have a rich and vibrant life in poetry, literature, and popular music and as a particular kind of political formation with a deep history in Buenos Aires. In many respects, these other manifestations of the barrio—as well-known cultural and political referents—provided important points of inflection for vecinos' efforts to slow down the smooth commodification of urban space, helping them draw out and hold present other forms of value in urban space that were broadly resonant in Buenos Aires. They, too, offer incitements to noticing and help cobble together a collaborative network of care for urban environments—environments in which living with the elements and living with histories of economic ruptures and dispossession always have to be thought together.

HUGGING THE LAKE: AMIGOS DEL LAGO
AND THE PARQUE 3 DE FEBRERO

Osvaldo used to notice the smell before he came within sight of the trash or the dead fish that would wash up on the lakeshore. This was back in 1989, when he used to jog in the Parque 3 de Febrero, commonly known as the Bosques de Palermo, Palermo Woods. I had met Osvaldo during fieldwork with a group called *queremos buenos aires*, an umbrella group of vecino organizations with environmentalist leanings that he had helped found (the group's name literally means "we want good airs"). In 2009, when I sat with Osvaldo in a nearby café talking about his early involvement in urban environmental politics, the park was one of the largest and most well known green spaces in the city, known for its rose garden, Japanese garden, manmade lakes, and other amenities typical of the early twentieth-century, French-inspired park design common in Buenos Aires. In 1989, however, the park was in a state of disrepair. The Lago de Regatas, or Regatta Lake, became a site of particular concern for Osvaldo and others. Large masses of aquatic plants stretched across its surface; trash floated alongside the bodies of dead fish; a foul smell emanated from the lake; and the water's volume had fallen due to the formation of large vegetative islands. The grass was not maintained, and cars parked on it all the way up to the border of the lake.

One day, Osvaldo told me, while he was jogging in the park, he encountered two men who had set up a small table where they were collecting signatures on a petition to improve the conditions of the park, and he stopped to talk to them. Over the following months, a group of people came together to form one of the groups for which Osvaldo served as president during my fieldwork, the Amigos del Lago de Palermo—Friends of Palermo Lake. The lake's friends continued gathering signatures, with demands that Osvaldo described to me twenty years later as naive: to cut the grass, install garbage receptacles, and return a sense of care to the management of the lake.

The Amigos also began to look more closely into the situation of the lake and gathered some lay experts to their cause. They learned that the lake, dug in 1906, had become home to an unsustainably high proportion of *Elodea densa* and *Ceratophyllum demersum*, water plants that are designated invasive in many U.S. states. Specialists diagnosed a process of rapid eutrophication induced by fertilizer runoff into the lake. Eutrophication overnourishes certain plant species as a result of phosphate increases in the water, making the lake uninhabitable for many other species of plant and animal.

Over time, the Amigos also expanded their efforts beyond petitions to denounce the lack of care of the lake and the park around it and to advocate for measures to take care of it. They wrote letters to government functionaries and to the newspapers. They also organized public events like the *abrazo al lago*, a giant collective hug of the lake, calling in all the people they could to gather around the massive, eleven-hectare lake, holding hands (see figures 3.1 and 3.2). Despite the large number of people they gathered for the hug, they couldn't hug the entire lake, Osvaldo explained to me: "There was a concessionary (a private business with concession to work on public land) who had put up a fence, claiming a bit of the lakeshore for themselves. So the hug stopped at the fence."

The fence wasn't the only thing the Amigos became more aware of in the course of their activities. They also determined that the eutrophication in the lake was the result of more than a generalized runoff of fertilizer: in the

FIGURES 3.1 AND 3.2. Vecinos hug the Lago de Regatas in the Parque 3 de Febrero in the early 1990s. Photos courtesy of the Asociación Amigos del Lago de Palermo.

southern point of the lake, they discovered a drainage pipe that channeled sewage into the lake, which they traced to two nearby private athletic clubs, the Club de Gimnasia y Esgrima and the Club de Caza Mayor. The fence and the drainage pipe would become for the vecinos a critical moment of recognition, in which their attention began to shift and they began to transform their arts of noticing beyond trash cleanup to encompass issues of private property that would later be seen as fundamental to their critical practice throughout the city. The lake hug was, in this sense, an expression of affective care, but also a way to channel physical bodies in a space, bringing them together around a smelly lake and up against a fence and a drainpipe in a way that produced new ways of noticing.

Meanwhile, the hug and the letters began the work of gathering media coverage to complement the Amigos' attention to the lake with that of a wider public consciousness. The publicity also had another, more surprising effect: soon after the hug, people began to approach the Amigos with rumors that there was a project in works by the government that would place half of the park in private concession. "[They said that] the lake was going to be converted into a permanent motorboat race-track," Osvaldo told me, "and that they were planning to build a five-star hotel on one of the park's plazas. All around the lake, they were going to build stadium seating and food stalls to service the motor boat races that were supposed to happen there. On the islands, which today are avian reserves, they were going to install the sound and illumination towers." The municipal golf course would be handed over to become part of the hotel as well. A shopping plaza, too, was planned. All told, sixty hectares of public green space would be diverted to the service of private commercial ends. Osvaldo and the Amigos wrote a letter to the editor of a major newspaper inquiring about the city's intentions for the park. They received no official response, but the rumors were confirmed when Amigos del Lago received a copy of the unpublished call for proposals through unofficial channels.

As these plans came into view, the state of neglect in which the Amigos had found the lake was cast in a different light. Hardly a benign form of neglect, it instead came to be seen as an active decision, part of a larger and more nefarious plan, one that would lay the groundwork for the eventual privatization of the park. If the park were ill cared-for, if no one used it, then the case for privatization would be that much easier for the authorities to make.

The Amigos began to publicize the secret plan, generating a public scandal and getting 11,000 signatures on a petition against it. In the end, they succeeded in defending the park against privatization. As Osvaldo explained to me, "We beat the government at a time when the entire country was being privatized. This was under the government of Menem, who handed over everything, who privatized all the state enterprises, a time when everything started to become private. But because of our efforts the park didn't enter into concession, the five-star hotel was not built, and the Planetarium and the Botanical Gardens remained public." In the end, only the zoo was handed over to private concession.

During this time, the Amigos continued to care for and attend to the park and the lake. In 1994 they began to enroll the assistance of various state institutions to address the lake's troubled ecosystem. Two-thirds of the plant biomass was removed, leaving the other third to compete with the phytoplankton that green the water and to guarantee the habitat and alimentary resources for various aquatic fauna. Trash and other solid waste were also removed from the lake. An aquatic weeding device was added to the lake to reduce the development of filamentous algae that alters the aesthetic of the lake. A spillway was constructed to bring in a constant source of fresh water, and the sewage pipe from the clubs was removed. The northern floodgate was reformed to minimize the entrance of sewage, though during southeasterly storms the long-buried and polluted underground Vega stream still occasionally floods the lake.

Animal life began to return to the lake as a result of these efforts. While only three species of avian fauna were present before these interventions, thirty-four species began to inhabit the lake, including the rare anhinga, which primarily feeds on chanchitas, one of the many species of fish that were able to reinhabit the lake. The Amigos also noted the nesting of the Macá Grande, which nests on floating vegetation near the lakeshore, returning annually to the same nesting place. The nutria, long gone from the lake, also returned.

But things were far from over for the Amigos. The arts of noticing they had cultivated in their experience had only deepened their sensitivity to issues of property, and they came to discover many other cases of private land grabs in the park, which they continued to fight years later. A brief inventory from 2010: the Club de Gimnasia y Esgrima makes use of 15,000 square meters for equine sports in what should be the Plaza Parque Olímpico and 30,000 square meters for parking and other logistical uses in what should be Plaza Haití; the Buenos Aires Lawn and Tennis Club built four tennis courts on 5,000 square meters of what should be Plaza Pakistán; the Panter company built a parking structure on 20,000 square meters of the Plaza de la Shoá, and was actively engaged in developing a chain "gastronomic hub"—including a McDonald's and a Starbucks—in the former Paseo de la Infanta. The list goes on, totaling nearly ten hectares of park space in which the persistent incursions of privatization have made these plazas endure only in name. All of these projects are illegal, prohibited under the urban planning code, and many making use of expired concessions from the city government that were not themselves legal in the first place. Discovering each of them depended on the difficult task of compiling plans, decrees, and concessionary documents, work that was often done, as with the hotel, through the assistance of discrete contacts embedded in certain sectors of city government who were willing to help when the possibility of generating a scandal for their political opponents presented itself.

The Amigos del Lago are part of what environmentalism might mean in an urban ecology. The lake—and its plants and animals—could not, for them, be conceived of or acted upon except to the extent that they were in relation with the dynamics of private property. The lake thus provided a crucial point of articulation between environmental politics and the politics surrounding real estate in Buenos Aires. Its plants and animals were not incidental to this project of recuperation, but instead provided ongoing objects of care and barometers for the effectiveness of that care.[6] They were central players in what became a struggle that included property, real estate, and development. I thus see the hug of the lake (and its affine quotidian practices, like jogging in the park and birdwatching) as marking the space of ongoing histories of relationality, creating an eventful presence among what could otherwise be thought of as a background for action. They offered ways of delineating, but also building outward, an embodied space of political concern, attention, and investment. It was within ongoing practices of care for the lake and the plants and animals around it that the Amigos helped give the dynamics of private property an eventful presence, developing a heightened sensitivity to the dark side of the market in urban construction.

Today, the lake is a living monument to a future that almost was. The image of the privatized park that came into view during the 1990s became firmly installed in the consciousness of the lake's friends, who continued to monitor and audit the park, seeing every encroachment from the standpoint of a possible future in which the entire park would be managed by private interests. Osvaldo remains among the proud enthusiasts of the lake's avian fauna and from time to time posts photos of them to the Amigos' blog and email list. In 2009, when a group of black-necked swans returned to the lake for the first time in thirty years, Osvaldo sent a picture of them to the group. In the message that accompanied it, he said, "Today, in the Parque 3 de Febrero, this show could be enjoyed without paying an entrance fee"—marking with proud irony the privatized history of the park that had almost come to fruition twenty years earlier.

BARRIO ECOLOGIES: PATIOS, TERRACES, AND GARDENS

Twenty years after the jog that introduced Osvaldo to urban environmental politics, in a barrio on the other side of the city, I stood looking at a much smaller patch of greenery in Abel and Nelly's backyard. Their yard was small—about four meters deep and eight meters wide. Meticulously cared for, the patch of grass was a vibrant green, interrupted only by some of their grandchildren's toys that were scattered upon it. The yard was surrounded by trees and shrubs bordering the wall that marked its limits. The *parrilla*—the charcoal grill that is a central feature of Argentine domestic life—was built into the wall on the left.

All of this had been visible from their large kitchen window, which opened onto the small yard. But there was also a shadow cast across it, obstructing the light that would have shone into the kitchen. They took me into the yard to show me its source, and together we craned our necks to peer up at the ten-story building whose corner directly abutted their yard, the building's ten rear balconies overhanging the yard of their next-door neighbor (see figure 3.3). The lateral side of the building was sheer—windowless, in preparation for the as-yet nonexistent ten-story building zoned to be built next to it, on the lot directly behind Abel and Nelly's house. The windowless side of the building afforded them a degree of privacy for the moment, but was a harbinger of more construction to come that would complete a ten-story wall of buildings behind their house that would cut off what sun they had left.

Nelly and Abel were part of a group of vecinos called Salvemos al Barrio (Save the Barrio) that was focused on slowing the pace of construction in the barrios of Villa Pueyrredón and Agronomía, on the western edge of Buenos Aires. I had been making weekly journeys from the center of the city to attend their street-corner *asamblea* (a popular assembly) for several months, joining a regular group of about twenty people who gathered under the banner that bore their name, crafted from a bedsheet and tied to a house on the corner. From our vantage point on the corner we could see, amid a sea of one- and two-story houses, several of the thirty-two ten-story buildings that were being

FIGURE 3.3. A building rises up behind a vecino's yard.
Photo courtesy of Salvemos al Barrio.

built along a sixteen-block stretch following the main avenue in the barrio, their "for sale" signs marking the recency of their completion (see figures 3.4 and 3.5).

Salvemos al Barrio wasn't the only organization in the city dedicated to stemming a tide of tall buildings. The construction boom that had begun in the years after the crisis was changing neighborhoods across the city, and such movements had become a well-known feature of urban life.[7] I had heard stories like Abel and Nelly's before: stories of how everyday life practices in barrios were disrupted and made precarious in the face of new construction. For many, the problem was the loss of the sun. For Mario, a vecino from Caballito, the gut-wrenching part of the ten-story building that went up next to his house was the sun it cut off from his garden: "I built this house with a lot

FIGURES 3.4 AND 3.5. New buildings rise up in Villa Pueyrredón. Photo by author and courtesy of Salvemos al Barrio, respectively.

of effort," he said. "I'm a worker—one with a fairly decent salary, but I'm not rich. This house is the fruit of a lot of work, of my savings and the apartment we sold to buy it. When I get home from work, I go out into the back and work in the garden, and it's like therapy. It's important to me." Lidia, from Villa Pueyrredón, told me she used to be able to dry clothes in a few hours, but now it takes all day: "There's no sun." Other stories were more ghostly. Silvana's bathroom door doesn't stay open anymore; a strange wind coasting off the building behind her and through her windows slams it shut. Elsewhere in the city, things could be much more severe: flash floods had become common, for many a result of the lack of absorptive terrain brought about by overconstruction.

The problems weren't just with the elements: others felt their lives change as they lost the intimacy of outdoor spaces that is an important part of barrio living. When I accompanied Patricia up to her terrace to look for some old newspaper clippings she had promised me, we dodged her clothes, which were drying on the line. "I used to come up here in my underwear to hang them out," she said, laughing shyly at her confession, as we looked up at the series of ten-story buildings whose balconies now had a prime view of her terrace (see figure 3.6). "Maybe it sounds silly," Jorge trailed off, as he told me about the loss of the intimacy in the small yard in the home his parents had lived in before him. "I'm not saying the balance of the world is at stake. There are people in this country who have to fight for much more basic things. This isn't a matter of life and death," he paused, looking into his coffee. "But it is a question of the life I thought I'd lead, in this house, with my wife, now with my kids and later when they're gone. To some people maybe it sounds frivolous, but I always thought I would die in this house. And then, one morning, I woke up, and they were pouring the fourth story of concrete over my yard."

Parks, then, are just part of the story. There are patchy bits of green with access to sun and sky throughout the city that are nestled within, but not overwhelmed by, concrete. But as with public parks, these patchy outdoor ecologies were made precarious by intensified private development. Buildings seemed to be taking over, and the winds had become fiercer, the sun scarcer, and the kind of dynamically manageable intensity described in Durand's poem less sustainable.

Urban gardening, drying laundry, and lives lived in intimate spaces close to the sun and the sky were practices through which vecinos developed sensibilities about good barrio life, a life in which the sun, wind, plants, and

FIGURE 3.6. New balconies, as seen from Patricia's *terraza*.
Photo courtesy of Salvemos al Barrio.

neighbors cohabited built environments that allowed for the composition of livable urban worlds. As with the Amigos del Lago in the Parque 3 de Febrero, they also produced a sensitivity to encroachment that helped vecinos attune to changing urban ecologies and intervene in their ongoing transformation as they worked to knit together concerns for good barrio life with the kinds of built environments that have long provided an environment for that life.

Built Environments: Barrio Buildings

I've landed in a marvelous pension house. The building threatens collapse from one day to the next, but the patio is so full of plants, vines and grapes, pigeons, chickens and birds, that I wouldn't trade my little room with iron bars for the entire Pasaje Güemes.

—ROBERTO ARLT, *Aguafuertes Porteñas*, 1993

As I mentioned earlier, a dictionary would translate the word *barrio* to mean *neighborhood*, which indeed it does. But barrios are not just generic spatial units through which the city is divided into parts. Instead barrios in Buenos Aires are spaces in which particular architectural forms, domestic life, and cultural values come together in a way that is typically contrasted to the dense, cosmopolitan urbanity of more elite sectors of the city. It was only in the last century that today's barrios became part of the city at all; prior to that, they were suburban hinterlands, more rural than urban. Then, in the late nineteenth and early twentieth centuries, the city's boundaries and the urban population began to expand dramatically: suburbs were annexed to the city, a modern street grid was laid out, and the population quickly expanded to fill these new areas of the city, typically buying lots in auctions and constructing their homes over time.

Today, barrios remain defined by their contrast with the urban center. As a relational category constructed through comparison, *barrio* is deployed as an adjective as often as it is as a noun: some barrios, and even parts of barrios, are considered "more barrio" than others. Places that are more barrio are typically more isolated, less sophisticated, and support a less transient population, in which several generations of a family might live.[8] Time is said to have a different rhythm in barrios, where change is slower than in the center; because of this, barrios are considered by many to be authentic preserves of a more traditional porteño life. As such, even while barrios are opposed to the bustling, dense, urbane city center, they are also taken to define Buenos Aires' urban identity: Buenos Aires is the "city of a hundred barrios," according to a popular waltz from 1945, and barrio landscapes feature prominently in tango romances carried out in muddy alleyways under lonely lamplights. Barrios are thus both other to, while also defining features of, urban life in Buenos Aires.

These characteristics of barrios are bound up with architectural forms of barrio life. Barrios are less dense than the urban center and are generally characterized by landscapes of low-rise buildings and quiet, more intimate streets (see figures 3.7 and 3.8). In many respects, these built environments also serve to carry something of barrios' more rural histories into the present through the ongoing importance of patchy outdoor spaces to barrio life. The typologies of buildings in barrios is hardly uniform, but nearly all of them feature a connection to the outdoors through rooftop terraces, patios, or open sky passageways.

In his genealogical study of porteño housing typologies, *Buenos Aires y Algunas Constantes en las Transformaciones Urbanas*, Fernando Diez (1996)

FIGURES 3.7 and 3.8. Villa Pueyrredón barrio landscapes. Photo by author and courtesy of Salvemos al Barrio, respectively.

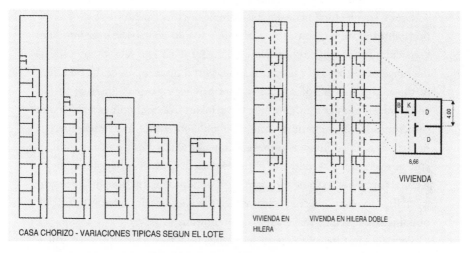

CASA CHORIZO - VARIACIONES TIPICAS SEGUN EL LOTE

VIVIENDA EN HILERA

VIVIENDA EN HILERA DOBLE

VIVIENDA

FIGURE 3.9. Variations of the Casa Chorizo show open space to the right of the lot and rooms or internal patios opening onto it; larger lots also have open space in the back. Image from Diez (1996, 43).

FIGURE 3.10. Vivienda en Hilera and Vivienda en Hilera Doble. Individual units open off of a shared open-air hallway. The individual units feature a semi-private patio uniting the other rooms. Image from Diez (1996, 51).

traces the transformation of vernacular architectural forms over the course of the city's history. His work reveals an architectural genealogy rooted in houses with large gardens and patios that, as the city became more densely built and populated, began to shrink and contort themselves while still retaining features of earlier typologies. In one line of the genealogy, for example, the colonial-era Casa de Patios became the Casa Chorizo at the end of the nineteenth century. Half the width of the Casa de Patios, the Casa Chorizo substituted the former's central courtyard with a four-meter-wide open-air or semicovered passage along one side of the lot, with rooms opening onto it (see figure 3.9). As densification increased in the first half of the twentieth century, the Casa Chorizo, too, was divided, this time not in width but in depth, such that two (and later more) units extended the depth of the lot with a common open-air hallway and semiprivate patios leading to the internal rooms (see figure 3.10). When buildings began to be built upward, this contact with outdoor patios was transformed but not eliminated; ground floors had physical access to them, while upper floors retained views of the patios below and access to the air and light they provided.

Diez's architectural genealogy is complex, with a great number of variations and transformations, some of which would be carried over into later vernacular forms while others would not. But what one sees looking across the range of history Diez presents is the central place, up until the buildings of the mid-1940s on, of structures that privilege gardens, internal patios, and terraces, even as they continue to shrink in size. Sometimes smaller and sometimes larger, sometimes collective and sometimes individual, there is nevertheless an endurance of these architectural features over time. And, of course, even in the second half of the twentieth century, when newer architectural forms began to be the main form of new construction, in the majority of the city, especially in barrios where the pace of rebuilding is less rapid, buildings that predate this era remain predominant.

Persistent features of the porteño architectural landscape, spaces of articulation with the outdoors have endured a long history of densification—an endurance that fostered, but also depended on, ongoing relational practices with plants, animals, and the elements. Consider, for example, the epigraph by Roberto Arlt, one of Buenos Aires' most famed chroniclers of urban life. His *Aguafuertes Porteñas*, originally published in 1933, remains widely read and offers humorous, acerbic, and touching sketches of daily life in Buenos Aires.[9] The epigraph is from an essay in which he describes in detail his relationship with two dogs owned by his landlady in a run-down pension house in the barrio of Flores. The patio, together with its urban flora and fauna, sets the scene of barrio life and stands in contrast to the Patio Güemes, a luxurious 1915 art nouveau building in the center of the city and one of Buenos Aires' first skyscrapers. The patio teemed with life: plants, vines, grapes, chickens, and birds—along with the dogs, their owner, and Arlt. The building was not luxurious, but even though it threatened collapse, Arlt says he wouldn't give it up for the entire Pasaje Güemes and the urbane luxury of the center it symbolized.

Today, patios like the one Arlt loved remain important parts of urban life in Buenos Aires and can be found throughout the city, but are especially prominent and important in barrios. Patios, gardens, and terraces are not only present in larger houses and apartments, nor are they the exclusive domain of the well-off. Instead, contact with the sky, sunlight, air, and plants are considered important elements of urban life even for the smallest and most basic dwellings. To enter the apartment of my friend César, for instance, one passes through the door of what looks from the front to be a house (the lot is some eight meters wide, the building one story high). On passing through the building door, however, the space opens onto a very long, open-air walkway that opens up on both sides to studio apartments, each of which has a small piece of patio in front of their door (a "Double Vivienda en Hilera," to use Diez's terminology, as shown in figure 3.10). The main room of César's studio measured about four meters squared, and the bathroom had neither a bathtub nor a separate shower (he showers straddling the toilet from a spigot overhead). Nevertheless, he had a small piece of patio filled with plants outside his front door, which, along with the walkway to the apartment, opened to the sky overhead.

Patricia's apartment in Villa Pueyrredón is similar, though larger: again, the street entrance appears to be a building of two stories, but the lot is deep, and many individual units open up off of it. The apartments in Patricia's building are all duplexes, and from the second floor you can access the rooftop terrace, which is used for barbecues, to hold plants, and to dry clothes. An internal patio descending from the terrace brings light and air into an open space on the ground floor (see figures 3.11 and 3.12). Two other friends of mine, Sergio and Adrián, have a small, relatively dark apartment but a huge terrace where they sit all summer long, and where Sergio keeps his plants—including a "norteño sector," with cactuses that he says take him back to his ancestral home in the Argentine northwest (see figure 3.13). My friend Pablo lives in a casa chorizo, with a patio sitting between his house and the shared passageway where he grows his plants and dries clothes (see figure 3.14). Another friend, also named Pablo, has only a tiny balcony in his second-floor apartment. It opens onto an airshaft between buildings, but it, too, is teeming with greenery (see figure 3.15). These spaces offer vital zones of engagement in which even small, dark apartments are allowed contact with sun, air, and plants.

The contact offered by such spaces was not just elemental. In my own apartment, especially on summer nights with the windows open, I could hear the near-deaf building association's president screaming at her husband; the couple on the third floor making love; and two young men I could never identify, whose conversations about politics echoed down from their windows into my ground-floor patio. These voices turned the patios into a kind of intimate social space, at once private and not, at times endearing and at times exasperating.[10]

New buildings are typically different. Lower-end models, like those built along the avenue in Villa Pueyrredón, often have neither patios nor terraces, and in some cases even lacked the balconies common in the rest of the city. My friend Nadia's small apartment was accessed via an elevator, then a windowless foyer; her balcony overlooked the tall buildings surrounding the back of the lot and the carpark located below. New higher-end buildings, too, are different. They tend to have luxurious, amenity-filled rooftop terraces, with

FIGURES 3.11 AND 3.12. Two views from a terrace in Villa Pueyrredón; the stairwell in the middle of the first photo leads down to an open-air patio on the ground floor. In the second, clothes dry on the neighbor's patio with new buildings in the background. Photos courtesy of Salvemos al Barrio.

(*clockwise from top left*)
FIGURE 3.13. Sergio and
Adrián's terrace, with a
hammock strung across the
foreground, plants around
the edge, a small table and
washing machine, and lines
for hanging laundry.
Photo by author.
FIGURE 3.14. The patio of
a casa chorizo. Photo by
author.
FIGURE 3.15. Pablo's plants on
a small patio in an airshaft.
Photo by author.

FIGURE 3.16. A collective rooftop terrace in a new building, with hot tubs and chairs for lounging. Photo by author.

hot tubs, pools, and collective decks (see figure 3.16). In these shared spaces, people are not allowed to hang laundry or tend their own plants. Neither lower-end buildings, which often lack such outdoor spaces, nor higher-end buildings with shared luxury spaces that feel like resorts, offer the kind of intimate, dynamically manageable intensity of urban life that was captured in Durand's poem, or that many people in barrios felt to be at stake in the face of new development.

Barrio Culture, Barrio Politics: A History

Barrio ecologies are historical formations that endure in the present in part through the ongoing presence of certain kinds of buildings that form the built environment. But buildings aren't the only means through which barrio ecologies are made to endure in the present. Deep political and cultural histories were also responsible for creating barrios as unique historical manifestations in Buenos Aires—political and cultural histories that remain part of barrio ecologies today, even as they are reconfigured in light of more recent transformations.

Vecinos in groups like Salvemos al Barrio and Amigos del Lago are the continuation of a long history of political formation in barrios centering on ecological concerns that bring the elements together with built environments. For some observers of Buenos Aires history, these politics are seen to be constitutive of barrio life itself. The historian Adrián Gorelik (2001), for example, has traced the intertwined cultural histories of the urban street grid and the park in Buenos Aires between 1887 and 1936. He finds Buenos Aires' peculiar barrio identities in the nexus of water and sewage networks, political geography, real estate development, and the modern urban grid that structured Buenos Aires' urban form at the turn of the twentieth century.

Gorelik argues that the concept of the barrio was one that could enter the Americas in general—and the flat Argentine pampas, or plains, in particular— only with a great deal of translation. In European cities, he explains, barrios were defined in large part by topological features of urban environments, emerging in relation to the mountains and valleys in which they developed. Cities and neighborhoods in Europe emerged tracing the contours of these variegated landscapes to develop intimate internal circulations, the specificity of which in turn produced the barrio as a social phenomenon. While in the European city, winding streets produced the physical and social medium of the barrio, neighborhood life in the Americas emerged through a different path. At a time when cities around the world were growing rapidly, observers looked to the expansive, flat terrain of American cities—including the flat Argentine pampa surrounding Buenos Aires—with an excited mixture of hope and fear. The hope came from the possibility of a new urban form—the modern street grid—that might break with the balkanized physical, social, and political traditions of European cities, hierarchically organized around castles and cathedrals. The regular, repetitive, and expansive pattern language of the grid, in contrast, brimmed with the possibility of egalitarian social inclusion, put into a physical form that couldn't be more different from the hierarchical earthly and architectural topographies of European cities. But there was also fear about what such a break might mean: what would society become without the moorings of topographical, architectural, and social differentiation to give people a place in the city and in society? The modern street grid, an emergent idea in urban planning, was felt by many to be poised to only reinforce the problematic social implications of the pampa's flat earthly topography. As much as the grid offered the possibility of broad inclusion, it was also seen (like the flat pampa on which it would be laid out) to threaten identity and community with the anomie of expansive homogeneity.

Buenos Aires' grid was laid out in 1898, incorporating 14,000 hectares of land to the city and more than quadrupling its size. The city would expand to fill this grid in only a few decades, transforming what had been suburbs into the emergent "barrios" of Buenos Aires. Initially, many observers doubted whether something like a neighborhood would even be possible in this new, undifferentiated natural-cultural topology of grid-on-pampa. In the end, barrios did emerge in Buenos Aires, but in a different way than they had in Europe, a historical emergence relevant to what barrios are today and to vecinos' political mobilizations around barrio life.

Gorelik traces the emergence of barrios in Buenos Aires through two intertwined phenomena. The first grew out of efforts to include barrios in the modern image of the good life, particularly in relation to urban infrastructural services. In the newly lotted areas of the city of the 1920s, basic infrastructure was often lacking. Residents of particular zones came together to advocate for water, gas, and sewage connections, creating *sociedades de fomento*, or development societies. These collective practices of advocacy helped create a social and political sphere in which emergent barrio identities could thrive (Gorelik 2001, 273–306). Thus while for some historians Buenos Aires' rapid expansion signaled the production of space on private economic terms through real estate development projects (e.g., Scobie 1974), for Gorelik advocacy around infrastructure served to produce the barrio as a public political sphere.[11] These institutions—together with schools, neighborhood social and athletic clubs, and urban parks that were meant to foster a new, egalitarian sphere of collective urban life—served as vehicles of particularity and identity within the undifferentiated grid of the modern metropolis, working to instantiate neighborhood identities on an otherwise homogeneous formal structure. Private concerns about infrastructure thus morphed into a new political public sphere, converting the homogeneous lotted grid into differentiated political environments. Gorelik calls this barrio, grounded in neighborhood advocacy for infrastructural inclusion and respectable life, the *barrio cordial*, or polite barrio.

The emergent barrios of the early twentieth century were not just the product of political advocacy for infrastructural inclusion and modern amenities, however. They were also the product of an emergent literary and musical culture that romanticized barrios' marginality. Barrios' unpaved streets, incomplete sewage and water networks, and a population of poorer, more recent immigrants had lent barrios a certain alterity that was both troubling and romantic vis-à-vis the more elite colonial city, which began to lose political and cultural hegemony as the barrios became powerful political and cultural forces in the city. While some sought the inclusion and respectable urbanity that came with being part of the city, others romanticized barrios' extra-urban marginality as picturesque reserves of the past. Gorelik calls this other manifestation of the barrio the *barrio pintoresco*. Part of an explosive literary culture of the margins (Sarlo 1988) that included journalists, playwrights, poets, painters, and songwriters, the barrio pintoresco spread and was sustained through barrio cultural institutions like popular theaters, popular libraries, and *peñas*, rustic cultural events that featured live music and poetry readings. In the barrio of tango music and marginal literature, Gorelik finds the other to the onward march of development and respectability that were central to the political and infrastructural improvements of *progresismo*, which called upon ideas of social ascent, innocence, and the social life of the nuclear family. If the barrio cordial was symbolically loaded with a drive for progress and a respectable, domestic, familial life, tango and popular literature romanticized barrios' muddy streets and poor, unemployed, depressed residents. This was the *barrio reo*, or rough barrio, which the barrio pintoresco romanticized, rejecting the barrio as a site of urban modernization and giving voice to the barrio's otherness and its power to erode the barrio cordial's pretensions of smooth inclusion in modern metropolitan life.

The barrios of tango, for example, opposed progressive modernity with descriptive urban scenography centered on dark, muddy streets that were sites of heartache, loneliness, and violence.[12] Consider the scene set by González Castillo's lyrics from *Sobre el pucho*: "An alleyway in Pompeya / and a streetlamp outlining the mud, / and there, a thug that smokes, / and a street organ grinding out a tango."[13] Other tangos, like the lyricist Celedonio Flores's "Corrientes y Esmeralda," tell grand tales of street fights and romantic encounters with prostitutes lush with urban scenography, while still others address the barrio itself as a woman with whom rough men have a profound affective relationship. Alberto Vacarezza's popular theatrical work *El Conventillo de la Paloma* is one example of this kind of love song to the barrio, in which the rejection of the barrio cordial is clearly evident:[14] "Villa Crespo! . . . Rough barrio, / of narrow streets / and little houses badly made / you were beautiful for your ugliness. . . . You're no longer what you were before / Villa Crespo of my dreams, / other laws and other owners have widened your streets, . . . and in building walls / you began to change your color. / What do you want with the posture / of your stores and your streets, / your cinemas and your cafes, / if the paint has taken hold of you? / You've been deceived by the architecture of the municipal plan." In these lines of verse, the speaker addresses the barrio as he might a woman, lamenting its transformation as a betrayal—the paint, like makeup, beautifies, but only superficially. Deceived by the architecture of the municipal plan, the barrio is no longer interested in humble stores and cafes. Underscoring the transformation, the words used to describe the old neighborhood are written in *lunfardo*, porteño street slang: *fecas* for cafes, *llecas* for streets. Tragic relationships that happen in and with the city manifest in these stories of love and loss, forming part of the encyclopedic compendium of sadness and betrayal from which tango narrates affective porteño lifeworlds.

Between the barrio cordial and the barrio pintoresco there was little consensus; instead, they produced almost contradictory manifestations of the kinds of things barrios were. These contradictions—between the middle-class barrio of respectability, social ascent, and infrastructural improvement on the one hand and the mythologized barrio of anti-progressive marginality on the other—would prove to be enduring, installing themselves as fundamental features of urban life as Buenos Aires became increasingly identified with the barrios that were both other to, while also the largest part of, the city. In "The Mythological Foundation of Buenos Aires," the author Jorge Luis Borges reflects on this changing cultural landscape, offering an alternative founding mythology to the consensus version of history, which locates the founding of Buenos Aires on the shores of the Rio de la Plata. Instead, Borges claims that Buenos Aires' origin was a square block in the middle of the pampa, on what would later become his barrio of Palermo. Borges's innovation, Gorelik argues, was in the way he was able to connect these contradictory impulses into a foundational mythology for the city. Neither purely nostalgic nor progressive, Borges's mythological barrio origin story united and poetically empowered both, allowing a barrio garden to be read as a "small square of pampa in the patio behind the wall" (Gorelik 2001, 381). Borges thus depicts the barrio block as the site that united both pampa and grid, archaic and modern, producing what Gorelik calls a "counter-progressive modernity" that defined, through the barrio, the contradictions of Buenos Aires.[15]

This contradictory history between the barrio cordial and the barrio pintoresco continues to endure in struggles over barrio life today, and Gorelik's cultural history helps me to draw together sites that may otherwise seem disparate. The hug of the Lago de Regatas and the sensibilities that the lake helped produce about encroachments of private property offer historical echoes of early twentieth-century ideas about urban parks as vehicles for the production of a public sphere in an urban topography that many saw threatened by the anomie of homogeneous extension. It was the communal space of the park—a space historically designed to produce collective life in opposition to the anomie of the grid—that formed, for Amigos del Lago, the staging ground for developing critiques about private property and its incursions into the park. The political mobilizations that came together around parks, gardens, and terraces in the work of Salvemos al Barrio and other organizations that gathered to stem the construction of tall buildings, too, can be read as rearticulations of the political activities that first produced barrios as distinctly American institutions founded on political advocacy. They remind us that barrios in the Americas have long been political entities, not simple geographic demarcations.

But at the same time, and in crucial contrast to the sociedades de fomento of the barrio cordial, contemporary barrio politics also draw heavily from the anti-progressive thrust of porteño barrios' multivalent history, working to hold on to the simple and humble features of the barrios they value. If today the streets are paved and services are more reliable, barrios nevertheless retain something of the unsophisticated romance forged in these histories of urban life, a mythological identity enshrined in tango lyrics, art, and the writing of people like Arlt and Borges. Nelly and Abel's backyard, Mario's garden, and Durand's terraza, in this sense, continue to be crucial sites for the maintenance of contradictory histories of the barrio cordial and the barrio pintoresco: they make the excessive remainder of these other histories endure within the urban environments of progressive modernity by holding on to the simple and humble features of the barrios they live in. Gardens and terraces, in an important sense, remain pieces of the pampa in Buenos Aires' urban landscape, holding on to something foreign to both the grid and to progressive modernity. Something of that excess remains, made to haunt modern urban life in the hands of vecinos, supported still by tango and barrio literature, which remain widely popular; they continue to inhabit built environments, are formative of the affective and political attachments of many porteños, and help make barrio pasts endure in the present.

These resonances signal the deep ground on which efforts to defend barrio life in the early twenty-first century were undertaken. The elements, infrastructure, the plan of the grid, and music, literature, and neighborhood political action have deep and entangled pasts. Their inheritances and inherences— reaching back into time and into one another—helped make barrios what they are today.

In 2009, I stood with a group of about fifty vecinos gathered at the corner of Avellaneda and Nicasio Oroño in Caballito, where they engaged in a partial blockade of Avellaneda, cutting off three of its five traffic lanes. There, vecinos stood with signs and banners, talked with one another, and made speeches into a bullhorn as the traffic rolled by slowly and a few independent media organizations filmed the event. The protest that night had been called by SOS Caballito, who had learned that a law to rezone former railroad lands in Caballito for the construction of a shopping mall may have been making its way to a vote in the city legislature. The corporation attempting to build the mall, IRSA, was responsible for various other large projects in the city, including two towers over thirty stories high in Caballito and a recently built shopping mall in Saavedra, a formerly quiet residential neighborhood on the border of the city. Vecinos themselves wanted the railroad lands to be used for the creation of a *corredor verde*—a chain of parks that would cut across the east-west axis of the city along lands adjacent to the railroad line. Proposed officially in 2001, the narrow park would stretch eleven kilometers long and increase the amount of green space in the city tenfold.

Although the proposal for the park had all the airs of an official plan, things were taking a long time. This might be expected for a proposal of this magnitude, but it was also possible, many argued, that they were taking longer than they should have: if it had been a project behind which the right people stood to make money, many said, things would have moved more quickly. Instead, the proposal was for a park. Large tracts of unbuilt land like those bordering the railroad tracks were prized targets not just for those advocating transforming the land into parks, but also for real estate development—and even more so in the boom years, when property was getting more expensive. If these lands were to be rezoned to allow for residential construction, they could support projects at a scale more difficult to carry out in already built areas of the city.[16] Like the project for the five-star hotel that Amigos del Lago had foiled in the 1990s, open spaces like the railroad yards allowed developers' imaginations to run free. A powerful developer like the IRSA Corporation was feared to have enough clout to get legislators to write them special regulations, allowing them to use these lands for private development. Indeed, some vecinos feared that the plan for the park may have been little more than a distraction, one that threatened to lull people into a state of calm while developers carved up the land among themselves: it was possible that the plan for the park would never actually come to fruition, and even that no one in the government had any real intention of following through with it, but were instead using it as a kind of screen for other, darker ambitions. The slow pace of movement on the park was thus also understood to be a time filled with the possibility that the park would be derailed completely or slowly eroded through the plan's persistent modification. Vecinos thus had to be vigilant, and even a rumor that the rezoning might be coming to a vote required quick mobilization.

In a political environment friendly to real estate and other corporate interests, the danger that the railroad lands would be rezoned for private development felt especially pronounced. Consider an image from a poster at the protest: Mauricio Macri, at the time the mayoral *jefe de gobierno* of Buenos Aires (who would become president of Argentina in 2015), looms large over the landscape, peering over a group of buildings at the park that lay beyond them, looking ravenous and sinister (see figure 3.17). Macri, who comes from a powerful elite family, led an administration that took a businesslike, managerial approach to running the city.[17] Another sign at the protest deepened this connection between the city government and real estate interests through a play on real estate brokers' signage: "For Sale: Exceptional Lots—Public Green Spaces for Towers and Shopping Malls—Rezoning by request—Macri and Associates Realtors" (see figure 3.18). Indeed, some large buildings had already been approved along the railroad lines, and their silhouettes towered on the horizon, reminding us of possible futures (see figure 3.19).

Nearly a century after the efforts of vecinos to obtain basic infrastructural services in newly lotted parts of the city consolidated barrios as political entities, contemporary barrio dwellers worked to articulate barrios' historical contradictions with new political and economic environments, in particular the burgeoning real estate market.[18] My use of the word *articulation* strikes at both senses of the term: on the one hand the "act of putting into words," of describing in a discursive political sphere the set of values they held in barrio environments, and at the same time the "act of jointing together to allow for movement," what Tim Choy (2005) has described as the "scaling, linking, and mobilization" of different types of knowledge with one another. What were the creative articulations through which vecinos worked to make the barrio ecologies they cared about intelligible within the specific economic and political atmospheres of post-crisis Buenos Aires? How did they work to articulate concern for barrio ecologies with politically resonant questions that could imbue changes in the barrio with an eventful presence capable of being noticed?

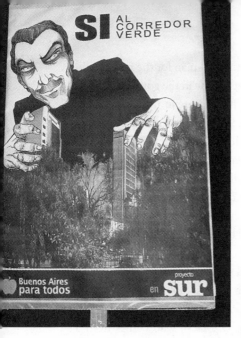

FIGURE 3.17. A protest poster depicts Mauricio Macri gazing ravenously at a park. Photo by author.

FIGURE 3.18. "Inmobiliaria Macri," a protest poster casting the administration as a real estate agency. Photo by author.

FIGURE 3.19. A tall building looms over the railroad lines in Caballito. Photo by author.

The protest on that night was one of the sites through which vecinos worked to articulate their concerns for patios, terraces, and gardens in their backyards with wider barrio ecologies that included green public spaces like parks. sos Caballito, who convened the partial blockade of Avellaneda that night, had not been born from concerns for park land and public green space. Instead, like Salvemos al Barrio in Villa Pueyrredón, the group had been founded around concern for smaller patches of green space in backyards, gardens, and terraces. Much of Caballito, which straddles the border between a richer north and a poorer south in the geographical center of the city, is solidly upper middle class and urbanized, with a shopping mall, a multiplex cinema, and a bustling commercial center where residential buildings can climb to twenty stories high. The areas to the north and south, however, are more barrio, and in the first years of the boom big changes were seen in these parts of Caballito.[19] I have already mentioned Mario, whose garden lost its sun when a ten-story building was built next to his home in the north of Caballito. Recounting the early days of what would become sos Caballito, Mario told me that he began gathering signatures on a petition to limit the construction of tall buildings. He suspected that the petition was going to end up as "toilet paper in an official's office," however, so he also hung a banner, which spanned the street in front of his house like those used in barrios to celebrate birthdays or proclaim love for a girlfriend. The banner read, "Here, they are trying to put up buildings that are going to change the characteristics of our barrio. We must band together and resist!" Several people came to an initial meeting, and legal battles, legislative action, and protests followed, making sos Caballito one of the earliest vecino groups to make headlines for their movement against tall buildings in the mid-2000s. They eventually achieved the zoning change they wanted, but several members of the group remained active, and it was they who learned in 2009 that the proposal to rezone the former railroad lands in Caballito may have been making its way to a vote in the city legislature.

....

Vecino political actions surrounding the barrio were more than a simple defense of private property. On the contrary, many vecinos saw their efforts as working against their own particular interests. Abel, Nelly, and Mario, for example, had already lost much of the sunlight, sky, and intimate space they valued to the tall buildings that had been built around their homes. The easiest thing they could have done, they told me, was to sell their land to a developer and move away. Furthermore, the zoning limits they advocated were unlikely to increase the value of their property and would probably decrease their property values, since restrictions on building height would make their lots unattractive to developers. Instead, barrios and the kinds of politics I witnessed unfolding in their name are steeped in a set of relations that problematize divisions of space between the private and the public. In the most obvious sense, this was manifest in the way vecino activism contested the unrestricted ability to build whatever one wants on a lot, drawing individual lots into an arena of public concern and debate. Their concern for the intimate, domestic life of gardens, patios, and terraces was also not reducible to concern for private property; their domestic life mattered to them, instead, as part of a broader ecology of barrio living that the private does not conceptually capture.[20] Several of the vecinos in Villa Pueyrredón, for example, had visited the new buildings going up in their neighborhood and told me they found the apartments there small, ill-equipped, and unable to support what they saw as a good life for the buildings' future inhabitants.[21] Rather than treating developments as a question of private property and individual consumption, vecinos treated them and the domestic life they created as an object of public concern. They gathered around a set of values in the built environment that were domestic but not private and worked to make those values politically relevant. The object of vecinos' care included domestic life, but always already as part of a broader ecology of barrio living; their approach to buildings was predicated on their relation to the barrio, a lifeworld that is more than a collection of fragmented pieces of private property, but that also extends into domestic life.

As they worked to make changes to barrio life noticeable within broader political spheres, vecinos experimented with several possible articulations—some of which would have more traction than others in enrolling interest in, and allies to, their cause. Historic preservation, for example, was one way to articulate concerns for changing urban environments that some groups in Buenos Aires were deploying with a degree of success. The city was undergoing rapid changes, and there was a widely held and palpable sense that a shared history embodied in architectural forms was slipping away as older buildings were torn down to build tall buildings in their place. In neighborhoods like Caballito and Villa Pueyrredón, however, historic preservation had to be substantially reformulated if it were to have any traction: unlike the Petit Hotels or arcade-like galleries of more central areas like Recoleta, the buildings of Caballito and Villa Pueyrredón were not recognized as historically valuable and worthy of preservation. In their efforts at articulating concern for barrios

with a discourse of historic preservation, vecinos in Caballito and Villa Pueyrredón worked to adapt preservationist forms of recognition to the barrio
by arguing that barrio life itself—the style of life given by a neighborhood
of low buildings—was part of Buenos Aires' *patrimonio cultural,* or cultural
heritage, and one that was being lost at the hands of development *en altura*
(lit. "in height," i.e., tall buildings). But barrios and their buildings did not
enter easily into this kind of preservationist politics, and historic preservation
remained a marginal articulation for barrio politics.

Environmentalism, too, offered possible articulations and was attractive
not only because many vecinos thought of themselves as environmental advocates (and were often involved in environmental politics more broadly) but
also because there was already a bureaucratic mechanism through which to
channel such advocacy: the environmental impact statement. But as with historic preservation, the effectiveness of describing changes to barrio life in an
idiom of environmental impact was more effective in some places than it was
in others. In Palermo, for example, talking about barrios in an environmental
register gained traction because the barrio faced flash flooding several times
a year during heavy rains, and open green spaces could be framed as valuable because they provided vital absorptive terrain for rainwater. Similarly, in
several barrios I heard people talk about excess cement as generative of *islas
de calor,* or heat islands, through which they sought to draw out the value of
green spaces for their cooling properties. As with historic preservation, vecinos also worked to push the environmental in new directions: SOS Caballito
achieved several early victories by arguing that the city's aging infrastructural
network was inadequate to the task of providing services if the pace of building continued. They posted videos online showing the low water pressure in
their homes and suggested that gas and sewage networks might be similarly
affected. They took the matter to court in a series of cases filed in 2006 and
2007. Many new buildings fell below the threshold of square footage that required them to file an environmental impact statement, but vecinos in Caballito argued that, taken together, the projects posed serious environmental
impacts. Despite developers' attempts to hold on to the individual building
as the bureaucratic object in question, the courts were sympathetic and ruled
that the state had to consider the effect of the total amount of building in
the neighborhood, granting a judicial stay on the issuance of construction
permits in Caballito in late 2006 in light of the impact on water services. The
city attempted to sidestep this requirement by asking the water company to
certify infrastructural capacity before awarding any new permits. Unable to

provide such assurance, the water company refused, and the issuance of construction permits ground to a halt, earning sos Caballito its earliest coverage on the front page of national papers, until the stay was overturned on appeal.

But talking about changes to barrio ecologies in a register of real estate speculation, as they did in the protest on that November night, appeared to offer vecinos in barrios the most traction in articulating their concerns for barrio life with wider structures of awareness and attention. Speculation offered the possibility to link up their concerns for their patios and gardens not only with public parks, but with historical forms of dispossession and urban environmental change that were resonant for a broad cross section of Argentines. What tied together their patios and gardens with parks and larger green spaces was, in no small part, a concern for real estate developers' (and in many cases the city government's) treatment of the city as little more than a giant machine for generating rents. Casting the city government as a real estate brokerage—one that would adapt zoning to the desire of developers— was one way to draw attention to governing attitudes toward open urban spaces that always saw them as a ground for more development. It was a way of making the quasi-event of persistent private real estate development in the city into an event that could be noticed and questioned.

These efforts, however, unfolded on a complex discursive terrain in which the going was not always easy. Some voices unsympathetic to Salvemos al Barrio's efforts in Villa Pueyrredón, for example, worked to portray their stance as retrograde, obstructionist, and standing in the way of "progress." For them, the neighborhood was changing, modernizing, becoming more of a center and less of a backwater, while Salvemos al Barrio was stuck in the past, too wedded to tradition and old values. In response, vecinos had to work to cast urban construction not as part of a progressive advance toward a better future, but as an outcome of a more monstrous drive for profit. They were able to do so in part by leveraging the deep historical contradictions that endured in the figure of the barrio to cast new tall buildings as the antithesis of barrio life, calling upon the ongoing romantic connection many porteños had with barrios as not completely urban places. In this sense, they worked to amplify the resonance between their contemporary real estate development and the urbanization of barrios that was decried in marginal literature and tango nearly a century earlier. These echoes helped attach the efforts of vecinos to deep structures of feeling that endured through tango music and other forms of popular culture that remained present in the cultural lexicon and valorized barrios as marginal, not quite urban, spaces.

Framing their struggle as one against speculation had more historically recent resonances as well, most centrally in the privatizations of the 1990s and the crisis that followed. Neoliberal discourses of development and progress had been used to justify selling off national resources, privatizing public goods, and sharply increasing foreign investment. The refrain that shared suffering from freed markets would be temporary and that good things would come to all at the end was a regular feature of claims made by politicians and economic experts during the 1990s: the nation would be made stronger and more agile the more it was exposed to market forces, even if the effects of liberalization appeared debilitating. But when everything came crashing down in 2001, this free-market discourse of development suffered a blow from which it would not fully recover in the following decade. When the dust settled following the crisis of 2001, it was clear to many that shared suffering had not resulted in a collective better future; rather, the benefits seemed to accrue to national and international elites. In the wake of the crisis of 2001, there was a widespread skepticism about finance, markets, and economic rationalization, making a conversation about speculation particularly resonant. In many ways the same arguments used to promote free markets in the 1990s were deployed in support of construction in barrios through the suggestion that building apartments would bring progress and prosperity to the barrio. To the extent that these arguments echoed the pro-market discourses of the 1990s in national politics, however, so too did they evoke the possibility of an impending collapse rather than a better world. What if, as with the national economy, letting market forces run their course didn't result in a better collective future, but little more than the extraction of wealth through financial speculation?

These sensibilities about the national economy were also present in popular considerations of the urban landscape. In the 1990s, real estate development had been characterized by the emergence of elite private gated communities in the suburbs of Buenos Aires, often built cheek-to-jowl with poor neighborhoods and informal settlements.[22] These developments had become emblematic of increasing inequality in Argentina and were critiqued as enclaves of privilege marked by fortified borders designed with the explicit purpose of excluding the poor who lived around them. After 2001, as development boomed within the city and began to transform many barrios, residents extended critiques of privatization developed around suburban gated communities in the 1990s to question the logics at play in the reconfiguration of urban life. In light of the history of gated communities, the construction of a fancy tower in a barrio could be read as the creation of yet another enclave of privilege, in which buildings with their own gymnasiums, common party spaces, and other amenities served to isolate them from the barrio around them.

Two images of the construction boom in the popular press, taken from the comic series *La Nelly*, point up the excessive, monstrous side of real estate development in the city and link it to broader structures of feeling operative in the years after 2001 (see figures 3.20 and 3.21).[23] In the first, Nelly, the main character, confronts the owner of M&M Brokers about the "express tower" that he's built in two hours while she sunned herself on her roof. "M&M Brokers," he introduces himself, "'we put a ceiling on your dreams!'" "Don't you know that this is a residential zone, and law 18743 states that you can't build more than 4 floors!?" Nelly asks him. "But there *are* only four floors!" M&M responds. "Three regular ones, and a fourth that's divided into 60 semi-floors!" Nelly rolls her eyes and asks him about flood risk, referencing an endemic problem attributed to overdevelopment in several parts of the city. M&M responds that she shouldn't worry—there are also plans to build water parks for swimming, aquatic sports, and regattas. In the excessive worldview of the corporation M&M represents, there is no problem for which "more construction" is not the answer: even urban ecological collapse can be leveraged for economic gain. Captured momentarily by his vision, Nelly imagines a future in which Buenos Aires' landmarks—the ecological reserve, the planetarium, and the iconic obelisk at the center of the city—are all transformed into new real estate developments. The Nelly series gains its comic thrust by recalling the excessive promises surrounding markets and unrestrained private development that characterized the 1990s. After the crisis of 2001, the discourse surrounding urban construction felt eerily similar to the promises of the 1990s, but they also fell on less receptive ears, coming at a time when the idea that free-market development would benefit all had already come under popular scrutiny.

Neighborhood groups leveraged these histories when they evoked real estate investment's excessive and monstrous manifestation, speculation, to characterize the transformation of barrios. Talking about real estate development as a form of speculation was a way to layer these recent Argentine histories onto barrios' enduring historical contradictions, articulating construction with shared historical experiences that resonated within broader cultural and social spheres. In the street protest in which I participated on that November night in Caballito, these histories were palpably present as vecinos worked to give real estate speculation an eventful presence in barrio ecologies and incorporate its critique into their environmental politics.

....

As I mentioned, the protest had been called by sos Caballito, who had learned that a law to rezone former railroad lands for the construction of a shopping mall may have been making its way to a vote. The situation, though, was murky. The land on which IRSA wanted to build the mall had allegedly been sold to them by a dummy corporation (*corporación fantasma*, lit. a phantom corporation) that had apparently purchased the land (perhaps illegally) from the Club Ferro Carril Oeste, an athletic club host to its eponymous national B-league soccer team. It was suspected that the phantom corporation had been set up by IRSA to obscure the identity of the true buyer and protect IRSA from the higher price the club might have sought if those responsible for the sale knew of the well-financed buyer behind the actual purchase. The phantom corporation was said to have bought the land and then turned around and sold it to IRSA within days, though the details weren't clear at the time.

With traffic on the Avenida cut to a trickle and the cameras rolling, one of the vecinos from sos Caballito spoke through a bullhorn: "Today, three years after the first popular protest that sos Caballito and other organizations held against cannibalistic buildings, we continue to fight for city legislators to legislate in favor of the quality of life of its residents, and we demand that they reject legislation that favors businesses dedicated to speculating with urban lands. Vecinos, too, are investors! We have the right, recognized by the Constitution of the City, to live in a healthy environment, and we have the responsibility to preserve and defend that life, because the environment is our common patrimony." With these words, the speaker recast the notion that corporations like IRSA invest in barrios, offering the alternative frame of cannibalistic speculation to characterize their activity; he argued instead that vecinos are the ones who are truly invested in barrios, an investment that is not only economic but part of a common environmental patrimony. He went on to recast IRSA's self-presentation through a close reading of their website: "[Quoting from IRSA's website:] 'As leaders in the development of urban enterprises, IRSA has sought at every opportunity to collaborate with the urban fabric, seeking the preservation or the development of assets that enrich citizens in the places where they live and work.' Well, we want to say to IRSA that we don't need their help—least of all given what they have perpetrated

FIGURES 3.20 AND 3.21. Scenes from *The Adventures of La Nelly*. Courtesy of Sergio Langer and Rubén Mira.

all over this city. IRSA doesn't want to enrich the residents of the city—they want to enrich themselves!" Urban enterprises, enrichment, and assets: their very language, he went on to explain, signaled the dissonance between IRSA's relationship with the barrio and those the vecinos wanted to defend.

Mario, from SOS Caballito, had expressed similar ideas in an earlier conversation with me: "This is an epoch in which real estate speculation has no limits. The entire juridical apparatus is at the service of indiscriminate construction. To such a point that if you have permission to build ten stories and you build twelve, you have to pay a fine of 3,000 pesos! Less than a thousand dollars to build 250 square meters that you can turn around and sell for 200,000 or 250,000 dollars. The profitability is monstrous." Nelly, from Salvemos al Barrio, had made a similar observation: "People's quality of life is something that they don't take into account at all. Here, the only thing that's taken into account is real estate speculation, that's the heart of the question for them: how do I speculate with what I have in order to earn the highest amount of money possible? This lot behind me, they paid 120,000 dollars for it. When they finish building it, they're going to earn more than ten times that."

These efforts to recast investment were widespread, gaining traction from histories of dispossession that were both recent and more distant. What for the speaker at the protest were cannibalistic buildings I had also seen described as "vampiric" in a barrio newspaper, an observation aimed to highlight how these developments are profitable precisely because the barrio around them is viewed as a good place to live: "In Palermo Viejo they are building a great wall of towers, all of which are sold as a 'new way of living,' rising up out of the greenery and with a good view. But it so happens that that greenery is the greenery of the gardens they overshadow, that the view is good because there are houses next to them, and that the lifestyle [they advertise] was built through those same houses. The towers come to vampirize what others have built. . . . They destroy elegance in order to sell it."[24] "The city of tango," the article concluded, "is not protected by legislators."

The vampiric and cannibalistic side of real estate development the speaker referred to is clearly evident in the rebranding of barrio living that was on prominent display in the marketing materials of the Dosplaza complex, two thirty-three-story towers being built a few blocks away, on a different piece of the former railroad lands in Caballito (the first of the buildings is pictured in figure 3.19). The marketing packet I gathered there features a series of artsy black-and-white photographs of old, decaying barrio buildings like the historic Mercado de Progreso, an indoor food market that continues to function in the late nineteenth-century building constructed by the Sociedad de Progreso de Caballito. The photos played up the barrio romance of the location of the towers, casting its proximity to historic barrio culture as part of its allure.[25] Another insert featured an extreme close-up of grass overlaid with the words "We return to the greenery," advertising the "10,500 m2 of park" associated with the complex. Inside are digital renderings of parents and children playing in a lush green environment: privatized green space that—if not for the development itself—might have been public park land (see figures 3.22 and 3.23). New developments like Dosplaza thus market barrio life, appropriating barrio value while simultaneously destroying it: on the one hand, a built environment they are in the active process of replacing with shiny new towers; on the other, green space transformed through the privatization of land.

Back at the bullhorn, the speaker continued to build connections between real estate, money, political power, and parks and gardens, reading aloud the lyrics from a song written by the Uruguayan songwriter Quintín Cabrera in 1979, "Los Asesinos del Paisaje," Assassins of the Landscape:

Witches that pull from their sleeves
permits and special laws,
they are present on all the street corners
and they have the keys to everything.

They kill parks, gardens, and hope.
Frightened streets are at their mercy.
Fabricating depressive cities,
They build giant nests with windows.

Unaccountable in years of fascism,
In democracy they do no worse:
They can be senators or ex-ministers,
Club presidents, whatever fits.

. . .

Their best ally is money,
They pay homage to gold, divine metal.
Their worst enemies, it is known,
Are the associations of vecinos.

As the protestors continued to build linkages between dispossession and development, on the sidelines of the protest others worked to sift through

FIGURES 3.22 AND 3.23. Marketing material from the Dosplaza apartment complex, 2009.

the opaque developments concerning IRSA's shopping mall and the possible rezoning of the railroad land that would make it possible. As with Amigos del Lago twenty years earlier, their concern with green space had taken them deep into the entangled worlds of money, politics, and property law.

Pedro, a lawyer and one of Osvaldo's long-time associates from Amigos del Lago, spoke on the sidelines with several of the people from SOS Caballito. He was encouraging them to pursue a legal path in addition to the political one of the protest. "You should hire an *escribano* [a notary] to do an investigation of the title," Pedro told them, "all the way back to when Ferro first got the land." Something about the phantom corporation that was rumored to have bought the land from Ferro and sold it to IRSA felt fishy to him. The vecinos from SOS Caballito weren't convinced at first; they didn't see the point in following the trail back that far, since Ferro had already sold the land. Operating from a perspective of markets in commodities, in which relationships between parties end after the transaction, this seemed like a fruitless path to follow. But what Pedro suspected was that the land had originally been transferred to Ferro as a gift from the state and that important restrictions on its use of the lands may have accompanied the transfer—for example, a requirement that they be used for the more collective ends of an athletic club. These old connections might be made to matter again, Pedro argued, if the vecinos could prove that Ferro's sale of the land to the phantom corporation was illegal in the first place. "This is how we finally stopped them from building that stadium in La Rural," Pedro explained, citing a successful episode in Amigos del Lago's ongoing fight over illegal transfers of land in the Parque 3 de Febrero in the 1990s, in this case to the powerful interests of the Argentine agricultural society that occupied several sectors of the park. "They wanted to build a stadium for 12,000 people and parking for thousands of cars," Pedro continued. "We investigated it, and it all went back to a telegram that specified the kind of use that they were allowed to make of that land. And there we had it—we filed a legal stay and we stopped it. Because the state doesn't just hand over land like it's private property—those lands came with conditions! But that's how we stopped it, with an investigation of the land title."

Both in the center and on the sidelines, then, vecinos continued the long project of cultivating sensibilities to the encroachments of private property on public lands, in the interests of defending the barrio from densifying development. As the member of SOS Caballito at the bullhorn worked to transmit and link issues of speculation in the barrio to histories of dispossession, vecinos taught one another about the legalities and bureaucracies that formed a central part of their barrio ecology.

Later that evening, in the middle of the protest, the organizers received a call from a legislator in the city assembly. The rezoning would not come up for a vote that week. Cheers went up from the crowd as the announcement was made over the bullhorn. Whether IRSA's efforts had been derailed because of the protest itself, because of political advocacy within the legislature, or because it was never going to happen in the first place was anyone's guess. But in the meantime, the members of SOS Caballito had made progress in the work of articulation that would help put the question of money and politics front and center in their struggle to hold on to livable barrio environments. A car creeping by alongside the protest opened his window to shout, "*Macri nos cagó a todos, eh!?*" Macri's screwed us all, hasn't he!?

CONCLUSION

A polluted lake in a public park facing encroachments by private sports clubs and a fantastic plan for a five-star hotel; gardens, patios and terraces overshadowed by tall buildings that generate gusty winds, floods, and problems with running water and sewage infrastructures; and a green belt in danger of derailment to build a shopping mall: three moments in which barrio ecologies face a conceptualization of space as little more than grounds for real estate development. But other features of Buenos Aires' barrio ecologies provide counterweights to the narrow forms of value embraced by ongoing development, not least of which are marginal literature and tango that have made the contradictory histories of barrios endure in the present, complemented by contemporary poetry like Durand's that offers evocative images of everyday barrio dwelling practices and holds present the possibility of a good life in barrio ecologies.

The partial blockade of the avenue in Caballito, like the hug of the lake, was part of an array of tactics through which vecinos engaged in performative public acts to intervene in their barrio ecologies. At other events I saw vecinos dressed as buildings, dancing in the streets to advocate for nine-meter height limits at barrio scale. There were also less eventful performances, like passing out pamphlets and gathering signatures for petitions, though vecinos tried to do these, too, with a bit of flair: vecinos from Salvemos al Barrio remembered with laughter the day they bought a bullhorn and rode through the barrio in a beat-up old jeep announcing the collection of signatures. Other vecinos installed a "civic robot" (a loudspeaker connected to a recording) that looped a long list of *denuncias*, or complaints, against the city government, which they installed outside the legislature on days of important public audiences.[26] Together with the hug of the lake and Mario's banner stretched across the street (which adopted popular forms of barrio communication between lovers to call vecinos to action), these tactics engage in the ongoing work of producing the barrio as a political space, leveraging barrios' long and contradictory cultural histories in the interest of making livable barrio environments endure.

Through their various activities, vecinos worked to articulate barrio ecologies with broader spheres of concern, drawing on recent histories of national economic dispossession and amplifying their resonance with post-crisis changes in urban life. These efforts helped to lend real estate an eventful presence, drawing it out and making it noticeable and open to public interrogation. But I also want to hold on to the humble, quotidian forms of care that underwrote these more overt political events, enabling a sensitivity to encroachment that helped vecinos mark changing urban ecologies and intervene in their ongoing transformation. Tending plants, hanging out laundry, jogging in parks, and looking at stars were vital incitements to noticing—grounds for developing a sensitivity to changing urban environments in a world in which money's centrality to shaping the city had to be noticed in order to be politicized. Attuning to the dark side of real estate development and making it eventful and noticeable was one way to begin to push real estate out of the realm of hegemonic common sense and make space for other dreams—dreams that are concretized in minor keys through the songs, poems, lake hugs, and protests that are also part of concrete's compound materiality in Buenos Aires. In the interest of helping such dreams endure, vecinos also brought their efforts into the halls of the city legislature, where they worked to translate the values of good barrio life into the concrete forms recognizable to the state and the regulatory tools it offered for remaking urban worlds—in particular, the urban planning code—a translation fraught with sticky questions of democratic participation and political voice that form the central concerns of chapter 4.

CHAPTER 4

Recoding the City

Plans, Codes, and the Politics of Voice

It's a rainy Tuesday night in Villa Pueyrredón, and the members of Salvemos al Barrio (some of whom I introduced in chapter 3) had moved their weekly assembly from its usual street corner to the cafe of a local athletic club seeking refuge from the rain. Seated loosely around a cluster of tables, Abel, Nelly, Patricia, Jorge, and others were discussing progress in their efforts to stem the tide of tall buildings that had been sweeping through the barrio over the past two years, when more than thirty ten-story buildings had been built along a sixteen-block stretch of the Avenida Salvador María del Carril. Like in other barrios in Buenos Aires, there was a stark contrast between these tall new buildings and the built environment that dominated the rest of the neighborhood: members of Salvemos al Barrio told me about gardens that wouldn't grow due to lack of sunlight; about strange winds that accelerated off the sides of buildings, slamming doors open and closed in the night; and about the new and unsettling kinds of intimacies generated by having ten stories of balconies overlooking their backyards. The new buildings had taken everyone by surprise. Aside from one tall structure on the avenue built in the 1960s or 1970s, everything but the trees were one or two stories high, and things had been this way for as long as anyone could remember (see images in chapter 3). The new tall buildings marked a drastic change in the barrio valued by vecinos, some of whose families had lived there for generations, while others had come more recently in search of a good home for their families.

In response, and inspired by the earlier efforts of groups like SOS Caballito, they had begun taking the organizational steps that would eventually draw them into the arcane world of state planning bureaucracy. Several vecinos had distributed pamphlets throughout the neighborhood and later began gathering signatures on a petition, setting up tables outside shops along the avenue and talking to as many people as they could. By the time I began attending their weekly street-corner assembly, they had used the petitions to secure meetings with several legislators and planners from the city government. The legislators had informed them that the new buildings were in compliance with regulations and that the only way to stem further construction was through a modification of the *Código de Planeamiento Urbano*, the city's urban planning code.

That rainy Tuesday night, several vecinos who had met with a legislator on the Urban Planning Commission were reporting back to the group. The legislator, who had said he would help them present a law that would address their grievances, had slightly altered the terms of the initial proposal, and the vecinos weren't sure why. Although none of them started out knowing much about urban planning, their language was already becoming laced with a halting, but increasingly fluent, use of the language of the code.[1]

"What I don't understand is why we're letting them go from R2bII to R2bI," Nelly said, leaning forward in her chair. "We agreed to R2bII in the first meeting, and they said they would respect that. So why are we talking about R2bI now?"

"He said R2bII would have trouble getting passed in the session, and that R2bI was almost the same thing," Patricia answered. "That the differences are like—if you had a laundromat that could be ten square meters, now it can be twenty. Things like that. And anyway, either one is much better than C3II."

"What about the differences in *altura maxima*, the maximum height?"

"For R2b1 it's 13.5."

"But is that the altura maxima?" Jorge asked, "because if it is, then it's 13.5 plus three, because of the floor that's set back."

Patricia flipped through her notes to see if she could answer his question.

"What we need is the 'planar limit,'" Jorge continued, "because *plano limite* and altura maxima aren't the same thing. Altura maxima is only for the part of the building that touches the municipal line. I don't think it counts the floors that are set back."

"Yeah," Ariel said, smiling, "and we want plano limite, because not even a TV antenna can go above that!"

Patricia started to answer thoughtfully, "I think that the antennas actually can, . . ." before she looked up, realized he was making a joke about the arcane complexity of the regulations, and cracked a smile along with the others.

Maximum heights and planar limits, R2bI and R2bII, the municipal line and other forms of technical vocabulary: this was the language of the code, a language in which vecinos became increasingly proficient in the course of their efforts. The code was the medium into which they worked to translate the values they held in barrio life in the hopes of making that life endure rather than see their barrio become a dense continuation of the urban life of the city center. Alongside learning the code's arcane language, vecinos also had to learn to navigate the structures of power and knowledge through which it worked—especially the nebulous field of authorship responsible for its production.

Salvemos al Barrio's initial encounter with city officials had already provided them with a glimpse of the murky complexities that would come to define their long experience trying to rewrite the code. When the officials had first come to the barrio to meet with the vecinos, vecinos had been prepared to argue with them about the urbanistic merit of tall buildings in the barrio. They had familiarized themselves with some basic concepts of planning gleaned from the internet and had also read some material on the history of the barrio. But when the officials arrived, few if any of them made the case that this was urbanism done properly. Instead, they pointed to a unique feature of the city blocks along the avenue in Villa Pueyrredón: namely, that the blocks were bisected by alleyways running parallel to the avenue, making the lots along Del Carril particularly shallow relative to standard blocks in Buenos Aires. In these shallow lots, ten-story buildings on the avenue rose up like a wall, much closer than normal to the houses behind them (like they did in both Abel and Nelly's as well as Patricia's cases). Del Carril was, the experts explained, a kind of exceptional avenue, one that never should have been zoned for ten-story buildings. "This zoning isn't right for this avenue," the experts had said. "There's no question about that. It's the alleyways! There's no way this should be C3II!" Though they may not have sided with all the demands of Salvemos al Barrio, they seemed to be in basic agreement with the vecinos that some sort of mistake had been made. Although vecinos' concerns exceeded those articulated by the officials, this was the issue the legislators and planners latched onto, and it was one vecinos were willing to go along with if it would get them the changes they sought.

With this meeting, vecinos had already begun to confront some of the particular characteristics of the code. Who was responsible for this mistake? The complexity of the answer has to do with the way the code functioned as a regulatory device. Although the officials framed the zoning as a "mistake," vecinos would learn that it was not the kind of strictly human error that could be attributed to a planner who had studied the neighborhood of Villa Pueyrredón and made a bad decision. Instead, it was an outcome that had a lot to do with the way the code as a medium does its work. Consider a sample of text from the code:

"R2bII," pp. 127–128 of the 2002 version of the Código de Planificación Urbana, City of Buenos Aires.

R2bII (see Official Interpretation 12, page 127a)

(1) Character: zones of residential character similar to R2a, with less intensity of total occupation.

(2) Delimitation: According to the Zonification Map.

(3) Subdivision: According to the general norms of Section 3.

(4) Building typology: Buildings between dividing walls, of free perimeter, and semi-free perimeter are permitted.

    (a) Buildings between dividing walls:
    Fabric: Will comply with the general dispositions of Section 4 such that:
$$R = h/d = 2.4$$
    Maximum height: 9 m counting from the base elevation of the parcel determined by the Division of Cadastre, permitting the construction of one floor set back at a minimal distance of 2 meters from the O.L. beneath an inclined plane set at 45 degrees from the height of 9 meters, with a planar limit [plano limite] at 12 meters from the base elevation.

    (b) Buildings of free perimeter:
    Only in parcels larger than 2,000 m2, or a quarter of a block, needing to comply in all cases with that set forth in Art. 2.2.2 of this Code. Total horizontal limit: 18m from the base elevation of the lot.

    (c) Buildings of semi-free perimeter
    Fabric: Will comply with the general dispositions of Section 4 such that:
$$r = h'/d' = 5$$
    Maximum height: 9 m counting from the base elevation of the parcel determined by the Division of Cadastre, permitting the construction

of one floor set back at a minimal distance of 2 meters from the O.L. beneath an inclined plane set at 45 degrees from the height of 9 meters, with a planar limit at 12 meters from the base elevation.

(d) Maximum F.O.T. = 1.2

(e) F.O.S.: that which results from the regulations of the urban fabric according to the general dispositions of Section 4 and of that which is set by the Chart of Uses Nr. 5.2.1. The L.F.I. will coincide with the L.I.B.

(5) Uses: Those that result from applying the dispositions of the Chart of Uses Nr. 5.2.1.

(6) Observations: Habitable constructions are permitted up to one horizontal plane located at no more than 3.5 meters of the natural terrain within the 30 percent which is occupiable in the free center of the block according to Art. 4.2.4.

(7) Special Cases: (7.1) In Sector 2 of the La Boca neighborhood, buildings of free perimeter are not permitted. When constructions do not rise at any point above 9 meters from the height of the curb, they will be liberated from the obligation to respect the I.P.: L.F.I. In the same fashion, when the pavement is not materialized in correspondence with the levels established by Art. 4.1.2.4 of the Building Code, it will not be obligatory to comply with the requirements for vehicle parking (Ordinance Nr. 43.319—B.M. Nr. 18.524).

The code is composed of line after line of regulations that pertain to all buildings in the city with that particular zoning designation. The "R" in R2bII stands for residential (the C in C3II stands for commercial), of which 2bII is a subset, within which still other subtypes are specified (i.e., buildings between dividing walls, of free perimeter, and semi-free perimeter). Within each subtype, specific regulations regarding height and volume are laid out. When any line of these regulations is changed, the change applies throughout the city, affecting all parcels with that zoning. Among other things, this means that no expert necessarily looked at Del Carril when they were making decisions about changes to its zoning. Instead, the emergence of tall buildings along Del Carril likely originated in a change to a few lines of the code in which the height limitations for buildings between dividing walls in C3II were changed from "FOT = 2" to "Avenues or streets of width greater than or equal to 17.5 meters: Maximum Height = 24 m, R=h/d=2."[2] In lay terms, this is a change in the calculus for how high you can build that is based not on the size of the parcel, but instead on the width of the avenue. The buildings along del Carril had been zoned C3II for some time, but the calculus for how high you could build in that zoning had changed, a change in a line of code that cascaded throughout the city, including the unusual bisected blocks along the Avenida Salvador María del Carril in Villa Pueyrredón.

As I listened to the members of Salvemos puzzle over the differences between altura maxima and plano limite, I thought about how different the code felt from the modern urban plans that are described by James Scott (1998), Timothy Mitchell (1991a), and James Holston (1989), all of whom underscore the ways in which image-centered regimes of urban planning were used to remake cities in the modern era. By representing the city pictorially and attempting to make the city conform to such an image, modern urban planners sought to order an otherwise chaotic urban world, making it rationalized, legible, and manageable, but also healthier, more livable, and more beautiful.

The code's long lines of opaque regulatory text were strikingly different from the ways modernist planners' dreams for the city were concretized. The latter relied in large part on visual media, in particular the drawings and models that marked modern planning's grounding in architectural practice. This is not to say that codes are new; on the contrary, they have long been part of the way that states regulate the production of the urban environment, and they were an important part of modernist planning's repertoire.[3] But during most of the twentieth century, codes operated as the bureaucratic actualization of plans constructed in other mediums, most notably the visionary practices of drawing that were imported from architecture as the means through which urbanism might improve life in cities that were being upended by processes of rapid industrialization. Vecinos would have little contact with such an imagistic set of practices, however. During my entire experience researching their involvement with contemporary planning structures, I never saw a single drawing like those I was familiar with from the history of planning.[4]

Later on, vecinos would learn about other intricacies of the code's workings, in particular regarding the mechanisms of its authorship, which, like the medium in which planning was carried out, were historically specific. At first, the apparent agreement from legislators and urbanists that the tall buildings along Del Carril were a mistake made it seem that getting the code changed would be a straightforward process. A host of institutionalized mechanisms for citizen participation in the code's authorship shored up the idea that city residents had a voice in the writing of the code. The ostensibly democratic authorship of the code reflected relatively recent changes in the structures of power and knowledge of urban planning. Modernist planning had been more properly the domain of experts, in many cases ensconced in bureaucratic structures to which everyday citizens had little access. But widespread critiques that problematized the undemocratic nature of modernist planning's interventions into the built environment led to the institutionalization of citizen participation through forums like public audiences, which were designed to make planning more democratic.

Yet while the conceptual thrust of democratization within urban planning has been to bring authorship of the city out of the hands of experts and into the public, such collective authorship has been anything but straightforward. Instead, efforts to make the people the author of the city have been haunted by questions about who is really writing the code and where power over the production of the city truly resides. As it turned out, getting the code changed proved to be anything but easy. Doing so required vecinos to become deft navigators of the structures of power and knowledge that underwrote the code and to look beyond the state's presentation of itself as a friendly bureaucratic space of citizen participation. Navigating these structures of authorship could be extremely disorienting. Vecinos rarely found themselves in a situation in which they were told that no one cared what they thought. On the contrary, they were constantly offered the chance to speak in public audiences, to meet with legislators, to draft laws, and to workshop those drafts. And yet despite all of this, attaining the actual legal changes they sought proved elusive. Perhaps more curious still was that only on rare occasions did state agents directly disagree with vecinos; instead, even in the face of much apparent agreement, things seemed to hang in limbo. Over time, despite all the fanfare surrounding their participation, vecinos came to feel that other voices were lurking in the shadows, less marked but perhaps more effective than those of public participation at authoring the code. The perspective held by many vecinos in Buenos Aires was that powerful economic interests, in collusion with key actors in the state legislative and bureaucratic structure, were guiding the authorship of the code and the city that came forth from it.

Translating vecino values in the built environment into the language of the code was a fraught process, and one that ultimately would have to take paths other than those proposed by the state as means of citizen participation. I see in the code one way to attend to the ways that changing terrains of urban planning have come to be felt in Buenos Aires—terrains through which questions of professional knowledge, the tools of that knowledge, and democratic politics were woven together. At the time vecinos came into contact with it, the code was a document of purportedly democratic authorship, part of an ethos of participatory governance that operated on historically emergent articulations of knowledge and practice in the production of the built environment. Things hadn't always been this way: both the code as a medium and the structures of authorship responsible for its production had changed in important ways, along with the planning field of which they are a part. In the rest of this chapter, I weave episodes from the history of planning in Buenos Aires into stories about vecino groups' engagement with the code. The historical moments I describe offer important perspectives regarding the historical specificity of the way the code operates today. Vecinos, in turn, deployed a variety of tactics to hold open questions of voice and authorship, imbuing apparently rational forms of statecraft with a set of market interests that are obscured from dominant narratives of progress and democratization in planning—narratives that would lay claim to the public as the democratic author of the city. Through various means—including formal political advocacy, but also less formal discursive media such as political gossip—groups of vecinos worked to eschew a discourse of democratic planning that would overlook the ways that economic interests come to take hold of planning as a process, and instead recast planning as a form of knowledge and practice situated in complex terrains of economic and political investment.

THE BIRTH OF THE CODE: MODERN URBAN PLANNING IN BUENOS AIRES

When Le Corbusier, one of modern urbanism's most well known advocates and practitioners, arrived in Buenos Aires in 1929, his first gesture was not to begin writing a set of codes. Instead, it was to pick up a piece of charcoal and paper on which he began to draw (see figures 4.1 and 4.2) (see Liernur and Pschepiurca 2008). Corbusier's visit to Argentina from France had been sponsored by several organizations in Buenos Aires seeking to revolutionize the way the city was thought about and intervened in. Cultural elites with powerful connections, his hosts were part of a burgeoning interest in modernism and the possibilities it offered to re-create a city that was rapidly expanding under the pressures of urban migration.

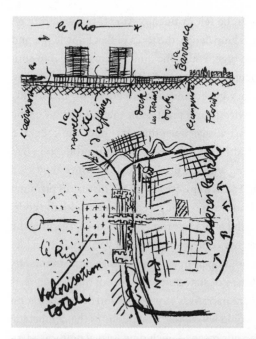

FIGURES 4.1 AND 4.2. Sketches for Le Corbusier's plan for Buenos Aires. In 4.2, perhaps Corbusier's most famous drawing from his visits to Buenos Aires, he reimagines the city by depicting a series of modernist high-rises rising up from the flat Argentine pampa, reflected in the Río de la Plata. Images from Liernur and Pschepiurca (2008).

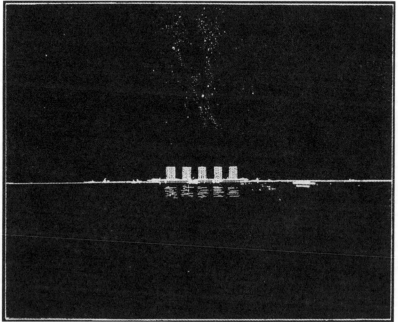

Corbusier and his hosts were not the first to attempt to intervene in Buenos Aires' urban form. The city's colonial foundation had been governed by the Laws of the Indies, which laid out guidelines for the founding of European settlements that stipulated the presence of a main plaza, a rectilinear grid surrounding it, and considerations for the locations of slaughterhouses, fisheries, and tanneries. During much of its early history, Buenos Aires would remain concentrated fairly tightly around this colonial center. In 1887, however, the city expanded drastically, more than quadrupling in area to include vast tracts of mostly rural land. This expansion accompanied a series of shifts in how the city was thought about. During most of the nineteenth century, immigration to Argentina had been directed primarily toward populating the interior of the country; national policies looked skeptically on urban growth, a skepticism grounded in elite cultural and moral norms in which Buenos Aires was imagined as little more than a beautiful but small bureaucratic and commercial portal for a vast national territory, home to a population grounded in rural life.[5] In spite of these ideals, half of new immigrants during the late nineteenth century stayed in Buenos Aires, where shortages in housing drove them to live in increasingly crowded, precarious conditions. The expansion of the city's geographical limits was one early indication that elite conceptions of the city and the nation were under pressure to change.

Buenos Aires' expansion was bound up with questions of the market in real estate and the state's relationship with that market. The years following 1887 saw a sharp increase in requests by landowners and speculators, often working in conjunction with rail transit corporations, for the city to approve road layouts and private urban extension plans within the city's new boundaries.[6] While some advocated growth driven by an unregulated market, the idea that urban growth should be regulated by the state gained increasing traction, particularly in the 1890s when real estate speculation began to face moral condemnation in a context marked by economic and political instability.[7] In response, a municipal commission laid out a grid, which was formally published in 1904. The grid, along with the electrification of tram lines, facilitated the vast expansion of a property market in which land was brought within reach of the working classes through a system of property auctions known as *loteos*, in which lots were made available for purchase in installments.[8] For many observers of this history, including Lewis Mumford, Peter Marcuse, and Richard Sennett, the grids that were laid out for American cities like New York and Buenos Aires represent the apex of market-driven, capitalist models of urban development in which nature and socio-natural histories were overwritten to achieve abstract, universal economic domination of urban worlds.[9] Adrián Gorelik has argued, however, that the grid was also a technology through which unfettered capitalist development was ordered and rationalized (2001, 37–40). The grid, in other words, did facilitate the real estate market, but it was also the heroic effort of technocrats working in a tumultuous economic and political environment to foster a more egalitarian city, imagined as a homogeneous extension of small property holders, which would refigure the sharp divisions between the rich and the poor that marked the already developed parts of the city.[10]

By the time Corbusier arrived in 1929, some more deliberate proposals to direct the city's growth in line with the emergent field of urbanism had been developed and debated. These included plans by the French architect Joseph-Antoine Bouvard in 1907 and the work of the Comisión de Estética Edilicia under the municipal government of Carlos Noel beginning in 1923. The invitation extended by local institutions to Corbusier was part of this growing local interest in modern planning. His visit included ten lectures, and while his visit bore little direct fruit in Argentina, his relationship with the country would be rekindled nearly twenty years later, in 1937, when he received two young graduates from Buenos Aires, Jorge Ferrari Hardoy and Juan Kurchan, in his studio in Paris. Over the following year, they drafted their *Plan Director para Buenos Aires*, which set out a series of basic ideas and would become the basis for continued efforts to influence urban planning in Buenos Aires.

....

As I mentioned earlier, the medium in which Corbusier and other modern planners worked was principally grounded in images and analytical texts that were different from the workings of the code. In both the *Plan Director para Buenos Aires* and Corbusier's (unpublished) book on Buenos Aires, the prominent place of drawings, sketches, photographs, and photomontage offer a sense of the importance of these tools for the way modern urban planners knew and intervened in urban environments. Le Corbusier's book, for example, was to be laid out in four columns, two for text and two for images, including analytical sketches, technical drawings, and photographs. Two pages from an abbreviated version of the book published in the journal *La Arquitectura de Hoy* give a sense of the prominent place held by images in this work (see figures 4.3 and 4.4). In the first, Corbusier makes a case for rethinking the scale of the city block in light of automobile traffic and the problems posed by intensifying traffic on existing streets. He does so through a series of analytical sketches de-

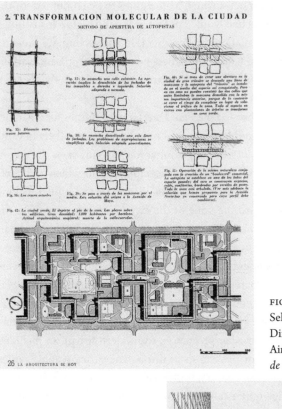

FIGURES 4.3 AND 4.4.
Selections from "Plan
Director Para Buenos
Aires," in *La Arquitectura
de Hoy*, 1947.

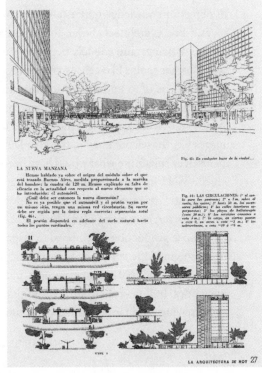

picting nine existing city blocks, which he imagines to be combined for the production of mega-blocks that would contain parks and high-density housing, with automobiles circulating outside them. In the second, he sketches out what life might be like within these new city blocks (top) and various possibilities to resolve vehicle and pedestrian traffic around them (bottom left).

Projective images like those in the *Plan Director para Buenos Aires* had become a central part of planning's technical repertoire as architects became its main practitioners. Modern urban planning was in many ways the culmination of nearly a century of professional development in which architects worked to adapt the tools of their discipline—drawing and model making prominent among them—to the scale of the city.[11] In distinction from the functioning of the code I was beginning to learn about with Salvemos al Barrio, modern planning was carried out as a natural extension of architecture, relying on the good judgment of the planner for the artful and effective execution of solutions to urban problems through highly visualized plans that were drawn to depict clear end-states that would one day be reached through a series of steps, not unlike a design for a building. Modern urbanists weren't the first to rely on visual media: precursors to modern urbanism included early efforts to survey and map urban space through new cartographic genres developed in the nineteenth century, tools that helped construct the city as an object of knowledge understandable through the natural and social sciences.[12] But as architects began to take on a more prominent role in urban design, drawings and models began to support, orient, and structure the host of other tools (like census and cartographic data) that urban planners also made use of to understand and intervene in the city. These other tools didn't disappear—indeed, no planner could do their work well without them—but projective images did become central to the practice. Projective images like those contained in the *Plan Director para Buenos Aires* did not in themselves constitute what would have been considered to be an urban plan, which would include a host of other data, legal frameworks, and plans for bureaucratic structures (this is why the document was not called a plan but a *plan director*, or guiding plan). But these images were vital to the eventual plan whose production they hoped to inspire: they were orienting directions meant to guide the sprawling bureaucratic undertaking that urban planning would imply and that would eventually include documents like urban planning codes. In this image-centric set of practices, codes were meant to flow from drawings and models as the bureaucratic actualizations of dreams that were largely articulated through these other media, translating projective images into the terms of bureaucratic regulation.

Drawings were not only technical tools, but political ones as well. As I mentioned earlier, modern urban planning was not a discipline famous for its democratic aspirations. It gave great privilege to the voices of experts, who typically took their own way of knowing to be a scientific, objective, and universal form of knowledge to which they had privileged access, which helped to make other ways of knowing the city—including those of the people whose lives they wished to transform—a significant blind spot to their vision. Thus de Certeau (1984) finds in urban planning a key example of the "god's eye view," or what Donna Haraway (1988) would call the "view from nowhere": a kind of knowledge that purports to universality, denying the situatedness of its techniques and the knowledge they produce. Politically, such an expression of objective knowledge often found its home in powerful, state-centered bureaucratic offices. James Scott, in *Seeing Like a State* (1998), thus refers to modern urban planning as "authoritarian." Urban planners were experts, and projective drawings were the medium in which they worked out solutions to the problems they sought to address. But while planning at the time was not a field with democratic aspirations, the visual media of planning did function as important pedagogical tools, means through which to entice and educate elites, but also the general public, about what urban worlds could become through modern planning. Imagistic media were one of the prime means through which plans for the future of the city were circulated and debated. They were presented in talks like the ones Corbusier gave in Buenos Aires, in books and professional journals, in public exhibitions, and in the popular press as part of the means through which modern planners worked to gather force and legitimacy to their practice, as well as the attention of the politicians who could make their visions reality. As Ferrari Hardoy (one of the young graduates who worked with Corbusier on the *Plan Director para Buenos Aires*) would later recall, the *Plan Director para Buenos Aires* was fabricated with the explicit aim of serving as a "wake up call" whose "objective was none other than to excite public opinion in order to achieve its fulfillment (cited in Liernur and Pschepiurca 2008, 177)." In this vein, Corbusier wrote to his associates in Argentina in 1940, urging them to form a civic committee that would foment public debate about the plan, noting that "a plan of such importance . . . must capture public opinion. . . . It is necessary that this be a movement of great enthusiasm" (188). Here, too, was an important difference between modern urban plans and the code I saw at work in Villa Pueyrredón: in contrast to the dense, arcane, and inaccessible language of the code, the drawings of modernist planners were meant to be pedagogical and communicative.

....

The production of a full plan based on the ideas of the *Plan Director para Buenos Aires* at times seemed close to becoming reality: in 1947, Ferrari Hardoy was named head of an office called the Estudio del Plan de Buenos Aires, or Study for the Plan of Buenos Aires. In his speech inaugurating the study, the mayor directly quoted paragraphs from the *Plan Director para Buenos Aires* of 1937. The idea of planning itself had become a prominent feature of Peron's political rise, from his early work as a junior officer in rebuilding efforts for the city of San Juan after a major earthquake in 1944 and, beginning with his electoral victory in 1946, as president of Argentina.[13] This plan never came to fruition as such, however; the short-lived Estudio was shut down following a change in municipal government in 1949.[14] Work toward a comprehensive urban plan for Buenos Aires would continue over the following decades, however, scattered throughout various state organisms. In 1962, a plan director was approved and, in 1968, published. The plan built upon the early work that had been laid out by the Estudio and is regarded as the most rigorous, in-depth study of Buenos Aires' urban development to date, incorporating analyses of the city's historical development, land use, and population density and distribution in order to set forth criteria for future urban growth.[15]

An early version of the Código de Planeamiento Urbano that vecinos from Villa Pueyrredón were trying to change was developed in the early 1970s and approved as law in 1977. Based on the guiding principles of the plan, it regulated what kinds of buildings could be built and where in order to allow for a city with varying but livable densities and architectural forms that would foster the presence of adequate air, light, and exterior views across the built environment. In the decades that followed, however, the code would come to take on a life of its own. Although stemming from a similar impetus to structure urban worlds, in many ways the plan and the code (as I saw it worked on that rainy night in Villa Pueyrredón) couldn't feel more different. Modern urban plans were the domain of studied experts who aimed to lay out a set of analyses about the present and goals for the future that depict urban problems through a highly pedagogic and communicative set of visual media. In contrast, the code vecinos worked on years later bore purportedly democratic authorship, but was written in line upon line of techno-bureaucratic language that was difficult for its purported authors to master. The code also contained little of the persuasive ideological thrust of modern urban plans, which worked to convince people about a better world to come. Instead, the code was overwhelmingly presentist, with no clear sense of retrospective diagnosis or prospective prognosis. And while many of the plans for Buenos Aires were the creations of at least some visible authors, the code's purportedly collective authorship, as we shall see, also worked to obscure some of the forces at work in its production.

THERE IS NO PLAN

"There is no plan!" Marta shouted to me, her head submerged in her closet as she rummaged for the documents she would use to teach me about contemporary urban planning in Buenos Aires. Marta was an old-school urban planner with a long history of urban activism in Buenos Aires. I had met her through Osvaldo from Amigos del Lago and other contacts associated with queremos buenos aires and APEVU, the Permanent Assembly for the Preservation of Green Urban Spaces—a group that had formed in the 1990s and was filled with a motley crew of environmentalists, neighborhood activists, and a fair share of architects and urban planners. Her conversation with me that day was steeped in thirty years of professional and civic frustration over the path urban planning had taken in Buenos Aires.

I had come to Marta confused. The neighborhood groups I was working with were all involved in efforts to change the urban planning code, and I had spent some time trying to learn about the broader set of urban initiatives the code represented—in particular, about the plan I presumed lay behind the code. I had heard talk of a document called the Plan Urbano Ambiental (PUA), passed by the city legislature in 2008 over the objections of many neighborhood groups I was working with. I had yet to understand what their problems were with the plan itself, however—nor was I even convinced that I had actually found a copy of the PUA; the document I had found read much more like a set of guidelines for an eventual plan than something that did the work I had expected a plan would do.

"This document," Marta told me, emerging from the closet and waving her copy of the PUA at me, "isn't a plan. It's a *mamarracho*, a false document that has nothing to do with a plan and even less to do with participation." She explained that the PUA had been passed in response to a mandate written into the city constitution in 1996 (when Buenos Aires transitioned from a federal

district administered by the nation to an "autonomous city" with greater inde-
pendence). Crafted in an ethos of participatory democracy and local control,
the city constitution envisioned the PUA as a tool through which urban planning could be democratized.[16] The PUA was passed in 2008 and purported to
satisfy this constitutional mandate, but for Marta and many others, the PUA
fell far short of the participatory ideals laid out in the constitution, a host of
public audiences and commissions to review it notwithstanding. For its critics,
the plan was a farce, a trick designed to legitimate systems of unequal power
over the authorship of the code through an aura of democratic participation.

For two years, Marta told me, she and many other groups of vecinos had
gone to the city legislature every two weeks, meeting with legislators and
making their case for a plan for the city that, in contrast to the plan that would
later be passed, would take its responsibilities to both planning and participation seriously. When, after all this work, a version of the plan was presented
in the city legislature that bore little evidence of taking into account what
they had been advocating for, they repeated their arguments in public audiences. Here, again, their opinions seemed to fall on deaf ears. The plan was
approved over their objections, complying with the letter, but not the spirit,
of the constitutional mandate. At the time, promises were made that, despite
all its shortcomings, the PUA was just the beginning of a process, and that
it was better than nothing. But for Marta, the plan did little more than provide political cover for the already existing Código de Planeamiento Urbano,
which had grown to monstrous proportions and been modified far beyond
the plan that it had originally been intended to enact in 1977. Gesturing again
to her copy of the Plan Urbano Ambiental, Marta told me, "This document,
mal llamado [misnamed] 'Plan,' is a pamphlet that serves no other purpose
than to prevent people from impeaching a group of functionaries for breach-
ing the responsibilities of public office."

One of Marta's principal critiques revolved around the relationship between
the plan and the code—a relationship that, for Marta, was perverse enough to
qualify this plan as an impostor. Marta took out her own copy of the PUA and
started paging through it, reading out sections to me. The PUA wasn't a real
plan, she explained, because it didn't plan anything. A real plan guides other
documents—it is a master document from which other documents must then
flow. But the PUA constantly made reference to documents that were supposed
to be inferior to it—particularly the Código de Planeamiento Urbano, whose
arcane language I had watched the vecinos discuss in the café. "Here," she
said, "look: 'Sector Plan: found regulated in paragraph 9.1.2.3 of the Código de

Planeamiento Urbano.' This is the plan, and it refers back to the Code! 'Detail plan: found established in chapter 8.4 of the Código de Planeamiento Urbano.' 'Areas of developmental priority'—this is where you should be putting all your intention!—'found regulated in the Código de Planeamiento Urbano'! The plan just refers back to the code!" she said, years of frustration rising in her voice. "The plan is supposed to *direct* the code! What is this plan for if we're going to continue falling back on old regulations?"

In a report she authored critiquing the passage of the PUA, Marta wrote, "The 'Urban Planning' Code is a misnomer, because a group of regulations does not produce urban planning. Planning is a process whose very nature makes its codification impossible. Planning is an interactive and interdisciplinary process that provides solutions to urban problems through the definition of programs of action agreed upon by various sectors of the citizenry. They are materialized in a variety of documents that include taxation plans for the redistribution of surplus value generated by construction projects, the integration of migrants to the city, and the preservation of local species in urban parks, just to give a few examples. Drawings (*planos*) and regulations (*normas*) are the instruments of planning, and only they are codifiable. A code is a legal document that materializes an urban plan—neither the only one, nor the principal one" (Dodero 2007). What Marta envisioned as true participatory planning was a far cry from the version of democratic planning that had been put in to practice in Buenos Aires in the previous decade. For her and many others, the PUA (and the code it left at the center of things) lacked both planning and participation: it involved neither the rigorous study embraced by modernist planning nor the participatory democratic authorship it claimed for itself.

URBAN PLANNING AFTER MODERNISM:
CODES, DEMOCRACY, AND THE CITY

The particular path through which Buenos Aires ended up with a code and an impostor plan is historically specific, but the ascendant place of urban planning codes at the expense of comprehensive planning extends far beyond the particular case of Buenos Aires,[17] owing in part to a set of transitions in urban planning that became particularly palpable in the profession during the 1960s and 1970s. During this time, modern urbanism entered into a series of crises and transformations that were at once epistemological (regarding how the field conceived of its object), technical (regarding the tools through which it worked), and political (regarding who was responsible for planning and to what ends).

Beginning in the 1960s, the epistemological contours of architecture and planning began to shift profoundly, as universal visions of truth that underpinned postwar modernism were increasingly questioned. Within architecture, postmodernism is typically cited as a shift in the ways that historical architectural forms were appropriated and cited in a context in which questions of meaning became a central axis through which to evaluate architectural form (opposed to modernism's emphasis on function). But while architecture led the charge into the questions of meaning and the collapse of universals that arose in the wake of modernism, planning took a different approach, embracing increased rationalization and objectivity through new systems of measurement and control that were different from the map-based visual representations central to the practice of modern urbanism.

Within this set of disciplinary reconfigurations, the city began to be reconceived as an object of knowledge. Modern urbanism, as described earlier, treated the city as a cohesive object and focused on the design of the physical environment by projecting a set of developments toward an imagined end point; this reflected modern urbanism's roots in architecture and the translation of the practices of architectural design to the practices of urbanism. In the late 1960s, this vision of the city came under mounting criticism internationally. Rather than stable, physical wholes, critics of modernist planning in the 1960s began advocating for understanding cities as dynamic systems of interconnected, interdependent, and interrelated parts.[18] Dynamism and change became keywords of planning, in contrast to the "end-state" plans of modern urbanism. Plans, too, were reconceived and came to be seen as trajectories rather than blueprints and planning as an activity based in ongoing processes of "monitoring, analysing, and intervening in fluid situations" (N. Taylor 1998, 63). The design of physical space became fragmented, and this fragmentation was seen as a productive alternative to the totalizing aspirations of modern planning.

For example, in *Buenos Aires: Una Trilogía Metropolitana* (2006), Alberto Varas argues that during the 1980s in Buenos Aires, visions for the future of the city moved away from the grand schemes of modernist urbanism to understand the city as a collection of articulated fragments. The goals of these newer interventions, Varas explains, was to recover the fragmented, local identities of the city. These fragments would not be static, but dynamic and flexible, servicing a variety of possible uses: a polo field doubles as a concert venue, former grain warehouses become lofts for living and working, restaurants are built below railway arches. Planning in the city took on the character of a chess game in which abandoned spaces could be endlessly reinvented, the buildings of the city treated as "the basis for a new and flexible habitat of programmed uncertainty" (Varas 2006, 223). Interventions thus worked at a much smaller scale, and city came to be regarded "as an entity that . . . requires *specific architectural proposals that do not call for a general plan*"[19] (222, emphasis added).

Within this context, codes seemed to come into their own as the importance of sketching out stable end points for the city as a whole fell from favor. The future, instead of being planned for in advance, would be the result of an ongoing process of measurement and tweaking in which dynamism rather than predictability were touchstone sentiments. Coupled with the developing rift between planning and architecture, one that was figured as science and the other as art, practices of drawing faded and media that were systematic rather than imagistic—including codes—took on a new importance.

New approaches to planning did not simply emerge from a reconsideration of the kind of object a city was, however. Political mobilizations against the destruction of neighborhoods under modern urbanism had made questions of democratization and democratic voice a key axis of these transitions. Grassroots political movements, dissatisfied with the visions of the good life built into and out of modernist urban planning, decried the technocratic and anti-democratic power structures that defined urban planning through most of the twentieth century. The urban activist Jane Jacobs's struggle against Robert Moses in New York is an iconic example of broader trends. Her book *The Death and Life of Great American Cities* (1961) expressed widely felt disillusionment about the destruction of neighborhood life at the hands of modernist urbanism. Citizen participation was seen to be the solution to the problem of professional planners operating in centralized bureaucracies with little public accountability.[20]

Following such critiques, it became common to embrace democratic and participatory forms of decision making in international planning circles. But democratic participation within planning did not escape the rationalized epistemological context of the 1960s and 1970s. Instead, the meanings that became attached to democracy within urban planning were highly instrumentalized, incorporated into a rationalized process of observation and assessment through citizen empowerment methods like public audiences, designed to channel citizen feedback into the planning process. This model of democratic participation meshed well with neoliberal concepts of democracy, in a broader context in which the scope and quality of visions for what government was capable of and responsible for were being reformulated. Urban planning, unthinkable in its modern incarnation without the welfare state and its vision of a universal good, was turning away from such universal and technocratic formulations of the good life at the same time democratization was made part of the agenda.

In Argentina, where the late 1970s and early '80s were a time of brutal dictatorship rather than grassroots democracy, the democratic ethos that had been infusing planning in other parts of the world did not become a topic of explicit attention until after the return to democracy in 1984. But even in the middle of dictatorship, the ideas that signaled the breakdown of the epistemic foundations of modernist planning were already being felt. Guillermo Jajamovich (2012a), for example, describes the exchange of urbanistic expertise with Spain in the 1970s (Spain having replaced France as a principal conduit for international exchange of urbanistic ideas through its efforts to strengthen Ibero-American linkages in the decade leading up to the quincentennial of the Columbian expedition). The project for the design of the Parque España in the city of Rosario—accompanied by a series of lectures and conferences—provides an example of the often complex forms of translation through which new planning principles were brought into relationship with Argentine planning. Working from a context of the recent democratic transition in Spain at the end of Franco's rule, the park's Spanish architectural team saw its park design as a fragmentary intervention that challenged the totalizing and authoritarian resonances of modern planning. The Argentine military government, however, treated the park as part of an integral plan that simply responded to a quantitative deficit in green space. And while the Spanish team proposed that limiting the height of surrounding real estate would help foment a more egalitarian public space, the market- and construction-friendly military government left this aspect of the proposal to the side.[21]

These tendencies toward fragmentation and a rejection of modern planning gained momentum and a more explicit connection to democratic politics after the return to democracy. Within post-dictatorship planning circles, critiques of modern urban planning were considered part and parcel of democratic transition. In the competition "20 Ideas for Buenos Aires"—organized through an agreement between the Municipality of the City of Buenos Aires and the Community of Madrid in 1986—the call for proposals specifically marked the concept of the city as a collection of fragments (Jajamovich 2012a). Contemporary Argentine observers saw in this a rejection of the "orthodox, abstract, totalizing, and homogeneous planning" (quoted in Jajamovich 2012a) of modern urbanism held aloft by the dictatorship, casting the fragmentary intervention as one that was less totalizing and therefore also more democratic.

The urban planning code was part of these debates. At its inception, the Código had a solid modernist pedigree and mission: as I mentioned earlier, it was written to be the bureaucratic enactment of the plan director for the city that was approved in 1962, after more than ten years of study and preparation undertaken at the height of postwar modernism. The passage of the Código de Planeamiento Urbano as law in 1977—one year after a military coup—finally provided a normative instrument for that plan. By identifying modern urban planning with the dictatorship, competitions like "20 Ideas for Buenos Aires" introduced early seeds of critique against the authoritarian pedigree of the code that was passed in 1977.[22]

Rather than disappear, however, the code has since been rewoven into the formalized democratic ethos of contemporary planning. In the 1990s, when Buenos Aires gained autonomy as part of a wider devolution of federal power to more local levels, the new constitution of the city not only charged the city government with elaborating a new urban plan that would be written with community participation, but also turned the authorship and modification of the code over to the newly created city legislature, a move through which the voices of vecinos, rather than career bureaucrats, were meant to be incorporated in the planning process through their elected representatives. As an additional mechanism for citizen participation, public audiences were required for any modification to the urban planning code. No longer tightly associated with the plans from which it was born, the code thus survived deep shifts in planning, woven into historically new technical and political registers.

THE CORPORATION AND THE PLAN

Marta and many like her found little of democratic value in the way the transition away from more modernist frames of urban planning was carried out, however. Instead of democratic participation, she found the pernicious erosion of state power and the surrender to market logics of a series of processes that would benefit from more—not less—comprehensive planning. Far from being part of a set of changes that made urban planning more democratic and sensitive to fluctuating social realities, the code's predominance was, for her, both the outcome and the enabling factor of tacit collusions between powerful market forces and the corrupt members of the city government that defended their interests. In contrast to earlier planning efforts for Buenos Aires that sought to

improve urban life for all by structuring and limiting markets in urban development, the contemporary Código seemed to work directly in their service.

Marta colorfully but seriously named these forces the Corporation of the
Industry of Real Estate Speculation. "You want a list of the agents of real estate speculation?" she asked me. Without waiting for my answer, she went on
to list a series of prominent Argentine professional associations: "The Central
Society of Architects; the Argentine Chamber of Construction; the Argentine Center of Engineers; the Professional Council of Architecture and Urbanism; the Faculty of Architecture, Design, and Urbanism of the University
of Buenos Aires. These gentlemen are always the same," she said. "They want
to build everywhere, because they see everywhere as empty—because it *is*
empty compared to what they would put there."

For Marta, the corporation was not only the author of the code, but also
of the process through which the code was maintained as the central tool of
planning: "The confusion [between planning and the urban planning code]
arises and endures because it is through this channel that the Corporation of
the Industry of Real Estate Speculation strategizes their business," she wrote.
"It's through the modification of the parameters of the Code that they increase
the yields on their investments. . . . It was the Corporation of the Industry of
Real Estate Speculation that decided, from the moment they began to consider the Plan Urbano Ambiental, that nothing was going to change. Their
speculative power rests on the Code of ill-gotten gains [*componendas*]. They
have manipulated processes, applied pressure, and confused languages to this
day" (Dodero 2006).

The notion that powerful economic interests were at the heart of the code's
authorship was understood to extend not only into these professional organizations, but also deep into the state bodies responsible for urban planning, especially the urban planning commission of the city legislature. Consider this story
I heard told at a teach-in I attended in the architecture school, in which a former
legislative aide recounted his efforts to look into the intense levels of real estate
development in the area of Puerto Madero, which was also home to an ecological reserve. He had been asked by a group of environmental activists to look into
the lack of environmental impact statements for all the towers being built there.
His office filed a request for information and never received a response. This was
strange, he said: as an aide for the minoritarian Partido Obrero (the Workers
Party), he was accustomed to filing unpopular requests that were in the sharp
minority—but never before had they gone without so much as an answer. He
went to speak to the chair of the commission, who asked him, "Why are you

sticking your nose in this?" The aide continued: "And then, with a tone halfway between reprimand and threat, he said to me 'Listen, this issue will never, ever be raised in committee.'" The experience provoked a moment of realization for the aide. He explained: "The key to everything was in the Urban Planning Commission. It was the Door of the Seven Keys, the unreachable place. At first I thought the important commissions were Education, Health, or Housing, where grand debates and battles occurred. But at least in those chambers, they *did occur*— they were explicit! This Commission was different: it was the location of the cashbox, where the business was quietly done, the home of the economic and political pact that's ruled over this city for the past twenty-five years. This pact, sealed by the interests of financial capital, marks not only the city that we have today, but is also a general reflection of the constitutional progressivism that was voted into place [with the constitutional reform] in 1996." Far from a straightforward instrument of democratic voice, the legislative commission was bound up with economic interests. It was a commission in which the big partisan battles were subdued, not because it was a place where nothing important happened, but because it was a place where economic interests greased all the wheels.

If the visualized plans of modern urbanism embraced a view from nowhere—the disembodied view of objective knowledge without a subject— then Marta and others who shared her perspective made a different claim about the contemporary workings of the code. While the purportedly democratized code bore all the hallmarks of participatory democracy and collective authorship, these claims to collective authorship wrote out of their account the powerful monied interests that were operating on sharply undemocratic terrain. These forces sat subtly in the background, foregrounding instead the rituals of participatory democratic participation through which they could lay claim to the public as the true author of the code. Marta, in her naming of the corporation, was part of wider efforts to pry open this claim to collective authorship by tracing the uneven contours of voice that peopled the shadows of democratic planning.

MANIFESTATIONS IN THE HALL:
OFFICIAL USES OF THE WORD

Looking around the large ballroom in the city legislature, I saw several familiar faces among the crowd: a group from Villa Urquiza, several people from sos Caballito, and several more from queremos buenos aires and Amigos del Lago. We were there, along with a few hundred others, to attend the public audience for the sale and rezoning of a small cluster of land owned by the city in the Buenos Aires district of Catalinas Norte. The city argued that the sale of the land was necessary to make up for budget shortfalls and that they would get a good price only if the land were also rezoned for high-rise development. The move required a modification of the city's Código de Planeamiento Urbano, which in turn required public audiences to be held so that the public could give feedback about the modification. The lots in question were small and located in a part of the city with little history of neighborhood activism. Located in the city center, in an area already dense with construction, supporters of the sale and rezoning painted the picture of an optimal business decision, one in which underutilized assets would be sold at the best possible price in order to fund needed city services—in this case, education. But the public audience had drawn the attendance of a loose coalition of neighborhood groups for whom the sale of these parcels instead laid bare a set of market logics that they saw as increasingly present in urban life in Buenos Aires. The apparently easy, businesslike logic of the government and its supporters was, for them, pernicious: if urban planning were reduced to the question of a balance sheet on a budget, the answer to the questions "should the city sell its land?" and "should the city zone for dense construction?" would always be "yes." By this logic, no parkland and no open space would ever be safe. That the government said it would direct the funds to school districts where infrastructure was needed (new roofs, etc.) was, for them, little more than a cunning effort to make opposition to the plan more difficult: who would place three small parcels of land no one cared about ahead of the needs of children?

The public audience was the mechanism through which such opposing ideas were meant to be debated. They have become defining rituals for the ethos of public participation that has imbued planning and other fields since the 1960s, taken to mark a shift away from the ways that urban planning decisions had been made during regimes of high modernism, when experts ensconced in protected bureaucracies made major decisions about the form cities would take and the lifeworlds that would exist within them. In the progress narrative of urban planning, planning has become more democratic and responsible to citizen concerns precisely through vehicles such as the public audience. The audience thus offers a glimpse into one of the code's spaces of authorship, one in which planning's democratic ethos was supposed to attain its fulfillment.

I had attended several other audiences like it, and the scene was familiar: the legislator or functionary presiding over the session sat at a table at the front of the hall, with two or more stenographers working to either side. Also present were a microphone and a podium. Speakers who had signed up to speak on an official register over the prior weeks were called up in order of inscription to speak for five minutes, after which they were given the option to leave the rest of their statement in written form to be incorporated in the file. Everyone would be able to say their piece.

But the actual practice of planning's democratic mechanisms was somewhat more complicated than this idealized image makes clear. Consider, as a way into these finer contours of voice in the political arena, the following exchange that unfolded in the course of the public audience for Catalinas Norte as it was captured in the public register. Señora Limia, who had spoken in favor of the sale and rezoning, drew her remarks to a close:

SRA. LIMIA: [concluding her remarks] Sirs: frankly, I'm given the impression that the opposition to the anticipated project seems more like an act of whimsy than a valid argument based in reality or reason.
MR. PRESIDENT (GONZÁLEZ): Thank you very much.
Protests in the hall.
MR. PRESIDENT (GONZÁLEZ): I ask for silence, please.
Protests in the hall.
MR. PRESIDENT (GONZÁLEZ): Silence, please. We have all listened to one another.

I cite this exchange and the way it was captured in the public record as one moment within a broader set of problems confronting the idea of democratic urban planning. The opposition that Sra. Limia characterized as whimsical consisted of several groups of vecinos who had gone to the audience to speak against the sale. The legislator presiding over the audience thanked Sra. Limia for her remarks, but the room—until then respectful—erupted in loud response to her characterization of vecinos as whimsical and operating outside of reality and reason. Sitting in the audience, I scrambled to record what they had shouted from the floor. Later, I looked up the stenographic record, hoping to find help piecing together what had been said. Instead, I found only the words *manifestaciones en la sala*—protests in the hall. This gloss was not simply a result of the difficulty of hearing voices from the audience. In other public audiences I attended, there unfolded sustained dialogues between members of the audience and the lectern that were easily audible to the entire room. In all occasions, if the speaker did not officially hold the floor, the conversation was recorded as "manifestaciones en la sala"—protests in the hall. Immediately following this gloss, there appears the statement by the commission president that everyone had listened to one another. I still laugh when I read it. We have all listened to one another, he says, while the voices of a multitude are transformed from signal into noise.

Reflecting back on this moment, I came to see both the demands for silence and the way nonsanctioned speech was glossed in the record as indicative of the limits of habits of state listening in the practical exercise of what are billed as planning's participatory democratic forums. Scholars such as Jacques Rancière (1999) and Chantal Mouffe (2005) have critiqued liberal democracy for the exclusions that travel unmarked within the purportedly inclusive form of democratic process. For Mouffe, the public sphere is not a common ground on which harmonious consensus could be reached through rational debate, but the battlefield on which divergent hegemonic projects confront one another. Introducing the Gramscian concept of hegemony draws attention to political assemblies' presence within sedimented histories of power. Rancière, in turn, focuses on the differential ability of voices to enter democratic debate as part of an order of the visible and the sayable, the maintenance of which he calls "policing": that which "sees that a particular activity is visible and another is not, that this speech is understood as discourse and another as noise" (1999, 29). In contrast to policing, Rancière defines politics as that which seeks to redistribute the sensible—the boundaries of what can make sense—and "make visible what had no business being seen, and make heard a discourse where once there was only a place for noise" (30). In Mouffe's and Rancière's concern for the uneven contours of voice in the political arena, I find a productive affinity with Isabel Stengers's "Cosmopolitical Proposal." Stengers seeks to incorporate in her politics a productive uncertainty about the capacity for voice and its place in political assemblies. Specifically, she looks with promise to the possibility of imbuing political voices with "the feeling that they do not master the situation they discuss, that the political arena is peopled with shadows of that which does not have a political voice, cannot have, or does not want to have one" (Stengers 2005b, 996). What Stengers helps me to find in the political work of vecinos is not just an advocacy for their own voices, but a sensibility about the efficacy of holding questions of voice open and attending to the shadows of politics.

The questions of voice that vecinos found haunting participatory planning concern feeling out who can talk of what and holding that question open. As I mentioned earlier, vecinos' situation was different from one in which they were told that no one cared what they had to say. On the contrary, they were constantly called upon to speak, told that their opinion mattered and that they were being listened to. The public audience was one such forum of state listening: any claim that the state did not have participatory mechanisms in place to provide for democratic participation in planning could be countered by the lists of people speaking at the audiences and the reams of paper their words added to the official project file. And yet vecinos became skeptical of such forms of participation, feeling not only that their words weren't being heard, but that other, powerful voices were also present in these forums, even as they went unmarked. Ostensibly endowed with political voice through public audiences and other tools of democratic planning, vecinos nevertheless found themselves exploring the shadows of voice in the political arena, feeling out the possibilities of their own voices while also attending to the often unmarked voices that peopled the halls of democratic politics.

When it comes time for a speaker to take the floor in a public audience, it is called "making use of the word"—*hacer uso de la palabra*. Making use of the word was something that vecinos did both within and beyond formal mechanisms of democratic politics, working to challenge official uses of the word and exploring uses of the word that might be made to effectively haunt the idea of a democratized urban planning to enact a politics of urban space otherwise.

Although the seasoned vecinos I was with approached their speaking role in public audiences with little sense of instrumental hope (i.e., that the state would take their words into consideration and change their plans), the audiences were nevertheless important moments when groups from across the city could come together and show support in a common cause, make connections to share advice and stories, and experience the solidarity of speaking in a united way against a shared set of problems. Incorporating such a collective ethos into the format of the audience required concerted strategy, however. The format of the audience presupposes that speakers speak as individuals, rather than parts of collectives (people sign up as individuals and are identified only by their name; it would be impossible for Salvemos al Barrio to sign up to speak, for example). Coupled with the five-minute time limit and the fact that people are called upon to speak in the order in which they signed up over the previous weeks, it was difficult for complex issues to be articulated by one person or for several people to speak with continuity without advance planning. Nevertheless, vecinos developed innovative strategies that would allow them to speak well in these sessions. To work against the restrictions of the five-minute time limit, several people would arrange to meet at the legislature to sign up at the same time, so their names would be called one after the other and they could share different parts of a prepared statement among three or four speakers. Vecinos wove together a variety of forms of speech in these interventions, including technical analyses, diverse forms of storytelling, and ethical injunctions, distributing them among speakers according to their abilities: architects interrogated the conceptual universe behind technical regulations about building height and urban density; environmentalists spoke of the depletion of green space and its impact on the city; and older vecinos told stories about barrio life in decades past or wagged their fingers at the legislators present, admonishing them about their duty as public servants, proclaiming that "the city belongs to all of us" and that "the city is not a business." They also learned to guard against signing everyone up together or as soon as inscription opened, however, because no one would be left to rebut ideas that were raised by the opposition. Instead, skilled orators who did not rely on prepared statements and could improvise well were often sent to sign up close to the deadline so they could respond at the end of the session to issues brought up by the opposition.

Vecinos used this voice to make the public audience into a space of the political, critiquing the terms upon which the audience took place. One of the central themes of vecino critiques was to highlight the ways in which market logics penetrated the process of urban planning. Vecinos constantly worked to recast planning as a form of knowledge situated in complex terrains of economic and political investment. By highlighting market interests behind even the most benevolent-sounding projects, they worked to conjure forth from the shadows of participatory democracy the unnamed participants in the room—the forces of private development that many saw as threatening participatory hopes for planning in the city. Abel Ali from SOS Caballito, for example, remarked that the government and its supporters' classification of the Catalinas Norte land as "underutilized terrain" could mean any lot without its maximal exploitation by real estate: "The unused asset must be transformed into a usable asset [they say], and with those little words it's as if we've touched the glory of the transformation! . . . No! This money will be pocketed by a gang of wise guys who live making money off of whatever spaces are left in the city, and have been doing so for years." His colleague Pedro Kesselman (the lawyer who advised vecinos from SOS Caballito in chapter 3), later returned to place this idea in a historical context stemming back to the neoliberalism born in the mid-1970s and deepened in the 1990s, situating the privatization of urban land today in the context of a history of privatizations that included the national oil company, airlines, and telecommunications networks. Their efforts to highlight the market's presence in urban planning decisions helped to interfere with the dreamspace of the public audience as the rationalized, transparent, and democratic peace terms upon which consensus about urban planning could be reached.

In addition to working to craft their own voices within the audience, vecinos also worked to feel out the commitments of other voices in the audience, which manifested themselves in ways that often went unmarked. It turned out, for example, that Sra. Limia was not just the concerned citizen she presented herself to be. She was also the legal operations manager of real estate in the Ministry of Economic Development, a fact she did not mention, but that was pointed out by several of the loudest voices that would be reduced to "manifestaciones en la sala" in the public record. Several others who spoke in favor of the sale also turned out to be employed by the city, casting a shadow of doubt over the interests to which they were beholden as they came to speak in favor of the sale. By pointing out the other commitments of people like Sra. Limia, vecinos thus worked to make manifest the economic and political interests at work behind the guise of participatory planning. Searching the shadows of the political, vecinos found market interests that would prefer to remain unmarked peopling the halls of participatory planning.

Like many of the other changes to the urban planning code that vecinos spoke against, the sale and rezoning of the land in Catalinas was ultimately approved by a broad group of legislators, including not only the liberal majority block, but also their political opposition, Frente Para La Victoria, and two socialists. Such defeats only served to confirm the assessment of one vecina, who articulated a common sentiment when she characterized the legislature as "Legislatura s.a.," or Legislature Incorporated.

STATES OF INTRIGUE, OR OTHER USES OF THE WORD

"He lives right here in the neighborhood!" one of the members of Salvemos al Barrio whispered to me in an aside during the weekly neighborhood assembly back in Villa Pueyrredón. I had arrived ten minutes late to the assembly and had already missed a lot. The man they were speaking about, as it turned out, was not unfamiliar to me. I had first heard his name months earlier, during the time I'd spent with a neighborhood group in another part of the city. I struggled to remember the details of what had been a complicated story.

"He's connected to some kind of union?" I asked in a whisper, trying to refresh my memory.

"Yes, him. And he lives right here in the barrio!" she repeated.

"Isn't that a strange coincidence?" I asked, still surprised.

"It is!" she said excitedly. Although my mind was whirring trying to remember the details, I was intensely aware of the excitement in her eyes, the intrigue that the story was understood to carry, and the exhilaration I felt at hearing it—the set of affects that I would later realize helps keep these stories on the move.

From what I could recall of my earlier conversations, the man was a relatively obscure city official, but with a connection to a powerful union of municipal workers. He was said to be responsible for moving construction plans through the city bureaucracy and getting them approved even if (or especially if) they failed to correspond to the necessary zoning requirements.

"They're all a bunch of *corruptos*," the vecina said to me, still in a whispered aside.

"Yes . . . ," I said, trying to move past the big picture. "I'm just not sure I understand how it works."

"They pay them off."

"Who? The developers?"

"Of course."

"Pay off the officials?"

"Yes!"

"And the plans . . . ?" I asked, glancing up at the meeting in progress.

"They get approved no problem!" she said. "They're all friends—the developers, the functionaries, the legislature. . . ."

We turned our attention back to the meeting, and I would have to wait until it was finished, some people rushing off, others lingering to share cigarettes and gossip, before I could get more clarity. It was nighttime, and dark, at around ten when most of the shops were closing up and people were headed home for dinner. As I began to ask more about the story, others began piping in with details, interrupting each other, laughing, and cracking jokes amid the intrigue.

Against the challenges of crafting a political voice in official realms, there were other uses of the word in which the political, economic, and social dynamics of urban construction overflowed the contained rationality of official discourse.[23] Gossip about corruption was one domain in which such overflows moved unencumbered by official uses of the word and in which the difference between speech and noise were blurred in a way that was productive of the political. Corruption stories were the focus of much of vecinos' time. They proved to be vital conduits for vecinos' energies and passions, but also did more than that by offering a way into understanding bureaucratic worlds that bore little resemblance to the smooth flowcharts the state produced about power and decision making; by telling these stories, they honed their skills at tracing the intertwined paths of politics, money, and construction in the city.

In Villa Pueyrredón, this journey into the shadowy world of construction bureaucracy had started with a simple placard, the *cartel de obra*, that all construction projects are required to display. They include the name of the architect and their license number; the number of the project dossier; the building's zonification (like C3II or R2bI); the size of the lot; and the height and total area of the approved project. The placards are meant to be the transparent link between the rules of the code and the specific buildings being built, offering a chance for participatory publics to monitor compliance. One of the first things that members of Salvemos al Barrio had done was to conduct a block-by-block survey of all the new construction in the neighborhood, gathering information and making spreadsheets, similar to what Kregg Hetherington (2011) has termed "guerrilla auditing."

While the placards are meant to be the transparent link between the rules of the code and specific projects being built, they proved to be an early gateway into the bureaucratically mysterious. Although the names of the architects of a project were always posted, for example, other important names, like the investors behind the project, were not listed and were difficult to ascertain through other means. Other pieces of information, like "FOT=5.2," were opaquely technical and communicated little to the uninitiated.[24] And though the number of the dossier ostensibly offered vecinos the ability to access the plans for the building, no one I know was ever able to lay their hands on project dossiers via official channels. The transparency offered by the placards often obscured as much as they revealed through the trick of bureaucratic transparency, in which people are led to think that everything is laid out before them, clear as day. Not that I knew anything about the intricacies of construction bureaucracy as I wandered the city streets peering up at new buildings, their placards proclaiming the required information. Nor did the vecinos I spoke with, until they began what they thought would be straightforward audits of the buildings in the neighborhood. The placards were the beginning of a longer journey in which it seemed that there was always something else to discover behind the transparency offered by the code and the bureaucratic tools and institutions that surrounded it. The intrigue-laden world of state corruption vecinos uncovered from there became a central feature of their interrogation into the code, who was writing it, and to what ends.

In Villa Pueyrredón, after trying to decode the placards themselves, members of Salvemos ended up hiring an architect from another neighborhood group to help them with their audit. She was able to confirm various irregularities suspected by vecinos. One building, for example, was registered as two separate construction projects, allowing the builders to circumnavigate rules pertaining to elevators and parking spaces; another building's second floor overhung the sidewalk too close to the street; another had two extra floors on top. In the end, of the more than thirty buildings along the stretch of the avenue they were concerned with, all but two had some type of irregularity.

The bureaucratic body through which most of these irregularities were said to slip was the DGROC—the General Directorate Registry of Construction and Cadastre, a bureaucratic arm of the city government through which all plans had to pass prior to being approved and from which construction permits were issued. It was widely rumored that a mid-level official—the man about whom I had shared the intensely whispered exchange during the meeting—was the man responsible for most of the malfeasance. He was said to be the son of the finance secretary of a powerful union of municipal workers, the organism to which it was understood the bribes paid to the official were eventually directed. The approval of plans beyond what was permitted in the code was understood not to be an exceptional act, but part of a well-oiled shadow bureaucracy: "They charge 1,000 U.S. dollars per square meter approved in excess of what's permitted," I was told by one vecino, "plus the 100 dollars you have to slip into the pages of the dossier!" another piped in, the specificity of amounts and the intimate knowledge of the process contributing to the drama of the story and helping to keep such stories on the move through vecino gossip networks.

Although the union said to benefit from this system was described to me as incredibly powerful—capable of shutting down the city, of getting mayors thrown out of office—the man inside the DGROC was described as an explicitly unimportant figure within the directorate. He did not hold a high post and did not appear on any of the state's transparency-driven organizational diagrams or decision-making flowcharts. And yet, he was understood to be the one that was calling the real shots within the DGROC. As the vecinos came to learn, the seats of power don't always proclaim themselves as such. Instead, his mid-level bureaucratic position was said to be the perfect cover for wielding power in a bureaucratic apparatus that was part of a democratic system. No one on the outside paid much attention to him, and if a scandal were to come crashing down, the political appointees at the top would be held responsible, not the career functionaries working beneath them.

Attempting to audit the buildings in their neighborhood thus brought vecinos into contact with the murk of state power, in which they had to gradually feel out where decisions were coming from, who their enemies were, and how they might move their own proposals forward. For this reason, much of their work was imbued with hypothesizing, gossiping, and conjecturing about where power came to rest, which was rarely in the places that the state's organizational flowcharts might have led them to believe.[25]

It wasn't just the bureaucratic forces surrounding the code's enforcement that had this murky quality. The same sense of not knowing where true authorship really lay also permeated the legislative process through which the code itself was written. Recall that early in their efforts, the vecinos of Villa Pueyrredón had invited several legislators to the barrio to observe the ways that tall buildings were impacting neighborhood life. The legislators who came to the neighborhood all agreed with the vecinos, describing the application of C3II as a kind of mistake. At first, this seemed to be enough: members of the planning commission drafted proposals to change the code for Villa Pueyrredón and limit the height of buildings in the area. Vecinos were hopeful. But time dragged on as the concrete around their houses rose ever higher, and construction permits continued to be granted for new buildings. Why did things seem to stall if no one had thought that this was the way things were supposed to be—if no one thought that this was good urbanism? Eventually, vecinos came to suspect that they had been placed in a legislative limbo, the proposals written and workshopped again and again, but ultimately stuck in a box in a legislator's desk.

At this point vecinos began to couple the kinds of rational urbanistic arguments they were making with other kinds of tactics—tactics that they described as political rather than technical. Jorge, a member of Salvemos al Barrio, explained this situation to me like this:

> I have no doubt about [the technical veracity of our claims, i.e., in the terms of good urbanism]. But in this country the technical crashes into

power. It dies there, it crashes and burns. . . . And so it doesn't make sense to just make technical arguments, because the guy who has to accept our argument doesn't give a damn about that. . . . Here, at the base of it all, it's about business, about profitability. Don't tell me any of this is based on some idea of urban development. You're kidding me, because in this city there are a ton of things that could use some development—the low areas that flood, the whole southern side of the city. So don't come to me with this idea that this is based on a technical argument about urbanism. If they're building on this side of the city, it's because there's money to be made. And if the technical arguments are always second to profit, then the whole thing is a fallacy.

Technical knowledge alone, in other words, was not a sufficient means through which to get their goals met. This was an effort they did engage in— vecinos tried to understand the urban design premises upon which certain decisions might be made, so that they could effectively articulate their own positions. But such efforts were not only not enough to secure the changes they needed, but might also result in pouring all of their efforts into a strategy that was doomed to failure if they were to ignore the kinds of tactics they referred to as political. Technical knowledge alone was weak unless it was augmented and supplemented by an understanding of power.

As they felt out the network of power surrounding the code's authorship, they became convinced that the code had ghostwriters—that its authors were neither democratic in the sense of having created a code built on popular participation in and concern for urban affairs, nor technocratic experts of modernist urbanism. They weren't even necessarily the politicians whose names appeared on the legislation. Official political regimes lay over and on top of another structure, a structure whose shorthand was manifest in corruption stories about bribes and mafioso unions, but that was also understood more broadly to be about the power of money to determine the future of the city—what Marta had called the Corporation.

Vecinos' political tactics to confront these ghostwriters of the code included street protests and the blockade of transit arteries to draw attention to their cause (like SOS Caballito's protest, which I described in chapter 3). For Salvemos al Barrio, it also meant something slightly different: on the one hand, they redirected part of their efforts from legislative to bureaucratic interventions, and at the same time they began to apply political pressure by threatening to expose the corruption in the DGROC.

In terms of their bureaucratic tactics, the vecinos in Salvemos had come to learn through political gossip that the DGROC had a tense relationship with another branch of the state bureaucracy, the DGFYCO, or General Directorate of Fiscalization and Control of Construction. While the DGROC reviewed plans to ensure that they were within code, the DGFYCO was responsible for making sure that the construction was executed in accordance with the plans on file. The splitting of the two branches of bureaucracy was a recent event, they were told—the outcome of a battle between warring political factions within the governing coalition, part of which was bent on stemming corruption. The DGFYCO, in other words, did not take orders from the DGROC and, if anything, was eager for a fight. As the vecinos in Villa Pueyrredón gained a better understanding of these internal conflicts, they developed a working relationship with the DGFYCO. Whenever they saw anything that might be cause for an infraction, they would place a call to their office, which would perform an inspection and at times halt construction, allowing vecinos to slow down the process of construction and on some occasions to stop it indefinitely. This tactic was effective but also limited, because the DGFYCO could only fault construction for being in violation of construction rules (about noise regulations and safety measures, for example) or not building in compliance with their approved plans; they had no oversight over whether the plans approved were in accordance with the code, let alone authority to change the code.

The more powerful tool ended up being the set of gossip-driven speculations they were able to generate around the corruption in the DGROC. The irregularities they had discovered in their audit of construction projects along the avenue were enough to get some high-profile media coverage. One piece of information in particular that emerged from this process had been as good as gold: the wife of the functionary at the DGROC was listed as a business partner on one of the construction projects. A crew from the well-known television program *Caiga Quien Caiga* (Fall Who May) interviewed the official's boss in the DGROC and tried to interview the official at his home as well. In addition to CQC, the scandal was taken up by several major newspapers. In response, the mayor himself called a meeting with the secretary of urban planning and a representative of Salvemos al Barrio. In that meeting, he ordered a junior legislator from his own party to present the law lowering building heights that vecinos had been trying to pass and in exchange demanded that the vecinos stop making a political ruckus. At this point the vecinos thought everything was finally resolved, but it wasn't: the legislator charged with getting the law passed couldn't get enough votes on the planning commission. Had the mayor chosen that legislator on purpose, the vecinos wondered, knowing that he wasn't powerful enough to get it passed? Had they once again been tricked by the false appearance of authorial power? Or was the mayor himself not powerful enough to go against the Corporation and rewrite the code? Once again, the vecinos of Salvemos found themselves wondering what their next steps should be and how and where they might locate the authors of the code.

But the corruption story that aired on television, meanwhile, had taken on its own curious circuit of power. At the next weekly assembly, word reached the group that the functionary's mother had gone to get her hair done in Villa Pueyrredón and had overheard other women gossiping about her son, saying that he was a *coimero*, a bribe-taker, and that she had rushed out of the salon, upset. Soon after, the functionary made contact with Marco, one of the vecinos who had been in the meeting with the mayor. He tried to point the vecinos back to the formal legislative apparatus. "I'm just a simple functionary," he told him, "What can *I* do? What you need is an *amparo*, a judicial injunction. The best thing for you to do would be to go through the court system . . ." But Marco stopped him and let him know that they had more information— another construction project on which his mother was listed as a partner, implicating her in a possible corruption scandal. As Marco would later to explain to me, it was ultimately a call the functionary's father (the secretary of the workers syndicate) placed to a powerful opposition politician on the planning commission that appeared to unclog the legislative wheels. They never imagined that it would happen like this, but the resolution to change the planning code was passed with unanimous support by all members of the Urban Planning Commission.

CONCLUSION

Within a broad context in which emergent forms of technical rationality have come together with the valorization of participatory democratic politics, the Código de Planeamiento Urbano has seemed not only to endure but to thrive. As a form of power with democratic authorship, however, the code has proven to be anything but straightforward. Instead, attempting to enact democratic authorship brought vecinos into contact with the murk of state power, in which they were constantly on the hunt for where power over the code, and the city that came forth from it, might lie. Feeling out the contours of the code's authorship required looking beyond the veneer of democratic planning and developing forms of voice that could work within complex terrains of economic and political investment. The technical proficiency vecinos developed with regard to the language of the code was not incidental to their efforts: it allowed them to suspect early irregularities, to slow down the progress of buildings in the back and forth between the DGROC and the DGFYCO; and it was the only way they could ultimately ascertain whether they were getting a good deal in the back and forth over R2b1 and C3II, plano limite and altura maxima, as they negotiated proposals with legislators whose intentions they rarely trusted. But their technical knowledge alone was not enough, and so they leveraged a variety of other uses of the word—from public audiences to street protests and corruption stories—to reinsert market and political interests as named forces at the heart of urban planning decisions.

After a year and a half of petitions, legislative meetings, marches, and other political maneuvers, what the vecinos of Salvemos al Barrio achieved was a few lines of code that marked an exception to the zoning parameters for C3II in a section of their barrio. For people like Marta, victories such as these are good news for some vecinos but, at the same time, an indication of the durability of the code itself and the power structures that author it. Getting more substantive changes made to the apparatus of urban planning—ones that would develop forms of authorship more responsive to vecinos' values in the built environment—would be a much longer fight.[26]

The vecinos of Villa Pueyrredón did not solve the problems of political voice in exactly the way that advocates for democratic planning might have imagined or that they themselves might have hoped. But by uncovering and holding open the question of authorship, vecinos achieved something more than a conclusive unveiling that would reveal an ultimate truth or arrive at a final author. Instead, alongside other groups in the city, the power of their interventions was in the way they wove questions of economic and political investment into the supposedly democratic fiber of contemporary urban planning. This is where I see the power of Marta's conceptualization of the corporation—that amalgam of political, economic, and professional interests that she finds holding up the code as a system of power and knowledge. With the corporation, Marta manages to give a name to the authors of the code while still resisting the final foreclosure that would be brought by a conclusive and finalized identification.[27] The Corporation is a name that points to its own mysterious identity, holding open the question of who the forces that threaten to capture urban planning are and where they may lie.

Although their most obvious concrete achievement was in a line change to the code, this was not the only outcome of vecinos' advocacy. At the same time that they worked to change the code, they also worked to question its efficacy as the concrete form through which dreams of democratic planning might be realized. By identifying the problem of voice in planning as a domain situated in complex terrains of economic and political investment, vecinos refused the suturing of the political implied in visions of urban planning that would point to the code as the realization of their dreams and identify them as its democratic authors. Instead, they made other uses of the word to explore the contours of the unspoken voices underlying the code, to lie in the way of the dreamspace of participatory planning, and to make the democratic process overflow with, rather than contain, disparate visions for the future of the city.

CHAPTER 5

Architecture Is for Everyone

Bodies, Drawing, and the Politics of Care

It was eleven-thirty at night, and I had hitched a ride with Santiago, who would drop César, Gaby, and me at the bus lines that would take us the rest of the way home after our class session of Design I at the architecture school at the University of Buenos Aires. Santi had saved me from a bus ride leaving the university that would be standing room only, packed with students and their large models and sheafs of drawings, the cardboard and paper lofted over their heads, occupying nearly as much room as the students themselves. The University of Buenos Aires is an enormous educational institution, the second-largest in the Americas, educating around 300,000 students per year, of whom about 25,000 study in the Faculty of Architecture, Design, and Urbanism (FADU). The teachers and students with whom I spent the year were part of a *cátedra*—an academic grouping within a subject area—supervised by Juan Molina y Vedia and Jaime Sorín, one of two dozen design cátedras in the architecture school.[1] It was fairly early in my fieldwork at the architecture school, and Santi, César, and Gaby took the opportunity to ask me again about my research. I told them that I was interested in studying architecture in the city in the context of the construction boom that had been in swing for several years. I was with them to learn, alongside students, how buildings were thought about and worked on by architects.

César's comment caught me off guard: "I'm not sure how much of what is being built today you can call architecture," he said. I would later hear the comment repeated in various conversations with practicing architects. The comment indexed more than a disparaging impression about the caliber of the buildings being built; it also spoke to the frustration many of them felt with regard to their professional lives, especially vis-à-vis their lives as students. Whether they worked as draftspeople in studios, as project managers on construction sites, or in their own small architecture firms, there was a sense that the market in construction had little place for the kinds of engagement with the built environment that they had been taught to value in their schooling. In the face of this dilemma, many returned to the university for limited opportunities for postgraduate study or, more frequently, as teachers. They don't do it for the money; many are unpaid, and those who are receive only modest honoraria. Instead, they travel to the school twice a week, after working a full day, to spend four hours teaching students because they find in teaching a way to hold present a set of values that doesn't always find a place in their professional lives. As one professor told me, he teaches because the university is the place where he feels like he's really doing architecture.[2]

Over the course of my fieldwork I came to understand this sense of disjuncture as one manifestation of a tension that has long characterized the relationship between architecture and the real estate market—a tension that seemed to be amplified in Buenos Aires in the years following 2001, when the hopes and dreams for a different kind of market for buildings had swollen and captured part of the architectural imaginary. Like the efforts of vecinos I described in chapters 3 and 4, the architecture school offers an opportunity to open some of the cracks in an analytic that would see architecture as the product of an always already commoditized form of production for the built environment. It is a place where the capture of architecture by market logics is placed in tension, in which alternatives have been nurtured, and where the idea of producing vehicles for investment has not always had easy tread.

This tension has a deep history: the architecture school has been a site of pitched battles over the heart of architecture and the bodies and souls of architects. The school has faced repeated and violent intervention from military governments as well as from neoliberal reforms that set out to make architectural education ever more amenable to market production. Within these contexts, many students and professors struggled to make sure that architecture would not be subsumed within the market relationships that defined architecture in professional practice, insisting on teaching a vision of architecture that was not limited to or defined by professional realities. In a world in which education in the arts and design is increasingly brought within the orbit of an entrepreneurial ethos geared toward market production, this is no small achievement.[3]

In this chapter I trace some of the values architects produce in their practice, the ways institutional homes are made and preserved for them, and the hopes that are held in making them endure in the face of other values that might overtake them. Building upon the insights of scholars who attend to shifting boundaries between commodity and noncommodity forms and to the multiple and divergent values that can inhere within capitalism, I leverage what I see as two key moments in the situated histories and practice of architecture in post-crisis Buenos Aires to describe the troubled and contested hegemony of market value in architectural worlds.

First, I describe the practices of drawing and model making that were the major focus of pedagogical practice in the architecture school. Every Monday and Thursday night during the academic year of 2008, I walked into the workshop in the University of Buenos Aires to find teachers and students scattered around the large room, leaning over sets of drawings that students had brought in early for extra help. As 7 p.m. rolled around, the students began to gather into smaller groups, each of which was presided over by three teachers. I rotated between the large tables and listened in on the lessons and critiques of student work. We would stay until eleven, sometimes later, the cigarette smoke curling up toward the ceiling and growing thicker as the hours passed. In these sessions, I was made conscious of the extent to which teaching students to design meant teaching them to inhabit their bodies differently: to become attentive to their inhabitation of space and the sensations evoked by different built environments—a skill that would foster their ability to evoke those sensations for others in their designs. Architectural education, then, is not just an epistemic enterprise unfolding in a disembodied mind; instead, architects learn to feel their bodies in space differently through their engagement with drawings and models. This cultivation of attention to human bodily experience was a far cry from other manifestations of buildings—for example, in the charts and graphs of market analysts I described in chapter 2. In the way that they focus attention on a different set of values than, for example, real estate investment, practices of drawing put into the world a form of value in buildings that operates in tension with, even while existing in the presence of, market-defined values. Putting into the world a reality that exists in tension with others is a political act insofar as architects are producing value in their drawings that diverges from others. I came to think of practices of drawing and model making as the matter of care in architectural education: they are materials that recalibrate bodies and minds and incubate certain forms of responsibility and obligation with regard to the built environment and its potential inhabitants.

But contemporary architectural education also reflects deep histories of more overt political struggle in Argentina. In the main atrium of the architecture school there hangs a large banner that bears the faces of students and faculty who were disappeared by the military dictatorship of the late 1970s and early 1980s. The banner offers an entryway into the second moment in the situated practice of architecture that I want to think with in this chapter—namely, the violent political history of architectural education in Argentina. I would learn only late in my time at the architecture school that the particular workshop in which I conducted fieldwork was intimately tied to leftist architecture movements that worked to reformulate architectural education in the midst of the political turmoil of the late 1960s and early 1970s. Political movements in the school at the time were explicitly concerned with reconceptualizing architectural education in a way that problematized architecture's existence within commodity society, and they made it their task to begin to imagine an "architecture of the pueblo" (of the people, as a collective body) in opposition to what they called the "architecture of the system." In light of these struggles, which many paid for with their lives, I then return to the workshop to ask how the more quotidian pedagogical exercises I witnessed in the school might inherit from this earlier political moment. Architecture students in the workshop in which I conducted fieldwork learned more than to draw from their own bodies; they also learned to draw from within a political body in which architecture might be something more than a luxury commodity and instead intervene in a world marked by ongoing relations of dependency, colonialism, and dispossession.

ATTUNING AND EQUIPPING BODIES: DRAWING "EN CARNE PROPIA"

"You have to think about the life of these spaces!" César implored his students one evening. "I want you to imagine all of this when you are drawing: When you draw this entryway, you look up, you see the house, you see the entryway. But also, you have to think through quotidian life. I need you to imagine more, to think more when you're drawing. You have to *live the house while you draw it*. You have to think: How am I going to design this space so that you can see the patio from the living room? When you draw the kitchen, you have to think to yourself: 'Now I'm going to put away the dishes' and imagine how that will be! Take the *Pastilla de Chiquitolina*,[4] the Tiny Person Pill, and *live it*!" Deby, one of his partners in the workshop, added, "When you begin to draw *en carne propia*"—literally in your own flesh—"you will realize things that you didn't realize before."

How do lines of graphite on paper come to produce lush built environments that are home to a diverse range of lived experience? How does the slow, intimate, and at times plodding work of design carried out in paper and cardboard get articulated with concrete urban environments and with bodies that see, feel, and move within them? César and Deby's comments to their students that night were in many ways a summary of the complex transformation that teachers were working to render in first-year students as they taught them the basics of architectural design. In later years, they would expand and deepen these basic practices; but for now, they had to learn to draw en carne propia—the art of being able to live a world while they draw it. Learning to draw en carne propia involves bringing together quotidian life and bodily sensation with specialized capacities to focus on human life in built environments using scaled models, collage, sketches, and drawings. Getting students' bodies to work together with drawings and models in order to articulate their designs with lived worlds was the principal achievement teachers in Design 1 sought to instill in their students.

....

"What's happening here?" César asks as he looks over Bárbara's design for a neighborhood cultural center before class. "I have to go through the courtyard to get to the bathrooms?" The courtyard the student wanted to place in the middle of the building had made it necessary to separate the multipurpose room from the bathrooms, and César wasn't convinced. "I couldn't make it work with the patio in the center and still maintain the views out to the park on the other side," Bárbara responded, referencing a dilemma they had tried to solve the previous week but that had continued to frustrate her. César interrupted her with his signature dramatic flair: "I'm in my senior yoga class doing my downward facing dog, and I have to go to the bathroom. . . ." He grabs his crotch and begins jumping up and down. "It's raining. You're going to make me put on my shoes. . . ." And then he begins to mime this while jumping ". . . put on my jacket, get my umbrella—it's freezing cold—and I have to go outside just to piss!?"

One of the ways that teachers approached the complex task of learning to draw en carne propia was to hold present the minutia of human daily life during their corrections of student projects. Students had to become attuned to the ways that buildings articulated with everyday life practices and experiences in order to learn to project these experiences in paper and cardboard

whose?

thinking comfort
out of different kids of bodies

environments. As César dramatically enacted—miming the feeling of having to use the bathroom, put on his coat and shoes, open his umbrella, and head out into the rain—this required paying attention to bodies and their everyday interactions with the built environment.

This was more difficult than it may sound for beginning students. The literal lines they lay down on paper or build from cardboard—of walls, windows, doors, and bathrooms—are of material things, and there was a tendency for students to approach them in isolation from the broader worlds of which they would be part. In fact, one of the pejorative descriptors that professors used to voice disquiet with student work was to say that it was _muy objeto,_ or "very objecty." Instead of designing buildings as objects, architecture was about designing buildings as integral parts of ecologies that included plants, the sun, and the sky, empty spaces and other buildings, and the human bodies that would circulate within and around them. The repeated work of returning students' attention to bodily presence in built environments was one way of making sure buildings were thought about as environments and not as isolated objects.

There were specific exercises designed to help students transition from drawing buildings that were muy objeto to drawing en carne propia. One such exercise was an assignment to draw and build models of their own homes and then redesign them. By having students redesign the places in which they lived, teachers were able to bring aspects of quotidian life into sharper relief. As the students brought in the plans they had drawn up for their houses, teachers interrogated them about the flows of people through their homes, the activities that took place within them, and how these aspects of quotidian life could be improved. "How do you get the meat out to the grill if the patio is so far from the kitchen? And if it's raining, what happens?" Flor asked one student. Similar questions were raised again and again throughout the year: "When I walk in, where do I put the groceries?"; "Why am I getting wet while I look for my keys?"; or "When I finish washing the dishes, where am I supposed to put them to dry?" In these pedagogic moments, human daily activities—breathing, cooking, cleaning, excreting people—are reinserted as central facets of the design process.

In addition to keeping present everyday life processes, student bodies were also trained in more specialized arts of noticing with regard to the environments around them. They learned to be hyperconscious of what they felt and to attend to how those feelings and experiences were generated by the forms and structures with which they interacted. In order to achieve this, pro-

how do architects [...] this [...] facade design? a broader public? → what does glass do here?

FIGURE 5.1. Blindfolded students describe sounds and tactile sensations to partners who take notes. Photo by author.

fessors took students on field trips or sent them to visit particular buildings, drawing their attention to the sensations the built environment generated in their bodies and teaching them to trace those sensations back to the material substrates that generated them.

One of the main ways this was done was through field trips. Each year the cátedra chooses a specific site in which the entire cátedra would base their final projects for that year. On one trip, I accompanied the first-year students on their site visit to a small park in San Justo, part of the municipality of La Matanza that sits just beyond the western edge of the city. At the site, professors guided students in their attention to the space, reminding them of the kinds of things that they should take note of as they sketched and took photos: "Pay attention to what this part of the city is like, how the layout of the lines of the streets helps determine the rhythm of the neighborhood," Arturo urged them. "What's this site like when I pass by in the train? What if I arrived in a car? What's it like to walk by?" To help them attend to senses beyond the visual, students were blindfolded and asked to pay attention as they sat in one place or were led around by a partner: "What do you hear? What is the air like? How does the ground feel?" (see figure 5.1). At their next class, they would be expected to produce a synthetic analysis of the space using photographs, collage, drawings, and small pieces of written text. There, professors pushed students into increasing levels of detail about the place they had visited: Where was there shade and where was there sun? What kinds of trees produced the shade, and do they lose their leaves in the fall? Did you notice that the colors of the flowers along the train track were the same as the colors of the train when it passed? Or that the stones laid out in this section of the park were larger than the ones on the other side?

I saw this cultivation of a heightened attention to urban environments on field trips to visit prominent architectural sites (like Le Corbusier's Casa Curutchet in La Plata) or to different neighborhoods (like Palermo, where upscale boutiques combined older buildings with high-end architectural design) (see figure 5.2). Walking students through the Casa Curutchet, for example, Deby asked them to pay attention to how a ramp encouraged them to travel up to a second floor and to feel what the ramp felt like while they walked along it. Did the material of the ramp make them feel like they were floating, or were on solid ground? Deby exaggerated her movements, clumping down on the actual concrete ramp, and then imagining another ramp, one of metal grating, which she floated up lightly, flapping her arms exaggeratedly as she coasted along the air that could flow through the grating. In one of the stores we visited in Palermo, they pointed out the materialities of the building and its impact on the experience of space: "Pay attention to how the interior space is segmented using materials—there is a zone dominated by wood and then another by concrete, differentiating the spaces without building walls between them. Notice how the openings in the walls permit you to see other spaces, inviting you to go to the other side, but also defining those spaces as separate," Debby said. In these pedagogic moments, students learned to experience their bodies differently, attuning them to the sensations evoked by their environments. Along with attention to the quotidian uses of spaces that are constantly reinserted in students' consciousness (like going to the bathroom), professors taught students to attend to these subtler feelings: the bodily lightness provoked by certain materials, the seductions of views that can call people into other spaces, the different ways to define and delimit spaces using light or changes in building materials.

Visiting sites in the world provided material from which to build these experiences into their own designs. In one class session, for example, Jorge was trying to help a student with her staircase. She had put in a basic staircase, and

FIGURE 5.2. Students, reflected in the window, observing a staircase in Palermo. Photo by author.

he pointed out that the solid staircase she had used would block light from windows on the other side, dividing the spaces rather than allowing visual communication between them: "You need to go to the Centro Cultural de la Cooperación and look at *that* staircase," he told her. "Look at how the sun passes through it, and how the light that is cast gets longer as the day goes on. Go and look at that staircase, and how it plays with *those* windows, with *that* light. You have to go there, and sit in that café, and look at the light, at how it makes the staircase dematerialize. This is what it means to do architecture!" Jorge was teaching the student how to feel a space and to pay special attention to how those feelings were generated by the architectural features that surround her. And he was then asking her to keep those feelings and that body present in her designs: to think beyond her everyday notions of what something like a staircase should be and keep present her sensibility to human experience in an environment in which concrete, light, and shadow have the power to make a staircase dematerialize.

....

One night, a professor from Design 2 came to the workshop with Juan Molina y Vedia (co-head of the cátedra) to conduct a guest critique of student work from Design 1. She had stopped to critique one of the students' projects for a house, picking up the model he had built at 1:100 (a scale in which one centimeter on paper represents 100 centimeters in real life). "At this scale, you really aren't going to be able to make certain decisions," she said to him and the group of students listening in. "For example," she continued, "the opening that you have in the roof here—should it be here, or maybe it would be better over here? How is it going to play with light and shade in the interior? Or, I'd like to consider a half-wall along here. But you're only going to be able to know if you build a model at other scales. *You're not going to be able to know, no matter how much you work on it, if you keep working at this scale. And you're not going to be able to know just by working on the model.* You have to do various sketches [*croquis*] if you're going to think through it properly. I'd like to see a photomontage. And maybe after you see it in 1:50, you'll decide that the roof isn't flat, that maybe it carries some weight. You're not going to be able to redo the entire project every time you make a different model, *but you will begin to think about other questions.*"

The art of drawing and building models en carne propia was about more than paying attention to quotidian life and bodily experience and then externalizing those insights into paper drawings and cardboard models. Instead, drawings and models are vital appendages through which students' capacities to feel and think are extended, reaching back into their bodies and minds to become essential tools of focus and exploration.[5] "Thought also has scales," Juan said, continuing the point of the teacher from Level 2. "You need to be always mixing and changing the scales at which you work." Getting their bodies to work with their drawings meant teaching students not just to feel and pay attention to the world in new ways, but to develop productive relationships with the complex set of imagistic tools in which architecture lives. These include different types of drawings, like plans (two-dimensional representations of horizontal space), cross sections (two-dimensional representations of vertical space), and elevations (two-dimensional exterior views); models; and work in other media like collage, photographs, sketches, and sometimes brief forms of text. Each of the types of drawings and models are

thinking w/
models – not a reproduction
of a perfect reality

FIGURE 5.3. A student awaits the correction of his elevation and cross section.
Photo by author.

themselves multiple, as they can be worked on at a variety of scales, including
1:1, 1:50, and 1:100 (see figure 5.3).

Different modes of analysis accompanied each of these tools, bringing to
bear different sets of questions for each kind of drawing or model. As they
learn to work with this range of media, they attune their own capacities to
think and feel what a building is about. Working with these tools en carne
propia is not so much about producing drawings *of* designs (i.e., the exter-
nalization of something already existing in the mind) as it is about learning
to draw as a processual form of engagement through which questions about
design are asked and answered.

Take, for instance, the different scales of drawing and model making refer-
enced by the professor from Design 2 on her visit with Juan to the classroom.
In his own more frequent visits to the class, Juan often made reference to
a lecture series on scale by the Argentine architect Jorge Vivanco, later published in the journal *Trama*, which explains the specific kinds of work that happen at different scales (1988). For example, Vivanco explains that 1:1, in which
one centimeter on paper is equivalent to one centimeter in real life, requires
and produces an intimate reflection on the materials of construction: "You

have to understand the quality of the material and how to draw it. . . . You have to express the marble, or the quality of the travertine stone. The travertine has cavities, a rough texture. The marble is smoother" (61). A 1:1 scale also provokes and requires attuning to a specific temporality, Vivanco explains. Unlike the depiction of an entire building, 1:1 is about instantaneous experience—you don't have to walk through it to understand it. It is not meant to convey the temporally elongated experience of passing through; rather, 1:1 works like snapshots of what one might see at instantaneous moments of experience.

A 1:100 scale, in contrast, is a scale at which very different questions are addressed. At this scale, models of entire houses fit comfortably on small boards, and drawings fit on poster-size paper. If 1:1 is the scale of the tactile, the intimate, and the directly perceived instant, then 1:100 is a space in which questions approaching the entirety of the building come into focus. A floor plan in 1:100 engages questions of the layout of rooms, of the flow of people through a building; it is a scale at which you can understand which rooms access which patios and how they relate to the space outside the building (see figure 5.4). This scale moves beyond the intimate closeness of one person's experience of material texture that can be expressed and considered in 1:1 and moves to a broader social environment of the building as a whole. As Vivanco puts it, "When we pass to 1:10 or 1:100, already we're talking about collectives, and other things enter in: it's about the organization of a society, there are many people" (1988, 61). The 1:100 scale also functions in a different temporality, one of processual time, focusing attention on how one moves through a building, rather than on instantaneous closeness.

The importance of different media for bringing certain questions into focus also applies to different kinds of drawings. One day in class, while thinking about the high ceilings in many of the older buildings I had visited, I asked Gaby how high the ceilings in a student project were. Gaby took the opportunity to teach me about the difference between cross sections and floor plans and the kinds of considerations that are developed in each of them: "The kind of spatial sensation you're talking about—that of verticality, of volume—is very difficult for students to learn to communicate. Have you noticed how few of them come in with cross sections or elevations unless we make them? They're very focused on the floor plan, because they still don't understand that it's within these other drawings that the kinds of sensations you're talking about are studied." It wasn't coincidental that I couldn't tell how high

FIGURE 5.4. Two professors discuss a student's floor plan in 1:100, asking about circulation. Photo by author.

the ceilings were, in other words; the student herself, Gaby wagered, hadn't thought the issue through, since she hadn't drawn any cross sections.

Different kinds of drawings and models thus serve to focus student attention on certain kinds of experiences and allow them to work through specific problems. Drawings and models are, in this sense, processual tools—parts of ongoing practice—and not final outcomes. The failure to draw in a variety of different ways—not just plans but also cross sections, not just 1:100 but also 1:50—were detrimental to students' ability to think through the wide range of experiences they learned to pay attention to when their teachers took them on field trips or talked them through the habits of daily life. Within the workshop, it was not possible for students to adequately think through the range of different experiences their designs would produce without the variety of media they were learning to use. The experiences they had learned to attend to were in this way tightly bound up with the practice of drawing and model making (see figures 5.5 and 5.6).

FIGURES 5.5 AND 5.6. Two professors study a student's implantation of a building on a lot in his 1:100 model. They are using the model to think with him about the uses of the space on each side of the building. Photos by author.

In the relationship between the architect and their media, then, it is not simply the case that the architect is the active agent who does the work of producing design. The practice of making drawings and models, encompassing various scales, perspectives, and media, also acts upon the architect, helping them feel and think about their designs in particular ways. Drawing en carne propia means being able to attend to a diverse range of lived experience, an attention that can only happen through a practice of drawing that is in turn bound up with bodies: the close tactile materiality of 1:1, the vertical airiness of a cross section, the movement through space of bodies that need to get to the bathroom in the rain worked out in a floor-plan in 1:100. The various media that architects work through are not, then, simply representations in the sense of putting down on paper something that is already known; rather, different types of media pose distinct sets of questions and allow certain types of thought and feeling to be considered. They are not the end products of a process, but are themselves processual. Architectural engagement happens through drawing rather than resulting in drawings.[6]

Holding present this processual aspect of drawing and model making was a central focus of first-year education. The visiting teacher from Design 2 I cited earlier was teaching students that their models in 1:100 were not finished products that they would then reproduce in other scales or through photo-montage and sketches. They were, instead, one tool among many to focus on a complex set of lived experiences that encompass various scales and dimensions. Teachers had other ways of encouraging students to keep their drawings and models in a processual register. Early in my year at the university, I sat with Marta and Flor as they examined a meticulously built student model. They asked him about the location of his staircase and, as he was working to formulate his answer, Flor interrupted him: "No, but what if we were to just...," and instead of finishing the sentence, she ripped the staircase off the model. The student looked distraught; he had been up most of the night working on making that model perfect. I must have seemed shocked as well, because Marta nudged Flor, pointed out my expression, and they both started to laugh. "Nico," they said, "tonight you're going to break a model too!" They sent me home with a fragment of cardboard and plastic that night, wrenched from another student's model.

Models and drawings can overpower students—especially younger students, who haven't learned yet to navigate the relationship: they had worked hard on something, they were devoted to it, and much of that work and devotion had been consolidated into the model or drawing. In so doing, they shut down the very forms of engagement that the models are supposed to enable. Students had to learn to manage the power their tools held over them if they were going to learn to be flexible enough to work within this expansive set of media and not allow any one tool to overpower the rest of the project. Keeping them processual, tentative, and as tools for thinking rather than passive representations of decisions already made was what enabled drawings to be a site of ongoing care for everyday life and embodied sensation in the production of built environments.

Through these everyday pedagogical practices, student bodies were re-equipped with sets of drawings and models that, together with new practices of noticing, made possible the work of architectural projection. Teaching students to draw en carne propia entangled everyday life and embodied sensation with specialized capacities to focus on that life using scaled drawings, collage, sketches, and models: students learned to live buildings while they drew them. Together, these practices enable a specific type of architectural care and a form of value in buildings focused on human experience and quotidian life in built environments.

ANOTHER ARCHITECTURE IS POSSIBLE

Drawing en carne propia is in many ways a reflection of the broad uptake of phenomenology within architecture globally since the 1960s and therefore something I wager would be present in many other architecture schools around the world.[7] But alongside teaching students how to draw en carne propia, there were other aspects of the architectural pedagogy I witnessed that were grounded more closely in Argentine history. Architecture in Molina y Vedia–Sorín was not taught as an abstract craft, but in an environment suffused with political inheritance—a political inheritance that works to hold together the bodily presence of drawing with national political, economic, and social histories. These histories, which I turn to now, and efforts to keep them present were one way of building a broader political and social body into the carne propia of architects' living, feeling bodies.[8]

Upon entering the large pavilion that houses the architecture school, students pass under a large banner bearing the names and photographs of students and faculty disappeared by the military dictatorship of the 1970s and 1980s (see figure 5.7). Most of those disappeared were engaged in efforts to reform their country along lines that operated in concert with movements

FIGURE 5.7. A banner (*in the upper left*) overhangs the central atrium of the FADU, bearing the names and photographs of students and faculty disappeared by the military dictatorship. The bottom reads, "Always present." Photo source: Elsapucai.

on the left that were sweeping through Argentina and many other places in the world in the late 1960s. Argentina's brutal military dictatorship is more or less well known, even beyond academic communities and Latin Americanists. But within and alongside these broad historical events, there were efforts to rethink aspects of life that played out in more particular registers. Among these were efforts to formulate a vision for architecture and for architectural education that worked to reimagine the field's role in a more just world.

The banner hanging in the architecture school does more than represent a past event of broad political relevance. It also provokes ongoing reflection about an unrealized future for architecture that was imagined and then pressed to within an inch of its life over forty years ago and asks students to consider their inheritance of that moment: to rethink the present through a past substantially reformed by bloody hands. The dictatorship and the disappearance of these students changed what architecture was and how it would

political movement directly impacts what arch. work be

arquitectos que no fueron

Estudiantes y egresados de la Facultad de Arquitectura y Urbanismo de la Universidad Nacional de Córdoba asesinados y desaparecidos por el terrorismo de Estado, 1975-1983

FIGURE 5.8. The cover of *Arquitectos que no fueron*—literally "Architects That Weren't," in the sense that their lives were cut short before they could exercise their profession. The book is a memorial published by the National University of Córdoba's architecture school, which provides biographical sketches of those disappeared during the dictatorship.

be lived in Argentina, and students today are living in the haunted absence of that once-possible future. The banner, along with the circulation of other texts and images geared toward sustaining memory of these events, calls on students to think through how they might inherit the work of rebuilding a world different from the one they live in: to hold open the claim that another architecture is possible (a slogan of one of the movements I will describe shortly) (see figure 5.8).

Like in much of the world, architecture in Argentina has been incorporated into an array of political projects.[9] These histories of struggle over architecture provide another perspective on the political significance of the architectural school as an institution that has been vital to the maintenance of forms of value beyond those of the market. In retelling some of this history here, I seek to give voice to a deep history of efforts to unsettle architecture's capture by capitalism and work to avoid the possibility that architecture might become simply another market commodity.

I enter a series of broader historical events through the particular history of the cátedra in which I did fieldwork: Molina y Vedia–Sorín. Within architectural circles in Argentina, both Juan Molina y Vedia and Jaime Sorín are well known for their affiliation with leftist architecture movements dating back to the late 1960s and early 1970s. In 1974, Juan was the head professor of the University of Buenos Aires' massive Talleres Nacionales y Populares— National and Popular Workshops, or TANAPO. TANAPO was a cátedra that had grown out of several years of underground student activism during the Onganía dictatorship in the late 1960s, specifically the efforts of a group called TUPAU (the Tendencia Universitaria Popular de Arquitectura y Urbanismo, or Popular University Movement of Architecture and Urbanism), in which Jaime, a student at the time, was a key figure. TUPAU's work focused on critically interrogating architecture and architectural education by working to problematize architecture's status as an elite cultural commodity, working instead to bring it into close relationship with the lives of the popular classes. These ideas were put into practice as TANAPO in a brief moment— only one year—before the intervention of the dictatorship of the Proceso, in which many involved in TANAPO would be disappeared. The story of Juan and Jaime's cátedra is in many respects an exceptional one. But it touches upon important and widely shared moments among those who have worked to keep architecture grounded in, and relevant to, the social, economic, and political life of a broad range of Argentines. Their story, and the story of the cátedra they run, are one way into this complex history.

With one influential exception, Juan didn't learn to think about architecture in relation to popular classes from his studies in architecture school. Instead, he traces his investment in popular architecture through a series of experiences beginning in his childhood. Juan's family has deep, elite roots in Argentina: his great-great-grandfather was a general who fought in the war against Paraguay in the 1860s, later being named the first governor of the newly conquered

Chaco Province; the general's daughter married an important financier, Octavio Molina, involved in orchestrating foreign loans from Baring's Bank for the republic. But one of their sons—Julio Molina y Vedia, Juan's grandfather— became an anarchist, renouncing his connections to the family and moving to a small shack he built of wood and corrugated metal on the outskirts of Buenos Aires. Juan spent a lot of time with Don Julio as a child in the early 1930s, while his parents finished their studies at the university. An architect and an intellectual who was close friends with the writer Macedonio Fernandez and the father of Jorge Luis Borges, Jorge Guillermo (the three planned to found an anarchist colony in Paraguay), Don Julio transmitted to Juan a set of values grounded in simple living, rebellious anti-authoritarianism, and social justice.

Juan's childhood was also marked by life in barrios. He spent his early years living off a dirt road in Villa Ortúzar at a time when it was a barrio of *quintas,* or small country homes, before moving to a street near a bustling market in Belgrano. Telling me about this time of his life, Juan called his years near the market his era of "street studies," when he hung out with the *reos del barrio,* or neighborhood delinquents (the reader may recall the barrio reo, romanticized in tango lyrics, from chapter 3). In the barrio, Juan's parents worked to incorporate their communist politics into their domestic life: they lived in a house without locks, let Juan roam the streets as he liked, and later enrolled him in the neighborhood high school rather than sending him to the Colegio Nacional or Carlos Pellegrini, the traditional schools of intellectual elites.

In 1950, Juan entered the University of Buenos Aires to study architecture like his father and grandfather (his grandfather had discouraged him: "Why would you want to make buildings for such a sick society?"). At the time, the UBA was an exclusive public institution, accepting a limited number of students by examination. In many ways Juan felt out of place there. Most of his classmates were traditional elites, and the course material was based on neoclassicism, which remained dominant at the UBA through the 1950s despite the global excitement surrounding modernism as a means of addressing the poor living conditions affecting the working classes in rapidly expanding industrial cities.

Juan felt an important political distance from his fellow students at the university. Perón had been elected president in 1946 and in that first term implemented many of the policies and programs that the Peronist left continues to hold dear: an expansion of social programs for the poor and important increases in worker's rights, protections, and wages. Juan's father remained a committed Communist, but his mother became a Peronist early on. The university, however, was a largely anti-Peronist environment. Juan's own political identity remained difficult to categorize; he supported Peronism's leftist policies, but was critical of its authoritarianism. This led to one of the most formative experiences of his life, when he was imprisoned in 1954 for protesting the imprisonment of Christian Democratic students organizing against the government. He spent four months in jail with them; when they were released, they asked him to join a group dedicated to the overthrow of Perón, but Juan, despite having just spent four months in jail at the hands of a Peronist government, refused. "If anything, those four months convinced me that I was anti-anti-Peronist," he told me. He was never convinced by Peronism's militarism and authoritarianism, but he remained committed to workers' struggles in a way that the anti-Peronists he spent time with in prison were not.

There were other formative experiences from Juan's years as a student. Though few of them came from within the classroom, a class he took with Ismael Viñas left a lasting impression for the way it approached Argentina's architectural history through the lens of its economic and political history.[10] On his own, Juan read Benedetto Croce on the theory and history of historiography; avant-garde Argentine artists and writers like Xul Solar and Borges; and phenomenologists like Merleau-Ponty and Heidegger, whose essay "Building Dwelling Thinking" had just been published in 1951 and was translated for him by a friend. Instead of going to the coast on his vacations like his classmates, he accompanied a friend from his soccer team to the poor province of Santiago del Estero, which he described as "105 degrees of dust, dirt, and poverty," where houses were made of mud and people pulled their beds outside to sleep at night. If his formal education focused on neoclassical architecture felt distant from the things he cared about, those summers in Santiago, his reading of phenomenology, and his engagement with leftist Argentine economic and political historiography spoke to him in a way that would stay with him for the rest of his life.

Juan began his teaching career in 1957, together with his friend and colleague Rodolfo Livingston, at the recently founded National University of the Northeast, in the poor, interior Chaco Province (the university has locations in both Chaco and Corrientes). Juan's experience in the northeast was the beginning of a pedagogical practice that would locate architecture within the historical and geographic specificity of everyday life in Argentine popular classes rather than giving pride of place to artistic avant-gardes, European architectural history, or even the national center of Buenos Aires for its definition of what architecture could be. "We began to construct a history from a different perspective," Juan recalled in an interview with the architectural supplement of one of Argentina's major papers: "the idea that the history of architecture could be seen from the standpoint of Chaco and Corrientes. The idea of creating a university that knows that one has to look at the world from the place where one is. Once you do that, you can study Greece, Rome, and everything else. But you have to know that the perspective is from *here*" (Ovalle 2014). This was not architectural education as usual, and a far cry from his own neoclassical education, which privileged famous works of architecture from Europe. The newness of the university and its distance from Buenos Aires allowed for pedagogical experimentation. Together with Livingston and his students, he studied the poor areas of Chaco's capital, learning how people constructed and lived within their habitat. In the process, they began the work of attuning architecture to the needs of poor people in a peripheral, rural province. "Architecture," Juan told me later, "has to be a cultural expression of a time and place; being in Chaco meant creating an architecture for Chaco." Crucially for Juan, this "time and place" had come to mean taking into consideration Chaco's history as a site of dispossession and ongoing relationships of dependency: between the poor villa and the city center, between Chaco and Buenos Aires, between Argentina and the world.[11] "I didn't learn this from my architecture classes," he told me, "but from Viñas and my engagement with the political left."

Juan calls this an architecture *desde aquí y ahora*, from the here and now—a geographical and historical location marked by power, inequality, and dependency. The value Juan placed on this aquí y ahora would situate him within an emergent tradition of rethinking architecture from the standpoint of the popular classes in Argentina that many today classify as *Nac y Pop*—national and popular. It was not without its antecedents, nor was it unthinkable at the time, but it was far from hegemonic.[12] And it was a kind of thinking, and imagined a kind of architecture, that was hardly politically neutral during the tumultuous and violent decades in the middle of the twentieth century.

In 1960, Juan and Livingston were (mis-)identified as Marxists and dismissed from their cátedra in Chaco. Shortly thereafter, Juan was invited to teach at the Universidad Nacional de La Plata in the province of Buenos Aires. He took leave from La Plata in 1963, however, when he and Livingston were invited to work in Cuba after a Cuban official heard a presentation about the work they had done together in the poor neighborhoods of Chaco. There, they joined Vivanco (whose work on scale I cited earlier and who was an important figure of the Tucumán School) in the heady years after the revolution, where they worked on urbanism and participated in collective labor details harvesting sugarcane. A year later, Juan's wife became ill, and they returned to Argentina, where he resumed teaching in La Plata.

In 1966, Juan's cátedra in La Plata was closed following the *noche de los bastones largos*, or "the night of the long clubs," when the military dictatorship of Onganía took over the university system.[13] Police raided the University of Buenos Aires, beating students and faculty who had occupied the university to defend a democratized educational system independent of the military government. The purge of faculty that followed the noche de bastones largos transformed the educational ethos of the country. Along with a vast number of professors from universities across the country, Juan was expelled from the university.

For many, what was at stake in the series of military interventions that would take place in the architecture school was a vision of the university as a place for the debate of ideas against a competing vision of the university as place for the production of depoliticized technicians. Jaime Sorín, later Juan's collaborator in the cátedra where I conducted fieldwork, was a student at the time. In a conversation he had with Juan for an oral history project at the UBA's Directorate of Archives of Argentine Architecture and Design (DAR), Jaime recalled that "after 1966 all theoretical discussion was left out. The workshops were terrible, they were places where nothing happened. . . . There was no interesting architectural thought left, and so one had to search for it outside. You took what you could find" (Sorín and Molina y Vedia 2005).

TUPAU, TANAPO, AND AN ARCHITECTURE
OF THE PUEBLO

The efforts of the dictatorship to produce a school for the education of technically capable but politically vacant architects did not go unchallenged. Between 1967 and 1973, Jaime and a small group of other architecture students in the FADU began organizing an underground group called TUPAU: the Tendencia Universitaria Popular de Arquitectura y Urbanismo, or Popular University Movement of Architecture and Urbanism.[14] Over the several years of their activity, TUPAU worked to rethink the mission of the architecture school in light of changing social and political landscapes in the country, a process that took them into collective consideration about architecture's place in both capitalism and leftist politics.

TUPAU began as a small study group. They read scholarship on politics, postcolonialism, capitalism, and inequality (the early work of dependency theorists was one strong influence) and wrote pamphlets and position papers that aimed to bring these ideas, as well as their own experiences in political movements, into dialogue with architecture and architectural education. The texts they wrote include inspiring messages of hope and dogmatic manifestos that were later compiled as the *Antología Pedagógica*, or Pedagogical Anthology (Departamento Pedagógico 1974). At just over 400 pages, the anthology is a polyvocal accretion from TUPAU's several years of activity.[15] I read the anthology as the record of a search for inroads by a young group of politically engaged students into how to conceive of and address a problem for which the typical solutions seemed inadequate: namely, how to think an architecture for the left in Argentina.

Articulating architecture with leftist politics was not an easy task. On the one hand, TUPAU saw in much of architecture and architectural history the trappings of an elitist art in the service of the dominant classes. But at the same time, they also sought to avoid a position held by some on the left (and occasionally voiced in the anthology itself) that an architecture in the service of the pueblo—of the people—could only emerge at some future moment, after the revolution (see, e.g., V1D15 and V1D17). These latter voices argued that it was impossible to reformulate architecture without first transforming society through the overthrow of capitalism: how could architecture place itself in the service of popular classes given its roots in academic elitism and a capitalist mode of production? For them, the best thing architects could do was fight for the revolution now, and worry about architecture later. Despite these doubts, TUPAU's texts indicate that for them, questions of the built environment should not be put off, especially when so much of the pueblo was living in substandard conditions. TUPAU thus worked to draw together architecture with a political stance on the left that was often uninterested in architectural questions, preferring instead to think in (major-key) revolutionary terms.

TUPAU sought to draw into question architecture's capture by capitalist forms of value and the forms of academic inquiry that value it—forces that together produce what the anthology calls the architecture of the system (*arquitectura del regimen*). The architecture of the system, TUPAU argued, is "architecture as just another aspect of the market economy, a generator of profit and multiplier of land rent; [it is] architecture that collaborates in the maintenance of a system of exploitation" (V1D4; see also V1D10). Escaping the architecture of the system, the anthology explained, was a tall order, for a variety of forces collaborate in its production and maintenance. For TUPAU, part of the task involved placing in crisis the central place afforded to European and American avant-gardes, both in education and in architectural publications like *Summa*, the Argentine architectural journal of record.[16] Valorizing the work of northern avant-gardes risked overlooking the particular features of Argentine realities, they argued; producing an appropriate architecture for Argentina would require architects to provincialize the Northern architectures that were valorized in the academy and in professional practice.[17]

Understanding the architecture of the system also required a theorization of architecture's place as part of a broader commodity culture. TUPAU was interested in challenging the commodification of architecture, through which it was turned into a "thing-in-itself" rather than a "being-in-society" (v1D7). The product of architecture, TUPAU argued, is "written into a process of commoditization, its value is determined by the demand, the ideology, and the culture of the dominant sectors of society. In such a society, the architect is limited to the production of obsolescent designs because they are oriented to the satisfaction of a distorted market, in which capacity for acquisition is restricted to those least in need" (v1D7). Only by reflecting critically on architecture's place within a changing economic and political order, they argued, would another architecture become possible. In response, TUPAU marshaled theories of imperialism and dependency to begin to build new criteria for architectural value distantiated from those of metropolitan centers (v1D7).

Against the threatening figure of the architect of the system, TUPAU also began to construct a hero: the architect of the pueblo. Imagining an architecture of the pueblo was a project that required a radicalized pedagogy, they argued, with a new sense of where knowledge could come from. TUPAU repeats many times throughout the anthology that their knowledge must not be born within university walls, but must come from beyond them: "The pueblo is not liberated from within the University; instead, the University is liberated from the pueblo" (v1D15). Marking a distinction with intellectuals who saw their role as that of educating the masses, TUPAU worked to imagine a place for architecture within a populist political movement in which they would be in close touch, and ideally at the service of, popular classes. Facing off against a vision of the luminary architect working from their studio and an education grounded in the big names and moments of architecture that they saw valorized by the academic establishment, the students of TUPAU argued that architects needed to "descend from their drawing pads to the pueblo to understand their lives, their problems, and the deformations provoked by dependency; in other words, to change their point of observation and ground it in [this] reality" (v1D4).

In the face of an architectural culture and educative system steeped in commodity society, dependency, and the universalizing pretensions of Northern avant-gardes, then, the students of TUPAU sought to create other openings, possibilities held out against probabilities: "Welcome to the struggle" (v1D10). The study of architecture, TUPAU states in a welcome pamphlet, is the history of the decision about what kind of architect one wants to be. "We welcome you to a new experience, the collective experience of a *búsqueda* [a searching]. This búsqueda—beyond the classes, the grades, the diploma— is the search for something that we don't have, that the institutions do not hand out, and that only our struggle could achieve." Architecture can be "the most beautiful course of study in the world, and also the most horrible. . . . It could lead to the achievement of a vocation, or sale to the highest bidder. . . . In what does this búsqueda consist? . . . As students, we simply want to be something. Facing the question of what, the University computer would answer: 'Architect.' But as students we know that this alone means nothing. What kind of architect do we want to be?" (v1D10). The búsqueda: a conceptual and political tool to hold open possibilities, even when the path ahead is uncertain and the answers are unclear.

By 1969, TUPAU had begun to grow beyond the small, underground study group it had started as a few years earlier. A major uprising in Córdoba that year marked a high point in collaboration between workers' movements and student movements against the dictatorship and served to galvanize many in the country, alongside more global events like the Cuban Revolution, May 1968 in Paris, and the frustration of American military efforts in Vietnam. Within architecture, student activism at the meeting of the International Union of Architects in Buenos Aires that year worked to articulate architecture with these global political events: students attempted to intervene in the official congress, held under the shadow of the dictatorship, and were thrown out by the police before hosting a counter-congress for which the honorary president was Che Guevara, killed two years earlier in Bolivia. The student congress drew large numbers of students and many architects from the official meeting and served as a politicizing moment for many architecture students in the FADU.

By 1971, the student body was highly politicized; many had joined the growing ranks of the Montoneros or the Ejercito Revolucionario del Pueblo and were involved in workers' movements and in organizing in poor neighborhoods.[18] At the same time, political restrictions by the dictatorship had loosened enough that assemblies could be held in the open. Massive assemblies and occupations of the university became common. In Mariano Corbacho's documentary about the architecture school in that era, *70 y Pico* (2016), Viviana Losada, a student at the time, recalled, "I remember enormous assemblies—I mean 3,000, sometimes 5,000 students! We ran the entire school in 1972." Through these assemblies and occupations, students advocated for some of the ideas found in TUPAU's statements: substantial modifications to the curriculum and the removal of entrance exams and prerequisites as a means of opening the university to the masses. In 1971, student occupations brought classes to a halt; they threw out professors, dismissed the dean, and in 1972 returned to classes under horizontal decision-making structures and an ethos of collaboration between students and faculty—among whom was Jaime Sorín, who had recently graduated and begun teaching in 1971.

In the face of ongoing protest and violence, the military government called for elections in 1973. Perón had been in exile in Spain and his party blacklisted since his overthrow in a military coup in 1955. He remained a potent national figure, however, and while he was personally prohibited from candidacy in the 1973 election, the military had been forced to allow the Peronist party to run a ticket. Perón's personal delegate, Hector Campora, ran as Perón's proxy and won the election. Less than two months after Campora assumed the presidency, Perón returned to the country and was elected in a special election.

Juan, meanwhile, had spent a few years after 1966 teaching in exile in Arequipa, Peru, until he was invited to teach at the National University in the province of San Juan ("another place of earth, dust, and poverty—the places in which I love to work," he told me). But the electoral victory of Peronism had allowed for formal curricular reforms within the UBA, and in 1973 Juan, who had a solid reputation as a leftist architect and a good teacher, was asked to return to the UBA to serve as head of a new cátedra along the lines TUPAU had begun to formulate. That cátedra would be called TANAPO—Talleres Nacionales y Populares, or the National and Popular Workshops.[19] At a moment of great enthusiasm for Argentine populism fueled by Perón's return from exile, in 1974 the cátedra enrolled over 2,000 students, with hundreds of faculty participating.[20]

Pedagogic practice in TANAPO centered on bringing architecture into proximity with the concerns of popular classes. Juan led the area of Human Sciences, in which architectural history was expanded to include pre-Columbian peoples, colonial dispossession and property relations, historical forms of vernacular architecture, and global structures of dependency. Through the Construction area and the Research Institute run by Mario Tempone, the school also began to establish relationships with villas, or shantytowns, where students worked alongside popular organizations to learn construction techniques and began experimenting with the development of new kinds of relationships between architects and the pueblo that valued nonhierarchical power structures and active, direct participation in design and construction. The transformations they were working to achieve between architects and the pueblo were illustrated in an educational pamphlet published by scholars at the Research Institute (see figure 5.9). On the left side, the system isolates the architect from the pueblo. He does not know what the pueblo needs and is more worried about copying foreign designs; the pueblo is unable to participate in the solutions of their problems. On the right, the politically organized pueblo argues with the architect and decides in popular assemblies the kind of housing they will have. If the architecture of the system isolates the architect from the pueblo and the pueblo from debates about architecture, an architecture of the pueblo imagined placing technicians within popular assemblies where the pueblo and the technicians could work together to debate solutions.

"We were always concerned with teaching architecture; in the university, our job is to produce architects," Jaime Sorín told me, responding to a prevailing dismissal of TANAPO as having been more concerned with politics than with architecture. "But we wanted to produce professionals who were aware of which country they were working in! In the 1960s, professors talked a lot about architectural 'quality,' but very little about what was going on in the world. With the Institute, we always had one foot outside the university, and that was a big change, because it changes the point of departure from which one thinks architecture." Placing their bodies in the presence of popular classes, expanding pedagogical sites beyond the university, and rethinking the architect's role vis-à-vis the pueblo were some of the pedagogical techniques that TANAPO put into place to reconfigure architectural education and bring it into the presence of what Juan called the "here and now," which I glossed earlier as a geographical and historical location marked by power, inequality, and dependency.

Things were far from perfect. Juan remembers vividly an episode in which a professor mentioned the British architect James Sterling and was jeered by students for favorably citing a foreign architect. Others took a hard line on the kinds of materials or methods appropriate for the architect of the pueblo: Jaime recalled that for some, it seemed that the architecture of the pueblo could only be realized in brick and fiber cement, or through self-construction

FIGURE 5.9. "The system imposes, the pueblo proposes." The image is from the pamphlet "Basics for a Political-Technical Project of Mass Construction with Popular Participation," which carries the authorship of the Joventud Universitaria Peronista's Region 1 Polytechnical team's Housing Area. It was prepared by Fermín Estrella Gutiérrez, who worked with Tempone in the Construction Area, and was nicknamed the "Little Red Book of Architecture," in resonance with Mao's Little Red Book. I thank Mariano Corbacho for sharing his copy with me.

methods, in which the poor build their own communities. Both Juan and Jaime were interested in these solutions, but not dogmatically. Juan, who was never comfortable with black-and-white distinctions, hated this posture and was never fully convinced by the starkness with which contrasts between the architecture of the pueblo and the architecture of the system were often talked about.[21] If things kept going in these black-and-white directions, Juan was determined to leave TANAPO.

TANAPO was a tragically short-lived project, however. Perón's return was marked by a violent clash between the Peronist right and the Peronist left, and it was the right that would gain control and power. In September of 1974, conservative factions of Peronism intervened in the university, placing a self-identified fascist in charge, and TANAPO was closed barely a year after it began. Political violence over the legacy of Peronism continued after Perón's death from illness in 1974, through the presidency of Perón's third wife and vice president, Isabel, who was overthrown by military coup in 1976. Her overthrow marked the beginning of the Proceso de Reorganización Nacional, Argentina's famously brutal military dictatorship, which carried out the abduction, torture, and disappearance of 30,000 Argentines, including the students and faculty whose images overlook the hall of the FADU today. Architecture was home to more disappeared students than any other school in the UBA, a fact Jaime attributes to their visible work with popular movements in the villas. "They hunted down and killed many of the people who were in the cátedra with me," Juan told me. Mario Tempone, along with many others, was disappeared; most of the faces on that banner were university students in their late teens or early twenties. Many others fled the country. Juan and Jaime each went into hiding in Buenos Aires.

Architectural education under the dictatorship, like in the years after 1966, was made to correspond to a different, more technical image of what architecture should be. "They took everything and taught it with a very closed set of criteria, in which a screw is a screw and two plus two is four, to produce minions who don't think, but who know how to build things that don't fall and roofs that don't leak," Juan told me. "It was technical practice pitched against the humanities and design, rather than with them. Because they were afraid, people just talked about technical problems—whatever they could do to avoid political connotation." Juan and Jaime would not begin teaching again until the return to democracy, when they won an open competition to found another cátedra in 1985—the one in which I conducted fieldwork more than twenty years later.

CALL: 30,000 compañeros detained and disappeared
RESPONSE: are present!
CALL: 30,000 compañeros detained and disappeared
RESPONSE: are present!
CALL: 30,000 compañeros detained and disappeared
RESPONSE: are present!
CALL: Now
RESPONSE: and always!
CALL: Now
RESPONSE: and always!

Today, the ongoing presence of 30,000 victims of state terrorism who were detained, tortured, and disappeared in the 1970s and '80s is a touchstone of contemporary Argentine politics for the left. Mass political rituals, like this call and response practiced at political gatherings, are part of ongoing practices of memory that hold present the ways past political struggles remain relevant to contemporary life. But alongside these major-key political moments, disappeared *compañeros*, or comrades, are also held present through other practices. I have already described the banner that hangs in the FADU atrium. I want to return now to the first-year design workshop to describe how these pasts may be inherited in contemporary architectural pedagogy.

First, a word on my use of the word *inheritance*. Like *holding present*, I understand the term *inheritance* to be a way of helping pasts endure. As I use the term here, I mean it as a form of passing-on that exceeds that of simple transmission or copy; TANAPO was a political event of a particular moment, and the inheritance of that event means something other than a duplication of its terms. Instead, I understand *inheritance* in the sense that Pignarre and Stengers do when they say that an event's power is the manner in which it makes the question of its inheritance endure (see Pignarre and Stengers 2011, 4). In this formulation, asking after how one inherits past events is itself part of the inheritance, and the ability to make the question of how to inherit present for those who respond to it is in turn part of the power of the event. That inheritance revolves around a question—the question of how to inherit—means that inheritance is not about being an authoritative spokesperson. Instead, inheritance is about being present to the obligations constructed by the event and to the possibility of keeping the questions posed by that event open and present.

Today, conversations about the pueblo, the architecture of the system, and dependency are far less present in the architectural lexicon of the FADU than they were in the times of TUPAU and TANAPO. Instead, most cátedras orient themselves toward more global architectural conversations about form, materiality, morphology, and sustainability. Juan and Jaime's cátedra is held to stand apart from others in this respect. They are widely regarded as running a "political cátedra," and it was not uncommon for professors from other cátedras to offer this to me as a qualification of my fieldwork with them: a way of staving off any impulse I might have had to see it as representative of Argentine architectural education more broadly.[22] Qualifying the cátedra as "political" leverages a dichotomy operative within the FADU between "political" and "professionalist" cátedras, in which the former are implied to be more interested in politics than architecture and the latter to produce architects concerned primarily with professional success (neither term is used for self-identification; both are caricatures used to disqualify the other).[23] Hearing Molina y Vedia–Sorín characterized as overly political in this sense felt strange to me, however. During fieldwork, it was in fact quite difficult for me to understand how the pedagogic practices I was observing in the workshop could be seen as political in a way that would correspond to the way others spoke to me about it. As I described earlier, I had observed students learning to draw and build models: to attend to quotidian life and embodied sensation and to communicate and evoke these experiences through practices of drawing and model making. Was this so different than what students learned in other cátedras? Architects who had studied in other cátedras, other universities, and even from other countries agreed that it was not unusual; for all of them, the kind of pedagogies that I described surrounding drawing en carne propia felt very familiar.

But Juan and Jaime, too, and not just those who would dismiss them, consider themselves to be engaged in a minoritarian pedagogical practice that works in the inheritance of TANAPO.[24] Where was this inheritance, if so many of the pedagogical practices I had witnessed seemed similar to pedagogies practiced elsewhere? My research into the history of TANAPO and TUPAU was an attempt to make sense of this question. After learning more about their histories, I began to see the pedagogic practices I had observed in the cátedra in a different light. Even if today they talk about architecture using a different conceptual repertoire than that of TUPAU and TANAPO, I nevertheless began to see the question of inheritance sit in Juan and Jaime's pedagogical practice in ways that were much subtler but that still worked to inhabit a set of questions and possibilities inspired by TUPAU and TANAPO.

I mentioned earlier that TUPAU had confronted the problem of how to articulate architectural practice with leftist politics. Some felt it couldn't be done, and that an architecture of the pueblo would have to wait until after the revolution, when the pueblo had taken power. But for many others, including TUPAU, holding architecture and politics apart was itself symptomatic of architecture's troubled existence in commodity society, an existence they took on the task of transforming. Today, I see Juan and Jaime's cátedra as one of several that carry on the work of tethering politics to practices like the drawing and model making I described earlier. Articulating national political, social, and economic histories with forms of knowledge like drawing and model making, which circulate more easily within architectural education in Argentina and internationally, is not straightforward. Focusing only on architecture runs the risk of detaching it from its social and political environments and producing a merely technical practice—the kind in which, as Juan put it, a screw is a screw and two plus two is four. On the other hand, however, is the risk of seeing architectural concerns eclipsed by other forms of political activity. One recent observer characterized the FADU of the TUPAU era as a time in which there was a tendency to "replace drawing with spoken discourse," which he saw as dangerous to architectural practice (Gutiérrez 2014). Navigating the dangers of abandoning politics for architecture or architecture for politics is thus a challenging practice, something that has to be achieved. Juan and Jaime each believe that teaching architects to be good architects is vitally important, but also that such efforts can be done in politically informed ways. How, then, did they work to inherit the obligations set out by TUPAU to articulate the work of architecture with the political body of a broad range of Argentines?

Ideological Orientations

As I have mentioned, in many ways the teaching I witnessed in the Design 1 workshop corresponds to phenomenology's broad uptake within architecture through the 1960s: a concern for bodies, what they feel, and how they live and connect to the environments around them. But in Argentina, political events within and beyond the school had placed into crisis the universalizing body of phenomenology, grounded in an abstract notion of sensation outside of a particular time and place, and instead placed architecture into relation with the geographical and historical contexts of the popular classes in Argentina. Part of what sets Molina y Vedia–Sorín apart from other cátedras in its efforts to integrate the phenomenological body of the carne propia

phenom body → political body

with the political body of the pueblo. In addition to being taught to draw from their bodies—en carne propia—students were also taught to attend to their bodies' presence within the particular set of relations that Juan called the aquí y ahora: political and economic histories formed by ongoing structures of colonialism, dependency, and inequality.

The general lines through which the cátedra situates itself within the aquí y ahora are outlined in two documents, a pedagogical proposal and the "9 points" of the cátedra, which together lay down a set of basic ideological orientations. These documents place architecture in tension with market value and the exigencies of professional practice, while not negating the importance of either for the formation of good architects: "Professional competency, which is indispensable, must not overshadow the need to see education as a problem of knowledge in which reflection plays a decisive role." The cátedra, in other words, seeks to produce architects who are professionals, but professionals whose understanding of architecture exceeds those defined by the profession and that seek to "foment consciousness of architecture as a cultural and historical occurrence."

Statements like these mark the cátedra's political differentiation from a standpoint that would see architects as building for an abstract market, outside time and place. Instead, they locate their vocation within Buenos Aires and in relation to broad classes of Argentines. "We begin from 'porteño' issues, from realities accessible to everyone, but without turning a blind eye to what is produced in the world today; . . . the history of our architecture is revisited as an inescapable referent alongside the international architecture of which we form a part," they argue. The kinds of international architecture recognized widely in the field are thus figured as relevant to, but not necessarily a model for, Argentine architecture. Working within Argentina's history in this way is a "practice of memory" that is "profoundly marked by a popular misery produced by the other 'misery,' that of the dominant classes." Though generally marked by an openness and a desire to foster an atmosphere in which disagreement and multiple viewpoints can thrive, a bold line is drawn here, with the question of architecture's relationship to the world around it: "The only limit to eventual polemical divergence will be the unavoidable reference to questions of our national reality and our particular role as architects."

This insistence on the historical and geographical situatedness of architecture in Argentina is a way to "return to architecture its everydayness" and imagine a quotidian architecture grounded in the everyday life of Buenos Aires. "We don't understand the practice of architecture as the creation of at-

situated architecture

vernacular styles?

tractive and sophisticated objects that are enclosed within themselves, without reference to quotidian life," they state. These kinds of objects, divorced from the city around them, might fit perfectly into a commodity culture or the glossy pages of an architectural magazine, but they do not produce good architecture, which for them "transcends mere commercial use." Instead, the cátedra argues that architects must remain "conscious of our responsibility as producers of cultural objects that are not limited by external values imposed by consumption rather than use."

The cátedra's statements echo the challenge articulated by TUPAU with respect to the troubled relationship between teaching drawing and social and political history. While drawings are the primary means through which architects work, they also threaten good design if they are treated as the end of architecture: "For too many years the tendency of architectural periodicals has been to publish and speak of drawings, accumulating an overabundance of theoretical information about drawn and photogenic images." But these same drawings, when built, didn't always serve the people who lived in or around them. Drawings can be *"engañosos,"* or tricksters, the pedagogic statements explain, when the work of design is separated from the street: "Drawings can be confused with habitat." Instead, students must be taught to treat drawing as "a medium, an instrument to foresee the construction of real buildings, with inhabitants that are also real." Foregrounding the quotidian, everyday lifeworld of architecture means not thinking of buildings as isolated, but as actors in a relational ecology: "The learning process cannot have as its end the production of a design with autonomous value."

These ideological orientations aim to produce a particular kind of architect, one that is a well-trained professional, but whose notion of the profession extends beyond the limits typically treated in architectural education. "We want to produce a professional that knows how to dialogue with popular classes," Jaime told me. "In general, the FADU prepares you for a professional practice linked to a different sector of the population [one with greater resources]. We want them prepared to do that work too. We don't know where their professional practice will take them. What we ask is that they know *dónde están parados*, literally "where they are standing."

For Jaime, there is a tension here with a model of architectural education that seeks to produce stars that will rise to the top of what the profession conceives of as excellence. "On the one hand you can train liberal architects whose objective is to be a star," he told me. "Or, you can think of your job as to produce a mass of architects, of whom a few might attain recognition, but the vast majority of whom are going to work in much more quotidian contexts. We want to produce architects that can work in the places where they live and do it well." In this sense, Molina y Vedia–Sorín embraces the mass-educational ideals that were behind university reforms fought for in the late 1960s and early 1970s, when the university began its transition from a university that was public but nevertheless elite (only the best students could get in) to a university for the masses. Today the UBA, like other national Argentine universities, is *libre y gratuita*: literally free and free, the latter indicating that there are no tuition or fees, the former that there are no entrance exams. While many individual cátedras put limits on the number of students they'll accept with the goal of teaching the best students to do the best architecture, Juan and Jaime's cátedra puts no limits on the number of students they teach. They also run all their classes at night, to allow working students to attend.

"Others think that's wrong, that the more restrictive, the better," Jaime told me. "But our concept of teaching is that the more massive, the better." This is not everyone's idea of a good education, if by *good* what is meant is the careful curation of students for the production of stars. Jaime chafes at this conceptualization of professional excellence: "Does excellence mean that you are really great at debating architectural problems, theoretical or experimental ones, but that the question stops there? Or does it mean you can produce architects with the capacity for critical thinking about the country they live in? We want to produce architects who can do both, who can think about architectural questions for those in our society who have the least. It's not that the architectural questions don't matter: something we've said is that poor people have a right to beauty. Because beauty is part of architecture, and if we're not conscious of that we're not doing it well. But at the same time, we hold on to our political identities. Politics is the means through which to improve the quality of life of the majority of the people. And we want to produce architects who understand architecture in this sense: that it's for the majority, not for the few. We are interested in an architecture for the majority."

Articulating "Carne Propia" with the "Aquí y Ahora"

Back in the workshop, the warm evening light radiates in through the ribbon windows that overlook the wetlands of the delta on the edge of the city. Students unfurl large drawings on the broad tables; cardboard models, the glue still drying, have survived their journeys on cramped busses, vaulted over students' heads. Around the workshop, some teachers perch on stools while others wander among groups of students scattered around the drafting tables.

In the workshop, there is little talk of political ideology, of national stand-point in global systems, or the question of the architecture of the masses. There is talk of the weight of drawn lines, the use of shadow, questions about a room's solar exposure, and ideas about how to use certain organizational schemas to stop the layout of rooms from spinning out of control. But politics is not just a verbal practice, articulated from the spoken word of ideological statements and manifestos. It is also something that can be built into and out of graphite lines, bits of cardboard, and architects' bodies. In Juan and Jaime's Design 1 class, I watched students begin to learn the basics, not only of draw-ing en carne propia, but of doing so in the aquí y ahora of inherited political histories marked by dispossession.

"Architecture is for everyone," I heard Gaby say one day to her students—a battle cry of sorts, I thought, in the slow but enduring pedagogical work that continues, if in a subtler register, to draw against the grain of the architecture of the system. The day she said this was at the tail end of an assignment for stu-dents to first draw their own homes, and then propose modifications to them based on the family's form of inhabiting their dwelling. I mentioned the assign-ment at the beginning of the chapter: the first stage offered a way for students to reacquaint themselves with domestic spaces they knew well using techniques of drawing and model making that were still new to them; the second stage, the redesign, was about unlearning the taken-for-granted aspects of that space and attaining the distance required to make a critical intervention. It was an archi-tectural take on making the familiar strange and the strange familiar.

When I first saw it, the architectural pedagogy about drawing en carne pro-pia was clear enough to me. What I realized after learning more about Juan's own history and about TUPAU and TANAPO was that by bringing students' own homes into the workshop, the assignment also pulled architectural pedagogy into relationship with the particular built environments of Buenos Aires and the diverse class backgrounds of students in this free, public university. The contrasts between these dwellings and the kinds of buildings usually taken as architectural referents could be strong. Years after my fieldwork in the cátedra, I asked Marta about this assignment, and she told me about some of the different houses students had come in with over the years. Some were lavish: Pilar came in with drawings of her four-story house in San Isidro, one of Buenos Aires' rich northern suburbs. Many others were not: Oscar, who would come to class with his hands stained by paint from his day job as a construction laborer, came in with a drawing of the two-room boarding house where he lived with his mother and six siblings in La Boca. Another student came in with drawings of his one-room public housing project; another brought in drawings of the shipping container he lived in, a five-hour train ride from the university, next to the apartment his father rented above a small manufacturing garage.

The exercise is a powerful experience for students, Marta told me. It was about more than learning to think differently about your own home, or about deploying a set of new technical skills to understand deeply familiar environments in new ways. It was also about putting your home—no matter what it was like—on the table alongside others from different social backgrounds and alongside the designs of Le Corbusier, Mies van der Rohe, Zaha Hadid, and other big names in architectural history that the students studied. So while the exercise is ostensibly about refamiliarizing students with their homes on newly learned technical terms, it also disrupts an education that might easily privilege elite architectures in global, abstract nonplaces and instead sets itself to work from the quotidian built environments of the aquí y ahora in Buenos Aires.

The exercise also makes incursions into conceptions about who is worthy of architecture. Gaby's reminder that architecture is for everyone was spoken in a conversation she and Jorge were having with a student who had added an extra room and a window for her proposed redesign of her house. Her piecemeal addition, without modifying the other spaces of the house, reflected a common error for design students to think additively rather than transformatively about the work of design. But it also failed to deploy the kind of passionate engagement expected from students. "This window," Jorge asked, "what is this? You could buy this on the corner at Tía María's Window World!" He began to pull architectural magazines from his bag, flipping through them and pointing out windows to present her with alternatives. "You have to design this, not just put in whatever," he explained. "What is the light going to be like in this room? How does the window open, ventilate the space, bring in air? What does this change about the other rooms of the house? And how does that light, that air, change how you live?" After a long series of questions and several possibilities, they propose turning the garage into a patio and redistributing the other rooms around this new space where light would pour in, filtered by the plants they imagined there. The house was transformed by architecture. "Architecture is poetry," Gaby said. And, suspecting that the student might have put less effort into her project because she never imagined her house as the kind of house architecture was concerned with, she added, "and it's for *everyone*." The professors' intervention provided a lesson in the technical execution of design, not unlike some of the moments I described at the beginning of this chapter. It asked the student to inhabit her body differently and to think differently about what she could feel and how to generate those feelings from the environment around her. But it was also, in this context, a lesson in rethinking who is worthy of architecture and where the homes of architecture might be—an exercise in pushing architecture beyond its troubled history as a luxury good. Despite her otherwise humble home, she, too, was worthy of architecture.

Other assignments also helped students to engage the aquí y ahora in ways that took them beyond the usual habitats of architecture. Each year the cátedra selects a particular neighborhood in which all five levels will locate their final projects. Leveraging techniques Juan used in his days in the Chaco and Jaime's experience working in Buenos Aires' villas, the cátedra locates many of its projects in barrios or lower-class suburbs, places on the margins or outside the geographical swath of privilege in which elite architecture more comfortably dwells: places like Liniers, Villa Pueyrredón, Parque Patricios, Barracas, and La Matanza. These are places, Jaime told me, with a low level of traditional engagement by architects. "These aren't the kinds of places where there are important works of architecture," Jaime told me. "Rather, they're the quotidian environments in which many of them may find work in their professional careers. And it's important for them to know that this kind of building is this way because of the particular history of this neighborhood, that these factories were built in this moment and closed down in another, and how that impacted the way the barrio has been inhabited." "We don't want them to become experts in a specific place," Juan told me, "but we want them to learn how to study specific places, to learn that no place is like any other." Bringing students to a place like La Matanza, walking around with them and teaching them to think through the sounds, the rhythms of the place, and the habits of life there, is a way to build into their own carne propia the aquí y ahora of a wide range of porteño lifeworlds. The programs they select, too, are diverse: in Design 1, cultural centers are common, but projects have also included things like the redesign of a recycling center for collectives of cartoneros, who make their precarious living gathering cardboard and plastic from the trash for resale.

These are simple but powerful tools for emplacing the work of architecture in the aquí y ahora for first-year students. Other areas of pedagogy were not that different from what one might expect in an architecture school: they still studied Mies van der Rohe, Le Corbusier, Hadid, Miralles. They still went to visit parts of the city where more elite architecture is concentrated. Theirs was not, in other words, a purified architecture of the pueblo, at least not in the ways that TUPAU had articulated it. They didn't only design mass housing, and their work hardly threatened to overthrow the commodification of architecture, let alone capitalism. But they did always return to something broader, to put their work into the tense presence of worlds where the architecture of the system isn't always concerned to go. And in that, they worked to inhabit the idea that architecture is for everyone—lying in the way of a reality in which architecture would be just another commodity, prolonging the question of what kind of architects they want to be, and holding out the possibility that another architecture is possible.

CONCLUSION: CARING FOR THE POSSIBLE

In the course of my research into the history of curricular debates in Argentine architecture programs, I found a report sponsored by the UBA in 1997, in the midst of 1990s high neoliberalism. The report argued that "the current teaching model in the FADU does not respond to the requirements of the professional exercise of Design today; the Facultad teaches architectural design in a way that is . . . disconnected from projects' productive aspects," including "the reality of the market, technology, costs, and other actors who intervene in construction" (Monti 1997). For the authors of this report, failure to engage architecture on the terms of projects' "productive aspects"—their money-making capacity in the housing market—means that the university is "disconnected from reality." Architects, they argue, leave the university with an education that does not correspond to professional practice. Instead, the project "stays in the drawing." As part of an attempt to reform the university in the mid-1990s, the report concluded that it was "necessary to change the mentality of the entire educative system of the FADU" or risk being left "in the margins of history."

The report marks another reality at play in conversations about architectural education. In some ways, the argument can appear to echo the critiques leveraged by TUPAU, Juan, and Jaime about the need to bring architecture into touch with the aquí y ahora of national realities. But the reality the report wanted to bring architecture into closer touch with was not that of life in the Argentine popular classes, but the reality of market production dominant in the professional practice of architecture. If architecture tends to live in a world of hegemonic market production, the report argued, then education should prepare students for that reality and only that reality. The proposed curricular reforms never happened, but they lay bare some of the tensions

educated for the market,
or to transform the market?

that architectural pedagogy faces in the context of demands for market relevance. Budgeting, negotiating labor contracts, and developing time tables for material orders: important skills for an architect, no doubt. But perhaps also a glimpse at what architectural education under the sign of real estate development might look like.

I want to hold on to, while also questioning, the "disconnect from reality" cited in the report. On one level, the students and faculty I've described worked to maintain exactly this disconnect from the hegemonic values of architectural production, in which architecture exists as just another commodity in the architecture of the system. Their interventions can, on some level, seem unreal—to be guilty of the charge leveled in the report that architecture in the university "stays in the drawing": the grand vision of the architect of the pueblo has, perhaps, not come to fruition, at least not in the terms proposed by TUPAU. Juxtaposed with TUPAU's radical vision, there is a way that the interventions I observed in the cátedra—having students draw their own houses or locating projects in humble parts of the city—can seem underwhelming: a minor inflection in a world nevertheless dominated by the architecture of the system.

But at the same time, drawing in a carne propia attuned to the aquí y ahora of national realities is itself far from unreal—a fact that many involved in TUPAU and TANAPO paid for with their lives. Drawings are not the opposite of reality, but part of the ongoing production and endurance of another reality that, with enough care and effort, can be made to endure in a body of architects. Juan, Jaime, and those who work to inherit alongside them may not have made TUPAU's vision into the dominant reality of architecture, but they have managed to carve out a marginal reality, incubated in the university, that maintains the possibility of emergence beyond it. For me, honoring architecture's dead—keeping the disappeared present—means recognizing the endurance of the values they believed in and fought for, however marginal those achievements may seem. The pedagogical practices I witnessed in Juan and Jaime's cátedra cultivated an alternative to the real estate development school I see proposed in the report, which I imagine to be the sweet fantasy dream of the architecture of the system—an education that responds to a real world defined by market demands concerning construction and profitability, rather than the real world of the aquí y ahora, of architecture for everyone. I want to reclaim, then, the "margins of history," which the report poses as a sign of ultimate failure or irrelevance. Managing to endure on the margins of dominant histories of the architecture of the system is, in fact, quite an achievement.

Drawing and building models is part of a practice of care at the center of architectural education. Care, in the way I have learned to think of it from María Puig de la Bellacasa, consists at the same time of "an affective state, a material vital doing, and an ethico-political obligation," conforming "tasks that make living better in interdependence, but which are often considered petty or unimportant, however vital they are for lived relations" (2011, 90, 93). This practice of care—produced in the articulation of technical practices of drawing and model making, sensory reformation, and political memory— offers the possibility of conserving a set of human-building relations in the face of market-based relational possibilities that threaten to overtake them. The future architects I studied learned to attend not only to bodies that need to get to the bathroom without getting wet, that feel the texture of travertine stone, or that see a staircase dematerialize in light; they also learned to draw from the carne propia of a political body, the body of a broad range of porteños in a country on the margins of world economic history. Teaching and learning to draw in this way are political acts aimed at reshaping reality through mundane practices. Practices of drawing and model making that articulate technical practice with this kind of ethicopolitical responsibility are ways of making dreams for an alternative world of architecture endure.

At the close of the year I spent in the architecture school, I stood in the workshop, empty of students but overflowing with drawings and models (see figure 5.10). The drawings and models were for their final project, a small community center on what was meant to be part of a green belt in Caballito, built on old railroad lands that many hoped would be turned into public spaces and not handed over to developers (it was part of a larger site that included the Ferro lands described in chapter 3). In addition to their final project, the students had built a large model that depicted the neighborhood around the project site. A space was cut out in this model, in which student models could be placed to envision how the building would fit in its *entorno*, or milieu. Deby placed one of the student projects in the slot and called me over. "Nico, do you know how to look at a model?" she asked me. Without waiting for my response, she foisted herself onto the table with just one leg touching the floor. She put her face down to the table, aligning her eyeball with the edge of the big model, gesturing for me to do the same. And there we were, our foreheads almost touching, peering up the street. It all snapped into vision, and I was in a cardboard world, with cardboard trees, looking up a cardboard street at a cardboard building. I had taken the Pastilla de Chiquitolina, the Tiny Person Pill, and I was in it. We had stepped into the world of the model,

FIGURE. 5.10. Final projects being graded at the end of the year. Photo by author.

and it reached back to help us to live neighborhood life in this newly designed environment. The architect and the anthropologist, squinting, contorting our bodies to adapt to the model, as the model's reality overtook us.

Deby's lesson brought me one step closer to understanding design as a project of attunement, an exercise of mimetic faculties that projected a body into a lifeworld constructed in cardboard and paper. Students had learned to attune themselves to the physical sensations of a place, to trace their sensations back to features of their environment, and to redeploy those sensations into a world projected in cardboard and drawings. But it was not just any world, and not just any body: it was a world in the aquí y ahora of a street in Caballito, where neighborhood political activism against private development worked to make it possible to think this space as a park instead of another development opportunity; and it was a body that had, with hope, inherited something of a history of struggle to enact another architecture, one that could ally itself with a set of values not bound to those of real estate development, and that could help hold on to the possibility of an architecture for everyone.

I want to continue to push against "for everyone" projects but I see how this function in this context as resistance.

Enduring Values

"We're all sad," Sergio and Adrián told me on the phone a few months into 2016. My two close friends, on whose terraza I had spent much time during fieldwork, were referring primarily to Mauricio Macri's recent assumption of the presidency. The former mayor of Buenos Aires, a free-market neoliberal, and the scion of a powerful Argentine family, Macri had won the election with promises to use his good business sense to make Argentina a "normal country" again by improving the climate for international investment and making the economy more "sincere" in the face of what he characterized as the distortions brought about by more than a decade of Kirchnerismo's redistributive economic policies.

The years leading up to Macri's election bore the markers of a troubled economic environment, one in which Argentine bricks were once again caught up in a series of political and economic events that reached through the nation and across the globe, entangling buildings in new ecologies of value and practice. Conditions, as they often do, had changed quickly, leading the post-crisis boom in construction to cool significantly in 2011. There was no dramatic crash in value, no bubble that could be said to have burst. Dollars, however, stopped circulating in quite the same way that they had before, and their new patterns of movement ended up having significant repercussions for the real estate market.

The global recession of 2008, which stemmed from the U.S. subprime mortgage crisis, had already marked an important inflection point for Argentina, bringing to a close several years of economic prosperity in which Argentina had been able to pay down a substantial portion of its defaulted debt, expand social programs, and grow its currency reserves. While the 2008 recession would impact trade balances and economic growth across Latin America, it posed a particular kind of problem for Argentina. Most nations in South America weathered the recession by taking on new debt and increasing foreign investment, but the political environment of Argentina, like that of Ecuador and Venezuela, was seen as unfriendly terrain for foreign capital. Argentina had a high country-risk rating and the low levels of foreign investment and high interest rates that go with it. In an economic environment in which new debt was not an option, Kirchner's government attempted to fortify state coffers through a variety of trade policies, including changes in the retentions levied on agricultural commodity exports, of which soy, at record high prices, was the most significant. A protracted domestic conflict over these retentions followed, bringing into relief mounting opposition by some sectors of Argentine society to Kirchnerismo's political-economic model. For supporters of the government, retentions offered a clear means to redistribute wealth from the large landowners and agricultural conglomerates who were the soy boom's most direct beneficiaries; for opponents, it was an example of government overreach that sought to accrue even more power to the state for redistribution to Kirchnerismo's political base. The conflict included road blockades and the delay of food shipments to the capital by agricultural producers, public demonstrations in favor of the retentions by supporters of the government, and a dramatic senate vote in which Kirchner's first-term vice president defected from the party and cast the deciding vote against the measure. In an economic environment in which the state was bringing in very little money, payments on reprogrammed debt from the crisis eventually had to be paid with Argentina's currency reserves, which Argentina continued to do through the rest of Kirchner's second term, succeeding in bringing debt to its lowest levels in recent history, but at the cost of placing the Central Bank's currency reserves, vital for maintaining the value of the peso, in jeopardy.

Currency reserves also faced more perennial challenges stemming from chronic high inflation and the well-worn habits it fomented of saving money in dollars. In 2011, capital flight (which includes the purchase of dollars locally) reached near-record levels. Such flight, even to domestic colchones, places an important drag on the national economy and on state fiscal accounts because the money never enters the formal monetary system. To stem these adverse effects, the government instituted sharp restrictions on the purchase of U.S. currency at the end of 2011, an attempt to *pesificar*—to "pesify," or de-dollarize—Argentine economic practices.

In this environment, sales of housing slowed. Sellers insisted on receiving cash dollars for real estate, which meant buyers who didn't already have them in their possession had to buy them on the black market (known by its euphemism as the *dólar blue*) at a much higher price than the official rates. In an attempt to address this situation (and giving a nod to the special relationship between real estate and dollars in Argentine investment ecologies), Kirchner's government introduced the CEDIN in 2013, a new bond strictly for the purchase of real estate and exchangeable for dollars at official rates (the instrument saw only limited adoption). Combined with dimming economic outlooks for the country, these new and more complex circulations of dollars and bricks brought the real estate market to a near standstill.

Political and economic landscapes in Argentina shifted further in 2015, when Mauricio Macri was elected president. Macri filled his cabinet with managers and businesspeople formerly employed by multinational corporations and invited the IMF to consult with the country after ten years of cold relations. Argentina began taking on debt again, a chunk of which was used to pay the vulture funds with whom the country had been in politically charged litigation in New York district courts for years.[1] Subsidies for domestic energy consumption were eliminated, and the currency market was liberalized—allowing once again for the free circulation of capital out of the country, as well as for the purchase of dollars domestically. Argentina once again became a "normal country."

....

Sergio's and Adrian's sadness was about more than the recent presidential election in Argentina. Across Latin America, political landscapes were shifting in a way that made it hard for them, like many of my other friends in Argentina, to find hope. One by one, the political leaders of the Latin American left who had gained power in the early 2000s were losing ground. Evo Morales and Rafael Correa remained in power, but others had not fared as well. Dilma Rousseff, Lula da Silva's political heir in Brazil, was in impeachment hearings that would end in her removal from office and the installation of an unelected neoliberal government that would curtail labor protections and reduce public spending. Da Silva himself would later be found guilty on corruption charges that, like those used to impeach Rousseff, were widely regarded on the left as politically motivated attempts to block his candidacy in the 2018 presidential elections. Hugo Chavez had died in 2013, and though his political heir Nicolás Maduro remained in power, Venezuela had begun weathering an economic and political crisis of catastrophic proportions.

Nestor Kirchner, whose supporters had hoped would run for reelection after Cristina Kirchner's terms, had died in 2010, a death Sergio, Adrián, and many others had felt deeply at the time and that took on new significance in the context of Macri's election. As Sergio and Adrián recited these events, they manifested a sense of loss made more painful by the big hopes that had come before them, when dreams for a future different than one dominated by neoliberal extractive capitalism felt closer than they had in a long time.

My words to Sergio and Adrián that day reflected some of the ongoing preoccupations that have structured this book. I shared with them a sense of loss and fear at the directions national, regional, and global politics were taking. But I also tried to hold present—for myself and for them—a sense of possibility that I knew endured alongside these major-key political events and that might give us hope in difficult times. I reminded them of Juan Molina y Vedia, of whom they had heard many stories during my fieldwork, and who had lived moments of great hope and tragic aftermaths, but had always stuck closely to the possibilities embodied in building a different architecture and a different world through mundane forms of pedagogy—pedagogies made all the more powerful for the ways they worked their ways into students' bodies and minds through the minor but politically vital practice of drawing—both in the presence of the dead and the lives of those living at the margins. I reminded them, too, of Osvaldo and the Amigos del Lago and the deeply embedded forms of attention they cultivated to market encroachments on urban life—forms of attention that helped make capitalism's chronic presence eventful in urban lifeworlds, even as hegemonic forces of participatory planning worked to capture their efforts in parodic simulacra of the kind of participation they envisioned. These stories, I told them, offered me comfort in these difficult times, placing hope in struggles for value that often play out in minor as well as major keys.

....

Of course, the lives of the people I had worked with had not remained stagnant, though they continued fostering forms of value even in less hopeful major-key political atmospheres. For pequeños ahorristas and market analysts, the real estate market remained embroiled in a complex macroeconomic panorama. Lifting restrictions on the purchase of dollars, one of Macri's first acts as president, did not bring construction surging back. More than a decade of investor-led growth, alongside the peso's ongoing loss of value relative to the dollar (especially sharp since 2012), had been bringing housing prices increasingly further out of reach for salaried workers. Macri's response has focused on efforts to reestablish a mortgage market in Argentina by allowing variable-rate mortgages to be indexed to inflation (prior governments prohibited indexation because it risks augmenting inflation). The program expands the ability of certain households to finance home purchases, but it does so by placing a lot of risk on the borrower. Unlike these loans, salaries are not indexed to inflation; they have to be renegotiated to keep up. The time frames are also different: mortgage payments adjust monthly, while salaries are negotiated annually, a lag that works to the detriment of those in debt. Though the market has begun to pick up again and real estate industry representatives seem enthusiastic, there are also many skeptics, and it remains to be seen how things will play out in a system dependent on variable-rate loans and in a context of ongoing high inflation.[2] In this environment, small savers like Mariela hold on to the bricks they have while looking for accessible but secure ways to save their savings in still-tumultuous economic environments. They also continue to tell stories, holding present rocky histories that offer important but limited guides for what the future might bring. Analysts like José Rozados, meanwhile, continue their efforts to understand a shifting market in which dollars and pesos operate in changing relationships to bricks, alongside new actors like indexed mortgages, and in changing economic and political environments.

Vecinos and architects, too, find themselves working on shifting terrains. The city government has been working to replace the Código de Planeamiento Urbano with a new code, called the Código Urbanístico. Billed as a ground-up rethinking of the Código de Planeamiento Urbano, promoters promise a city that is more harmonious, plural, and sustainable. The new code proposes to do away with FOT, the calculus of building height based on lot size, and replace it with six morphological categories that define maximum height regardless of lot size. Advocates say that doing away with the opaque, complex calculations of the FOT will improve transparency and prevent buildings of radically different height from existing alongside one another—the *torres sorpresas* (or "surprise towers") they say caused so much strife in previous years. The new code is also billed as encouraging sustainability and protecting barrio identity and historical patrimony and is seen as both the outcome of and a vehicle for ongoing public participation.

Vecinos are less optimistic. They continue the work many of them have been engaged in for years, highlighting the dubious forms of authorship claimed by the state while formulating and advocating for their own dreams of what the city might become. Members of SOS Caballito, Salvemos al Barrio, Amigos del Lago, and others turned out for a participatory forum in 2017 in which they once again drew attention to the market interests that occupy the space of authorship of the new code, just as they had for the Plan Urbano Ambiental. For them, the new code is yet another missed opportunity to engage in a real, honest, and deep process of rethinking urban priorities. In the forum, they characterized a series of state planning activities surrounding the new code (which state representatives had pointed to in order to characterize the new plan as the outcome of a participatory process) as little more than information sessions, pseudo-participatory acts in which meaningful response was impossible. Once again vecinos were told they had a voice, only to see their years of deep engagement with urban issues reduced to a series of five-minute presentations to be logged and filed by the state.

For vecinos, the true goal of the state's proposal was a net increase in constructive capacity across the city. Decoupling building height from lot size and then "harmonizing" the block, they predicted, would serve as little more than a vehicle for more construction as lower buildings are renormed to match the taller buildings around them and secondary markets in unused air rights are expanded. Vecinos also pointed out that the new code's claims to sustainability and increased green space are spurious: green spaces in the new code are defined to include landscaped rooftops and vegetative walls while reducing the restrictions to building footprints that allow for absorptive terrain within city blocks and allowing no provisions for a meaningful increase in park land. For these vecinos, it is unsurprising that a city government that has worked to sell off public land at an incredible pace would read buildings themselves as green spaces while doing little to advance the more direct solution of expanding park lands: as a member of SOS Caballito reminded those at the forum, vecinos have proposed converting former railroad lands into a park for over twenty-three years while the city has, instead, repeatedly tried to rezone those lands for the construction of a shopping mall, supermarket, and residential towers—efforts that the vecinos of Caballito managed to thwart for the sixth time in only eight years in 2017 (the first of which I described in chapter 3). As Pedro Kesselman (the lawyer from Amigos del Lago) put it in the forum, "The only green these gentlemen care about . . . is the green of the U.S. dollar." The vecinos of Salvemos al Barrio have returned to holding weekly assemblies on the street corner, since the passage of the new code will invalidate the clause they had worked so hard to insert in the old one.

Juan Molina y Vedia passed away in 2019. Though his ability to teach at the university waned in recent years, he continued to run workshops out of his home, and his plans for future publications on architectural history and politics in Argentina showed little sign of slowing down. Jaime Sorín, meanwhile, has been named the dean of the Architecture School at the National University of Avellaneda, one of nearly a dozen new national universities opened in the Buenos Aires metropolitan area as part of Kirchnerismo's efforts to make university education more accessible to the conurban area's poorer population. He has a cátedra there, where several of the teachers I worked with at the UBA now teach. Jaime is enthusiastic about his new students, who typically have a different profile than those at the UBA: two-thirds are first-generation college students, he told me, and almost all of the students work and have families to support. The university is experimenting with different ways of reaching these nontraditional students, modifying prerequisite requirements and offering extra help in passing the introductory courses that often function to filter underprepared students out of the UBA. He considers his teaching in Avellaneda to be a natural continuation of the political work he has been engaged with since his own time in TUPAU and TANAPO. When I asked him to describe the kind of student he dreamed would emerge from the program, he said that he wanted to produce professionals who could work in close dialogue with popular sectors of the population—professionals capable of understanding how they live, what they want from their environments, and how to build those dreams with them. He knows that most of the students will work in the private sector "for the market" rather than designing for the poor or working for the state. But he sees preparing them to do so as an important part of his commitment to building a better kind of architect for a better kind of world. "We ask them to know where they are situated, and to be able to think critically. They have to be ready to serve different publics with different necessities," he told me. "They have to be ready to get their shoes muddy. They have to learn not to be afraid of going to the kinds of places where popular classes live, to learn to talk to the people who live there, and to appreciate that not everywhere is like the city center. This is what will allow them, if they choose, to be able to work with cooperatives, with mutual aid organizations, where you have to be able to work in a different way. I believe being able to do this kind of work is important."

ENDURING VALUES

One final story. In August of 2007, while the initial idea for this project was still coming together, I read a roundtable interview with several small architectural studios in the latest issue of the Argentine architectural journal

Summa+ (I mentioned the article in the introduction). The piece was heady with hope for a different market in buildings, in which architects might accrue to themselves a greater say in the kinds of buildings that would be produced in Buenos Aires. At that time, as I mentioned, architects were taking on new roles channeling real estate investment into construction projects, doing the work of gathering investment capital and managing construction themselves instead of simply designing a project for an outside developer. In their emerging place in the post-crisis real estate market, architects had imagined themselves forging a new place for architecture through the avenue of private development. Tristán Dieguez, one of the architects interviewed for the article, said that the building his studio had built in this way (and that was featured in that issue of the journal) was "the first project we actually built in which we could truly explore questions that interested us architecturally" (Mercé 2007). Others around the table concurred with this experience. They used the language of the *búsqueda*—the search, which I described in chapter 5—to describe what they were able to do now that hadn't been easy before. Being in charge of their own business, they felt, just might allow them to pursue this kind of vocational calling and to continue improving, refining, and discovering new architectural possibilities through their craft.

There was, however, also a sense that transforming the market in buildings would be an uphill battle, because the búsqueda seemed to run against market logics that favored mass production and repetition. Marcelo Lopez commented that 50 to 60 percent of buildings in Buenos Aries are built by engineers or construction companies that don't share the same value in the búsqueda: "Across the street from our studio there's a building that I've seen in other neighborhoods; for the builder, the neighborhood didn't matter. For them, it made no difference whether their building was going to be in Flores, Palermo, or Belgrano." In contrast, part of what the architects spoke about as the búsqueda involved buildings that were appropriate to their barrio and the development and valorization of building typologies that worked well at smaller, barrio scales. The architects around the table that day acknowledged that if they were really going to be profitable, they would have to work at larger scales. But for López, their dedication to the kind of work they were doing had to do with something more than the search for profit: "We've all had to convert ourselves into business people in some way or another. But I don't know if the kind of work we do is the best way to make a profit. The most profitable thing is probably to build towers, or a tall building of 9 or 10 floors." "Repeating all the floors," Mariana Cardinali said, continuing López's thought. Part of the reason they didn't work at these scales had to do with the amount of investment they could pull together; but in their conversation it was clear that it also had to do with something else: with that part of the búsqueda that was not reducible to market value.

Three years later, toward the end of my fieldwork, I reached out to several of these architects. While in general the projects they spoke of in 2007 had been commercially and architecturally successful (they both made money and received professional recognition), and while some of them had gone on to develop sustainable business models, others were less taken with this model of architectural production. Dieguez told me that while it had allowed his studio to build something they wouldn't have been able to build if they worked for a developer, the work also required an attention to business in a way that felt like it took more away from his architectural practice than it added to it. Neither he nor his partner really had an inclination for business, and they had gone on to do other things, designing some smaller projects, entering (and winning) some competitions, and working on proposals and feasibility studies for developers. Cardinali and her partner Montorfano were still in the business and had a few projects in the pipeline. One was a ten-story apartment building that they spoke about fondly; they had done what they could to build a building they were proud of while filling up the space the way they had to in order to make a profit, repeating all the floors, as one does in this kind of a project. But their eyes lit up when they told me about another large lot they had been able to buy that had an unusual zoning that allowed them to be more creative.[3] Cardinali and Montorfano had designed forty-seven units for this lot, each different from the others. It was an enormous undertaking that consumed not only a great deal more time to design, but also to construct (since the repetition of one design is easier for builders to execute). Though they felt personally gratified by the outcome of such efforts, they were unsure if it resulted in any economic benefit for them. In fact, they were skeptical about whether those who purchased the units cared very much one way or the other about their design: "What people were often buying was a certain quantity of square meters in a determined area," Cardinali told me about their experience selling the units. "To many of them, it would have been the same if they were buying an apartment in the building across the street." She laughed a tired laugh and shrugged. They still love that building, but they also make other buildings that they love less, but that are more profitable.[4]

In both Dieguez's dissatisfaction with the business side of the practice and Cardinali and Montorfano's building of less profitable buildings that are nevertheless important to them, I find the endurance of values that are perhaps all the more remarkable because of their close proximity to market value. Even here, in the heart of private development, there was something excessive to their practice, something that eluded capture by hegemonic modes of valuation—minor moments in which they insist on a value to their practice beyond that of economic gain.

Of course, stories like theirs could be understood as marking the limit of what's possible in a world where economic value will always prevail: despite all their efforts to understand human habitation of built environments and to articulate that with specific urban contexts, their work is reduced to a quantity of square meters in a certain part of the city. They end up building repetitive high-rise apartments or getting out of the game altogether; the dreams they had for a different market in 2007 remain unrealized. At the end of the day, capitalism wins, as other forms of value are pushed to the margins. The same could be said for more politically oriented architects, or for neighborhood groups who dream of a different kind of urban planning, or pequeños ahorristas who dream of a world of economic stability. This reading is not wrong; we live in a world in which capitalism has a deep hold on our lives and continues to strengthen its hold on many practices.

In this book, however, I have aimed to foster attention to the endurance of other forms of value in a world in which they have not quite been overrun, but instead continue to haunt hegemonic forms of value from the margins. I remain committed to attuning to the ongoing presence of minor values that may not win out against—but are at the same time not fully captured by—hegemonic forms of value and by the ways such values inhere in practices, even in what can feel like the totalizing presence of market value. Attuning to these minor forms of value is a way to hold on to the possibilities present in the world around us, possibilities that are made to endure through people's everyday practices.

Concrete dreams help me hold these values present. They offer a foothold for feeling out divergent sets of aspirations for what buildings are and what they might become across a variegated, historically developed topos of practical engagement, attending to diverging values through the social and material forms in which they are articulated and worked on. They help me remain alive to the ways that buildings are more than one (they are not the same thing for each practitioner) but also less than many (they do not exist in harmonious plurality); they are partially connected entities that reach across divergent worlds. In the work of architects who hold onto their búsqueda, in vecinos who work to protect their barrios, and even in investors who look for long-term stability rather than short-term profitability, I find the endurance of values that evade totalizing capture.

Capture by capitalism and the forms of value that it recognizes can threaten these divergent forms of value; its parasitism has a capacity to redefine practices. The endurance of other forms of value does not spell an end to capitalism or the problems it poses for the creation of more livable worlds. But their endurance can be an important part of cultivating ways of living that are excessive to, other than, or against the grain of capitalism. For this project, their endurance matters. Fostering attention to them is a descriptive (and political) project that nurtures possibilities in a way that is different from major-key dreams of commonality and unified resistance, which, as I described in the introduction, frequently imply leaving behind divergent obligations in the name of consensus.[5]

Attention to divergence is one way to build minor-key political projects grounded in what Donna Haraway has called significant otherness. "How," she asks, "can people rooted in different knowledge practices 'get on together,' especially when an all-too-easy cultural relativism is not an option, either politically, epistemologically, or morally?" (2003, 7). The answer, she writes, "can only be put together in emergent practices; i.e., in vulnerable, on-the-ground work that cobbles together non-harmonious agencies and ways of living that are accountable both to their disparate inherited histories and to their barely possible but absolutely necessary joint futures. For me, that is what *significant otherness* signifies" (7). Significant otherness resonates with the slow and difficult work of what Verran and Christie (2011) have described as "doing difference together": fostering encounters in which it is possible to attend to incommensurability in an accountable way capable of producing new ways of living together. For me, attending to divergent values is part of this work.

I saw this kind of on-the-ground work to cobble together nonharmonious agencies in both fleeting and enduring encounters in the field: moments in which the striations of different practices were interrupted by flashes of encounter. At times, such encounters unfolded on tense terrain, like in some of the real estate seminars I attended in which the political activity of vecinos to rewrite the urban planning code appeared literally as a "threat" in Power-Point slides about current market conditions, the divergence of their values in buildings making a brief, but not particularly productive incursion into a world of price per square meter. At other times, however, divergences were the project of ongoing efforts to produce possible, partially connected futures.

The presence of architects as prominent members of some groups of vecinos (like SOS Caballito and Amigos del Lago) or the collaboration of vecinos with architects (Salvemos al Barrio collaborated with an architect in the audit they conducted of the barrio) are two examples in which at times uncomfortable copresences unfolded. Architects affiliated with vecino groups also made attempts to bring their experience into the architecture school, including one teach-in I attended that was sponsored by QUEREMOS BUENOS AIRES, the umbrella organization of vecino groups run by Osvaldo from Amigos del Lago. Marta, the dissident urban planner, was there, as were several other architects—alumni of the school involved in urban environmental politics through organizations like APEVU, the Permanent Assembly for the Preservation of Green Urban Spaces, and the group of vecinos dedicated to defending the city's ecological reserve. There, they spoke to a small group of students, telling them stories about the connections between money, power, and architecture that they had encountered in their work—Marta's Corporation, or what TUPAU would have called the architecture of the system. Through their stories, they cultivated a space for the work of inheritance across divergent ecologies of practice and value.

....

As my conversation with Sergio and Adrián wound down, I cited a lyric from "Por qué cantamos," or "Why We Sing," a song that puts to music a poem by the Uruguayan poet Mario Benedetti and was popularized under dictatorships in Argentina and several other Latin American countries in the early 1980s. The poem is addressed to one who would ask how it's possible to go on singing in difficult times, when hope is scarce and so many suffer. "Usted preguntará por qué cantamos," I said to Sergio and Adrián—you sir, will ask why we sing. Sergio and Adrián, who taught me many of the songs I learned in Argentina, picked up my cue and continued the song. "Cantamos porque el grito no es bastante," Adrián quoted—we sing because crying out is not enough. Sergio followed "Y no es bastante el llanto ni la bronca"—and neither are weeping nor anger enough. We found ourselves laughing, despite our sadness, at our dramatic rendering of the moment. We didn't continue, but the song goes on:

> We sing for the child and because everything
> and because some future and because the people
> we sing because the survivors
> and our dead want us to sing.

The song serves for me as a reminder that we live in a world that requires so many kinds of care to get by in, and that if outcry, weeping, and anger at major-key political environments can be an important part of our projects of care, it's also important not to lose sight of minor forms of value and the politics of making them endure in practice. Because I learned these words as a song sung by singers about the importance of singing, it has always carried for me a reminder about the power of minor-key practices even in the face of major-key worlds in which hope can seem difficult to hold on to. Like the verses I cited in the epigraph of this book—cada cual con sus trabajos / con sus sueños, cada cual / con la esperanza adelante / con los recuerdos detrás (each one with their work / with their dreams, each one / with hope before them / with memories behind)—the song helps me hold a place for quotidian, habitual practices and to keep present the power of those practices for remembrance, endurance, and dreams. If there is value in singers continuing to sing, it is important, too, for other practitioners to continue producing the divergent forms of value they make through their practices in the interest of building better worlds. My own hopes for the future, even in times when they seem unlikely to triumph against more hegemonic forms of value, are grounded in these minor values and the practices in which they are produced and maintained.

It is my hope that my own practice as an ethnographer—telling stories of concrete dreams as a way to sit with the vital differences of a diverse group of practitioners and foster attention to divergent forms of value in buildings—can also make a contribution to the project of getting on together. In holding present some minor-key practices of value in the face of major-key horrors and hopes, neither I nor my informants can promise bold and definitive breaks from the past. But I do see in the work of storytelling a means to lend a bit more presence to these minor-key dreams, part of the work of cobbling together an incremental divergence, a way to nudge things in a different direction, or at the very least to allow for possibilities to be sustained in the face of the debilitating capture of probability.

NOTES

....

INTRODUCTION: CONCRETE DREAMS

1 In anthropology there is a long history of thinking value in this register and of attending to the ways that value is created in practice. In *The Fame of Gawa* (1993), for example, Nancy Munn studied the ways that Gawans, through practices like gardening, canoe building, and *kula* exchange, imbued the world around them with value and in turn derived value from them. Kula exchange and gardening are different practices that both produce and rely on different forms of value: while kula travel is about lightness and extension, gardening is about heaviness and concentration. Different ritual practices produce these values, ensuring good kula and good gardens. On the different valences of value in the history of anthropology, see Graeber (2001).

2 A long history of scholarship has worked to problematize the image of the subject as pure mind, divorced not only from subjects' bodies but the world around them and the tools they use to engage it. I come to this work through Science and Technology Studies, where the importance of machines, instruments, and experimental setups has been treated as a central feature of scientific knowledge production. See, for example, Callon (1986), Hacking (1983), Latour (2005), Law and Hassard (1999), and Pickering (1995). Recently, scholars (including many anthropologists) have deployed a similar approach to analyze the importance of documents in understanding bureaucracy (Hetherington 2011; Hull 2012); of drawings, models, and imaging technologies in various forms of knowledge (Dumit 2004; Kaiser 2005; Latour and Yaneva 2008; Mialet 2012; Mol 2002; Myers 2015; Raffles 2010; Rheinberger 2010; Taussig 2011; Vertesi 2012); of charts, graphs, and algorithms in international finance (Lépinay 2011; Zaloom 2006); and even the particularity of certain forms of speech, like jokes and rumors, in political life (Das 2006; Nelson 1999). This work has shown the ways that forms of knowledge are entangled with the tools of practice and that fine-tuned attention to these tools is critical to understanding how knowledge and values are produced and circulated.

3 Michelle Murphy has described this as the production of "regimes of perceptibility" in which "arrangements of words, things, practices and people [draw] out and [make] perceptible specific qualities, capacities and possibilities" (M. Murphy

2006). On requirements and obligations, see Stengers (2010). See also Bourdieu (1977) and de Certeau (1984).

4 I take the word *situated* from Donna Haraway (1988), who proposed situating knowledge as a powerful tool for producing accounts of knowledge that do not ignore the broader power dynamics of which they are a part. Along with other feminist scholars of science, she pointed out limitations to the ways that certain laboratory studies circumscribed practices within the laboratory without taking into account the ways that structural forms of inequality get built into and out of scientific knowledge production. She saw situating all knowledge as a way to disrupt the "view from nowhere" of masculinist, universalizing science by showing how all knowledges are situated, and not just those of women and others who have long been said to have a particular perspective or standpoint. Haraway thus situates the knowledge practices of Western science within sets of power relations including gender, race, colonialism, and capitalism. Showing how knowledge is situated socially and technically is a means of approaching relationships between knowledge and power and of producing responsible accounts of their relationship.

5 My initial fieldwork plan for this book was to hold the one object with which my various sets of actors were concerned—the building—at the center of analysis and to follow buildings through the different worlds in which they played a central role, a method based on tracing the chain of production of contested objects, mapping the conflicts and struggles over them and the social worlds that unfold around them. As Anna Tsing (2005, 51) has argued, each step in these chains can be seen as an arena of cultural production; analyzing the frictions between these often divergent cultural economies, which can be linked in awkward, uncomfortable ways, allows for a thick ethnographic understanding of the social lives of the objects and the cultural worlds that surround them (see also Appadurai 1986).

And yet, as I moved between different groups of actors in the field, I realized that the building that I was attempting to follow was not in any way stable. Rather, its materiality shifted in ways that made it nearly unrecognizable between the different sites in which buildings existed. Indeed, over time I began to question whether I was following one object at all. Was a building one thing that moved between worlds, or was it many different things? To what extent was there an "it" to follow? When and how did it appear, and how did it seem to both be the center of everything, and yet so difficult to pinpoint at the same time?

This dilemma, and the question of how to express it ethnographically, was one impetus behind conceiving of this book as an ethnography of practices. On the one hand, buildings can be many different things—investments, objects of design, environments for living. In this sense, they are multiple. And yet, this multiplicity is not the kind that enables a conflict-free coexistence in harmonious plurality: buildings are fraught terrains on which practitioners with diverging requirements and obligations make claims, and they can and do press in on one another. In this sense, John Law (2002, 3–4) has described objects as existing neither within a single dimension nor in multiple independent dimensions; instead, they are drawn together without being centered, cohering in a state that hangs between singularity and plurality. In this sense, buildings are "more than one and less than many," to borrow Marilyn Strathern's phrase (2004, 35).

Different instantiations of buildings can come together, but not in ways that necessarily resolve or overcome their differences. Practices offer me a way to hold present the various material manifestations of buildings, blurring the focus of the perceived stability of objects and instead building toward a form of perception in which buildings "come into being—and disappear—with the practices in which they are manipulated" (Mol 2002, 5). Practices allow me to place the different media in which buildings are instantiated front and center, and begin to think contextually from there. I came to think of buildings not as stable entities, but as a kind of flickering set of layers that moved in and out of focus, always in the presence of others.

6 Deleuze and Guattari (1987) have written about this as the virtual. See also DeLanda (2002) and Massumi (2002).

7 I describe these measures in detail in chapter 1.

8 On narratives of crisis, see Roitman (2013).

9 See, for example, Klein (2007).

10 On neoliberalism and the years after the crisis in relation to it, see de la Barra (2009), Faulk (2012), Gutman and Cohen (2007), Levitsky and Roberts (2011), Masiello (2001), Rock (2002), and Shever (2012).

11 It's hard to overstate the extent to which conservative factions in the country tried to purge Peronism from the country: one of the military leaders, Aramburu, made it illegal to speak the names of Perón or Evita; Evita's body was later exhumed and secreted to a foreign grave, a story dramatized in the novel *Santa Evita* (Martínez 1997).

12 The concentration of both left and right factions of Peronism at the airport to receive Perón on his return to Argentina in 1973 ended in a shoot-out, with estimates placing the death toll in the tens and injuries in the hundreds (the episode is explored in depth in Verbitsky [1985]). Perón would make his allegiance clear in a major May Day rally in which he threw his support behind conservative trade unionists. The left withdrew their columns from the plaza, and violence against them escalated, presaging the actions of the dictatorship in 1976. Despite Perón's own disavowal of the left, in the years to come Peronism would remain a multivalent political category in Argentina, which many describe in terms of a contradictory copresence of left and right tendencies within the Peronist party. Today, Perón remains a poignant figure for those on the left. While many reject Peronism for a variety of communist and socialist parties, others continue to identify (often in ambivalent ways) with the legacy of Perón. On some of these legacies, see Daniel James (1994).

13 The military government's liberalization of the economy coincided with a new phase of U.S. imperialism driven through foreign loans. The OPEC oil crisis, stagflation in the United States, and a deal brokered by the U.S. with OPEC countries to filter petroleum profits through Wall Street investment banks, together with a dearth of profitable investments in the U.S. led to a surge of lending to foreign countries (D. Harvey 2005). The military government in Argentina accrued heavy debt. In the 1980s, U.S. economic measures against stagflation (the "Volcker Shock") effectively cut off credit from the developing world, provoking debt crises throughout much of the developing world (Branford and Kucinski 1988; see Roddick 1988). Argentina, by the end of the 1980s, was one of the fifteen most severely indebted countries in the world.

14 In his notes on the translation for *A Thousand Plateaus*, Brian Massumi explains that Deleuze's use of *milieu* is a combination of the word's three meanings in French: "surroundings," "medium" (as in chemistry), and "middle" (Deleuze and Guattari 1987, xvii).

15 Erin Manning describes the minor in this sense as being tightly connected to "the event at hand," even as it exceeds its bounds: "Each minor gesture is singularly connected to the event at hand, immanent to the in-act. This makes it pragmatic. But the minor gesture also exceeds the bounds of the event, touching on the ineffable quality of its more-than. This makes it speculative. The minor gesture works in the mode of speculative pragmatism. From a speculatively pragmatic stance, it invents its own value, a value as ephemeral as it is mobile" (Manning 2016, 2).

16 For example, Marilyn Strathern noted in the late 1980s, "There are other metaphors today on which the anthropologist draws: communicational field, ecosystem, social formation, even structure, all of which construct global contexts for the interconnection of events and relations. Their danger lies in making the system appear to be the subject under scrutiny rather than the method of scrutiny. The phenomena come to appear contained or encompassed by the systemics, and thus themselves systemic. So we get entangled in world systems and deep structures and worry about the 'level' at which they exist in the phenomena themselves" (Strathern 1988). Understanding events and relations as "contained or encompassed by the systemics, and thus themselves systemic" gives little room to the attention to minor forms of difference that is, for many of us, one of ethnography's hallmark strengths.

17 Manning offers the following in this regard: "The unwavering belief in the major as the site where events occur, where events make a difference, is based on accepted accounts of what registers as change as well as existing parameters for gauging the value of that change. Yet while the grand gestures of a macropolitics most easily sum up the changes that occurred to alter the field, it is the minoritarian tendencies that initiate the subtle shifts that created the conditions for this, and any change. The grand is given the status it has not because it is where the transformative power lies, but because it is easier to identify major shifts than to catalogue the nuanced rhythms of the minor. As a result, these rhythms are narrated as secondary, or even negligible" (2016, 1).

18 On intellectual currents that operate in tension with critique, see Anker and Felski (2017); on the limits of critique as an intellectual practice, see Latour (2004); on finding promise and possibility in practice, see Muñoz (2009).

19 In *The End of Capitalism* (*As We Knew It*), Gibson-Graham work to decenter capitalism's hold on our economic imaginaries and the way we view the world around us. Their examples are humble, like looking to child-care reciprocity networks to unthink the idea that we are living in a world completely characterized by market exchange. As they describe their project, they seek to "discover or create a world of economic difference, and to populate that world with exotic creatures that become, upon inspection, quite local and familiar (not to mention familiar beings that are not what they seem)" (1996, 3). More recently, Anna Tsing (2015) has

shown how even in the midst of market interactions, other forms of value endure, like the divergent ways that mushroom foragers value their practice and the mushrooms they collect. For Tsing, mushrooms in the markets of the Pacific Northwest and Japan are not pure commodities, because they carry these other values along with them. See also Paxson (2012) and Weiss (2016).

20 On striation, segmentarity, and territorialization, see Deleuze and Guattari (1987).

21 Stengers's use of ecology in this sense corresponds to thinking "par le milieux" or with the surroundings, as I explained earlier. Throughout this book I make use of the words *ecology* and *environment* in different ways, at times signaling the social, technical, political, economic, affective, and embodied surroundings of practices, at times referring to the buildings, plants, sky, and social life of the city. My sense of playfulness here is deliberate. My own thought is indebted to the work of many environmental anthropologists, and my play with these terms is an insistence on that relation. Environments, as these scholars have shown, are hardly passive backdrops in which action takes place. And they are never only green but, like the city I study here, meticulously worked-over and cared-for compositions of organic and inorganic materials, human and other-than-human beings. *Ecology* is a word that I find useful for drawing out the tense and dynamic sets of relations that are involved in the composition of environments; as I explain in chapter 1, I draw on the double valence of the shared root of economy and ecology, the Greek *oikos*, or the home, and again at times transgress what may seem like the most straightforward use of these terms.

22 On endurance, see Povinelli (2011).

23 See especially Zaloom (2003, 2006, 2009) and Lépinay (2011).

24 See Guyer (2004), Hayden (2003), Kockelman (2016), Munn (1993), Roitman (2005), Weiner (1992), and Zelizer (1994).

25 On the political ontology of doing difference, see also Blaser (2009).

26 On capture, see Pignarre and Stengers (2011).

CHAPTER 1: CRISIS HISTORIES, BRICK FUTURES

1 On the economic practices of Argentine elites, see Abelin (2012).

2 An excellent explication of the subprime mortgage crisis in the U.S. can be found in a collaborative podcast, "The Giant Pool of Money" (2008), by *This American Life* and *NPR News*. On the mortgage modification programs that followed and the ways debt and reciprocity inhere within contemporary financialized mortgage markets, see Stout (2016).

3 Major developers who could leverage financing for large-scale projects without recourse to Argentine banks were also largely absent from the market after the crisis, with the exception of a few concentrated zones of the city, like Puerto Madero. On Puerto Madero, see Guano (2002).

4 Deposits were converted to pesos at a rate of 1.40 pesos per dollar, nearly half the free market rate in March of 2002, and even less than half by May when the dollar was trading at close to 3 pesos.

5 An earlier version of this chapter was developed in D'Avella (2014).

6 Smoki Musaraj (2011) has described a similar attentiveness to materiality with respect to pyramid schemes in Albania in the 1990s.

7 See especially Mauss (1966), Munn (1993), Strathern (1988), Praspaliauskiene (2016), and Weiner (1992).

8 See Ho (2009), Lépinay (2011), Miyazaki (2013), Riles (2011), and Zaloom (2006).

9 See, for example, Page's (2009) consideration of depictions of economic crisis in Argentine cinema, Martin Kovensky's (2002) artwork surrounding the crisis of 2001, and the depiction of the bizarre side of Argentine economic life in the comic work of Langer and Mira (2006). Sarah Muir (2015) has described the extensiveness and depth of everyday Argentine talk about money, economics, and crisis as a form of critique that draws on various interpretive genres, including psychoanalysis and conspiracy theory, to try to make sense of economic-historical events.

10 See especially Diana Taylor (2003) and Julie Taylor (1998); from a different context but with important resonances, see Klima (2002).

11 See Povinelli (2011, 175–76); see also Trouillot (1995).

12 The Rodrigazo in 1975 was an example of the former and La Tablita in 1979, of the latter. The former was designed to shock the economy back into health. The latter was based on the idea that slow and predictable devaluations (known as a "crawling peg") would contain expectations and reduce inflationary drives. Neither functioned to curb inflation effectively.

13 This was especially true after 2007, when the government intervened in the method for measuring inflation used by the National Institute of Statistics and Census (INDEC).

14 The austral was Argentina's national currency between June 15, 1985, and December 31, 1991.

15 See Fridman (2010) and Neiburg (2006, 2010).

16 On economic practices across scales of value, see Guyer (2004) and Maurer (2005).

17 Convertibility worked by limiting the number of pesos in circulation, tying them directly to the supply of dollars entering the country from abroad through exports, loans, or foreign direct investment. But a high currency value for the peso also limited the country's ability to generate export surpluses, since production in Argentina was made more expensive. Coupled with a recession that began in 1998 and a downturn in foreign direct investment, eventually the only way left for Argentina to maintain convertibility was through loans—loans that became more and more difficult to repay without an economic surplus. A similar issue confronts indebted countries in the European Union who cannot devalue the euro. See Marshall (2008) for a detailed analysis of convertibility's role in consolidating the influence of international banks and lending institutions in Argentina.

18 The series of events that led up to the crisis and the particular role of Wall Street institutions in exacerbating the default and the crisis are well detailed by Blustein (2005).

19 Pino Solanas's *Memoria del Saqueo* (2004) is another documentary that closely follows the events of the argentinazo. See also Chronopoulos (2011).

20 Bondholders could also sell their bonds on secondary markets to entities with debt (either individuals or corporations) to be used for debt repayment.

21 See Ballent (2005, 215). Perón's election in 1945 was preceded by a military coup in 1943. Some of the measures I describe here, including the rent freeze, were initiated under the 1943 government. See also Elena (2011).

22 Data are from Gazzoli (2006). I thank Eduardo Reese for his help in understanding some of these shifts.

23 Savings and loan programs were fomented across the Americas through development programs in support of homeownership, underwritten by U.S. financial interests and channeled through agencies such as the U.S. Agency for International Development. See Kwak (2015). These programs were part of broader efforts by the U.S., in concert with governments across Latin America, to stem social upheaval (and its associated Cold War specter of communist expansion) by expanding access to homeownership on different terms than those posed by populist governments. See, for example, Benmergui (2009) on the Alliance for Progress.

24 The peso moneda nacional was Argentina's national currency from 1881 until 1969.

25 One exception to this stability in pricing occurred in the era known as *plata dulce*, or sweet money, in the early 1980s, in which an influx of foreign capital (financed through foreign debt to the military government) drove prices sky high, only to see them fall sharply to their previous levels in a subsequent devaluation. (This may have been what happened to the character in *A History of Money*, though the exact timing of the events he described are difficult to pinpoint.) Circular 1050, mentioned previously, was part of this era. The other exception is the dip following the crisis of 2001, which lasted about two years before real estate prices recovered.

26 One study carried out in 2011 by the Real Estate Chamber of Commerce of Rosario estimated that 70 percent of units constructed in that city were destined for investment rather than direct use. See Reese, Almansi, del Valle, and Juan (2014). Again, I thank Eduardo Reese for helping me draw together this data.

27 Juan José Cruces has argued in the press that the rate of return on an apartment over ten years (including rental return and eventual sale) is 3 percent, comparable to U.S. Treasury bonds for a similar time frame (Lendoiro 2014). Argentine real estate investors, he argued, are making economic decisions based on prejudice against finance and an unreasonable economic affinity for real estate that is both driving up prices and keeping rental profitability down. Others, including the Argentine Central Bank (BCRA), have disagreed, showing that in the long term bricks outperform saving in cash dollars or investing in fixed-term deposits like CDs (Blanco 2016). I examine these kinds of analysis more closely in chapter 2.

28 In the 1990s, purchases in Buenos Aires financed at least in part with mortgage loans hovered between 25 and 35 percent. In the decade after the crisis they dipped below 4 percent and then hovered around 6 percent.

29 On the dollarization of the Argentine real estate market, see Gaggero and Nemiña (2013). Dollars are also an important part of the agro-export economy, a topic I return to in chapter 2. On the use of the U.S. dollar in Argentina more generally, see Kaufman (2013).

30 This is a popular-knowledge riff on the concept of performativity, which scholars of the social study of economics have typically applied to the ways more authorized forms of economic theory help to shape markets. They have argued that

economists don't just study markets that exist beyond their practices of knowledge, but that their practices of knowledge are formative for the markets that they
study and that economic theories are used to remake markets in their image. See
Callon (1998) and MacKenzie, Muniesa, and Siu (2007). Like these scholars'
observations about economists, I see the stories told by Argentines as more than
reflections on economic life, but as a defining feature of that life.

31 See Luzzi and Wilkis (2018).

CHAPTER 2: A MARKET IN SQUARE METERS

1 Building on the tradition of Marx (1990) and Simmel (1990), one of the powers
found in modern money has been its ability to commensurate, flatten, and homogenize difference, allowing for comparisons of different things on the same scale of
value. In this analytical tradition, money works to bracket other forms of difference.

2 On Tarde, see Candea (2010), and Latour and Lépinay (2009).

3 I'm thinking here specifically of the work of Vincent Lépinay (2011), who traces
the production of derivatives through the physically written contracts in which
they are materialized, and of Caitlin Zaloom's (2003, 2006) evocative ethnographic depictions of the different material manifestations of numbers in commodity trading, on the one hand through the vocalized and embodied shouts
and gestures of pit traders and on the other in the digital screens of computer
trading terminals. Similarly, Koray Çalışkan (2010, 18) has argued that the market
in cotton is not a geographical entity but a graphical one, made up in indices and
reports. His work is part of a growing body of work that seeks to attend to the
ways that graphic tools and technologies bring markets (and their subjects and objects) into existence. See also Knorr Cetina and Bruegger (2002), various authors
in MacKenzie, Muniesa, and Siu (2007), and Poovey (1998).

4 See Guyer, Khan, Obarrio, Bledsoe, Chu, Diagne, Hart, Kockelman, Lave,
McLoughlin, Maurer, Neiburg, Nelson, Stafford, and Verran (2010) and the other
articles in this special issue. See also Hacking (1983) and Latour (1988).

5 Bill Maurer's (2006) review of the literature on money sketches out this long arc
of scholarship. Building on Jane Guyer's call to "incorporate attention to thought
and calculation [in order to] 'think other' precisely about number, measurement, and money" (2004, 174–75), Maurer argues that whether and how number,
quantification, and money allow for abstraction should be treated as a research
question rather than as a foregone conclusion.

6 See Ballestero (2012, 2015), Chu (2010), Mitchell (2002), Muehlmann (2012), and
Searle (2013).

7 Caitlin Zaloom (2006), for example, building off of the work of William Cronon
(1991), has described the process through which grain was made fungible in
Chicago, allowing it to be traded on the commodity trading floor of the Chicago
Board of Trade, far away from the actual product in question and without ever seeing the actual bundle of grain being traded on the trading floor. See also Espeland
and Stevens (1998).

8 On the durability of such forms of knowledge and the market structures they help
maintain, see Besky (2016).

9 My logic here loosely follows that of Annelise Riles (2000), who has shown how tracing a network is also a way of remaking a network.

10 See Luzzi and Wilkis (2018).

11 "SWOT analysis" is a common tool of global business culture.

CHAPTER 3: BARRIO ECOLOGIES

1 Typically translated as *neighborhood, barrio* has a variety of other connotations I return to shortly.

2 *Porteños* is the term for residents of the port city of Buenos Aires.

3 On noticing, see Choy (2011) and Tsing (2015). On attunement, see Myers (2015), Shapiro (2015), and Stewart (2011). See also Michelle Murphy (2006) on perceptibility.

4 On the vecino as a political figure in a different urban context, see Corsín Jiménez and Estallela (2013) and Estallela and Corsín Jiménez (2014).

5 See Choi (2015), Graeter (2017), Lyons (2016), Mendoza (2016), Procupez (2016), Zee (2017), and Zeiderman (2016).

6 I am thinking here with McLean (2009), who points out the often overlooked place of nonhumans in collectives and related work on conviviality, relational ecologies, and entanglement across species lines in urban worlds. See Archambault (2016), Hinchliffe and Whatmore (2006), Nading (2012), Poe et al. (2014), Porter (2013), and Stoetzer (2018). I explore the ways that bird watching and animal census-taking are articulated with urban environmental advocacy in D'Avella (2018).

7 Most of the neighborhood movements I worked with were on borderlands between richer, densely built parts of the city in the northeast and poorer, less dense barrios to the west and the south of the city. In some of them, like Caballito, there had long been a section of dense, upper-middle-class apartment buildings in the center of the barrio, and both development and vecino movements regarding it were focused in the more southern and northern parts of the barrio, where single-owner lots provided easier opportunities for development. Many of these neighborhoods, like Villa Urquiza, Palermo, and Villa Pueyrredón, were of mixed class, and the composition of the groups of vecinos I worked with reflected that. Core members of Salvemos al Barrio, for example, included a secretary, a teacher, a medical lab worker, a mid-level bank employee, the proprietor of a sand and gravel yard, and a business executive and a lawyer.

The boom provoked changes to some neighborhoods in the city that took on the characteristics we associate with gentrification—namely, the displacement of a certain class of people by wealthier residents. Such was the case with the barrios of Abasto, San Telmo, and La Boca, for example, and on a few occasions I saw the word *gentrificación* used in these contexts. Changes in the social composition of barrios was not a salient issue in the cases I studied, however, where there was little sense that new residents were of a different social class than those who had lived there for a longer time. For more on displacement in Buenos Aires, see Centner (2012). Concurrent with my fieldwork, there was also a large amount of construction happening in the former port district of Puerto Madero that was qualitatively distinct from the transformations this book focuses on. For more on Puerto Madero, see Guano (2002).

8   Villa Pueyrredón, where Abel and Nelly live, is widely regarded as "muy barrio," very barrio. In the area of Villa Pueyrredón where Salvemos al Barrio was centered there is no bank; transport to the center takes longer, and bus lines, dense in the center, can be distant; none of the supermarket chains common in the center are close by, nor are the national café chains; and convenience stores are often operated out of the open window of someone's home. The hub of social activity is the neighborhood sports club and neighborhood cafés. Caballito, by comparison, would not be considered muy barrio when taken as a whole: the center of the neighborhood has a bustling commercial district, several major cinemas, and a shopping mall. But further afield, to the north and the south, are parts of Caballito that would be considered more barrio than the rest. And of course, almost any place can become less barrio than it was as construction gets more dense, traffic increases, and the lifestyle begins to feel more like that of the center.

9   Writing on barrios remains an important part of Argentine literary culture; see, for example, Terranova (2007).

10 See Ghannam (2002) and Ring (2006) on managing the intimacies of cohabitation in different built environments.

11 On infrastructure as formative of material but also social and political environments, see Anand (2017), Carse (2014), Jensen (2015), Larkin (2008), Simone (2004), von Schnitzler (2016), and Whitington (2016).

12 On the histories and contemporary endurances of tango, see Miller (2014).

13 "Un callejón en Pompeya / y un farolito plateando el fango, / y allí un malevo que fuma / y un organito moliendo un tango"; cited in Gorelik (2001, 367).

14 Again I follow Gorelik (2001, 372). "! Villa Crespo! . . . barrio reo, / el de las calles estrechas / y las casitas mal hechas / que eras lindo por lo feo. . . . / Ya no sos lo que eras antes / Villa Crespo de mis sueños, / otras leyes y otros dueños / te ensancharon las veredas, / y con manos chapuceras / el grébano constructor / clavó en los güecos en flor / del andamiaje las redes / y levantando paredes / te fue cambiando el color. / ¿Qué querés con la postura / de tus tiendas y tus llecas, / tus cinemas y tus fecas, / si te agarró la pintura? / Te engrupió la arquitectura del plano municipal."

15 Gorelik (2001, 382). On Borges and the built environment, see also Grau (1989).

16 Though not quite as valued for development as unbuilt land, a similar situation applied to large warehouses, former factories, and single-family homes, all of which were prime targets for developers because they provided an ease of acquisition that multi-family dwellings did not. Since the Ley de Propiedad Horizontal of 1949, which allowed for the ownership of individual apartments in larger buildings, a developer trying to purchase a smaller multi-unit building for redevelopment faced the challenge of convincing all of the owners to sell—multiplying the amount of effort and money that might be spent negotiating the purchase of a property. Properties with no owner (like the lands controlled by the state along the railroad yard), or with only one owner (like a warehouse or single-family home), thus had great logistical appeal. This was one of the reasons that del Carril, the avenue that

ran through Villa Pueyrredón, and the northern section of Caballito, where Mario lived, were prime sites of densifying construction: they were all valuable as sites for redevelopment because the land was mostly occupied by single-family dwellings, which were much easier to buy for redevelopment than multi-family units. In the case of the railroad yard, rezoning did require legislative efforts to rezone, but the payoff was potentially great, since the lands were so extensive.

17 PRO, the name of his political alliance, officially stands for "Propuesta Republicana," but it also consciously evokes the term *professional*.

18 On the ways relational practices can be used to hold historical relations present, especially in built environments, see Fennell (2015), Gordillo (2004, 2014), Grant (2014), Pandolfo (1997), and Srinivas (2001).

19 The Avenida Pedro Goyena, in the south, received an almost wholesale renovation, with new fourteen-story apartment buildings going up on both sides of the street and spilling over to Avenida Directorio even further south. When the north side of Caballito began to densify, too, the political environment for new construction began to heat up.

20 Ann Cvetkovich, in speaking about depression as a "public feeling," captures some of the ways that the domestic can exceed what is understood as the private: "The intimate rituals of daily life . . . need to be understood as a public arena . . . that is, a location that doesn't always announce itself or get recognized as public but which nevertheless functions as such. My Public Feelings fellow traveler Kathleen (Katie) Stewart is very adept at capturing what she calls the private life of public culture, which holds out the dream of a cocoon-like domesticity as a sanctuary from the anxiety and terrors produced by economic crisis, war, and cultural conflict. But as the private life of public culture, the home becomes the soft underbelly of capitalism, a place where the current state of things is experienced through a complex range of feelings" (Cvetkovich 2012, 156). Argentine domesticity is not the same as the North American versions Cvetkovich and Stewart (2007) describe. Nevertheless, Cvetkovich's observation about the ways that domesticity can both buffer and refract broader social and cultural phenomena, upsetting the stability of the border between the public and the private, is particularly helpful for thinking through vecinos' struggles, which are simultaneously about their homes and about something more. To invert the formulation regarding the private life of public culture, vecinos articulated their domestic life with and as objects of public concern—giving a public life to domestic culture. They did so, as I will argue shortly, by placing domesticity into dialogue with the dispossessions of capitalism that were the object of widespread popular critique during the crisis.

21 This was reflective of broader attitudes toward new construction. As I mentioned in chapter 1, the vast majority of new housing stock was comprised of studios and one-bedroom apartments, inadequate to family life. But even for single occupants or couples, many of the new spaces were deemed insufficient by local standards. In one episode from the cartoon strip *La Nelly*, which ironized the ways that developers spun buildings that were small, dark, and cramped as luxury dwellings, the main character is taken to see an apartment by a developer who wants to trade her house for an apartment in a building he proposes to build on her property. He shows her

a studio apartment in which the bed is crammed between a microwave and sink on the one side (there is no stove) and a toilet on the other. "Look," he says to her, "you barely have to move, everything is at your fingertips!" I describe this comic series more extensively in D'Avella (2016). These judgments are not only aesthetic. They are also political judgments about what good life entails; see Elinoff (2016).

22 See Auyero (2001), Ciccolella and Baer (2008), Dubois (2005), Grimson (2008), and Svampa (2001).

23 This comic series is explored more fully in D'Avella (2016).

24 "Protestas de Palermo Despierta," June 1, 2008. https://palermonline.com.ar /noticias_2008/nota255_palermo_despierta.htm.

25 Fernando Diez remarks on a similar process that unfolded in the barrio of Belgrano in the 1970s, in which real estate developers used the slogan "Belgrano is a Garden" as their marketing campaign to sell apartments in towers (1996, 84). What they were selling was a view of other people's gardens and the image of suburban life that they were in the process of replacing. Today most of Belgrano is dominated by high-rise buildings.

26 These audiences and the kinds of speech they entail are considered in detail in chapter 4 and in D'Avella (2016).

CHAPTER 4: RECODING THE CITY

1 Many other groups, including sos Caballito and queremos buenos aires (the umbrella organization of vecino groups run by Osvaldo from Amigos del Lago), counted architects among their core members, providing a literacy with urban planning regulations to which Salvemos al Barrio did not have regular access.

2 As far as I was able to determine, this line change to the code was made in Law 449, published in the Official Bulletin of the City on October 9, 2000, and is itself seven pages of code modifying the urban planning code. The code's structure, in particular its lack of historical narrative, makes such determinations challenging. The current version of the code is online, but prior versions are not; by combining an array of sources (including, for instance, a detailed search for laws that modify the urban planning code in the weekly Official Bulletin of the city government), I identified Law 449 as the probable place in which the height limits for C3II were implemented. However, the line change in question doesn't appear in the text of the law, but is probably located in the annex, which my copy of Law 449 says can be viewed on the ground floor of a building at Avenida Rivadavia 525 in Buenos Aires. In the end, several experts I knew confirmed this as the likely source of the change, but I narrate the difficulty of clear historical attribution here as one of the code's particular features as a medium that, despite its appearance of clarity, can nevertheless be opaque, a topic I return to later.

3 On the long history of codes, including those used before the development of modern urban planning, see Ben-Joseph (2005).

4 Matthew Hull (2012) describes a similar experience in relation to his research on Islamabad.

5 My narrative here follows that of Liernur and Pschepiurca (2008), especially chapter 1.

6 On these expansions, see Scobie (1974); see also Sargent (1974).

7 Argentina faced a major economic and political crisis in 1890 that would have repercussions throughout the world when it defaulted on debt to the London-based Baring's Bank.

8 As I mentioned in chapter 1, credit for homeownership in Buenos Aires for the working classes was not a state priority at the time, geared as it was toward populating the interior of the country, and was thus facilitated mainly through developers themselves or private building and loan companies. See Scobie (1974, 182–91). Workers would typically build precarious shacks or small homes on these lots and improve them over time. Between 1904 and 1919, the population of the western half of the city grew fourfold, with most living in poor conditions without basic public services like running water, sewage, and paved streets. Advocating for these services became a prominent focus of political mobilization in these emergent barrios, as explained in chapter 3. In 1929, roughly one-quarter of the western half of the city remained ambiguously rural or unbuilt, but by 1937 the city was urbanized up to (and beyond) its borders.

9 See Marcuse (1987), Mumford (1961), and Sennett (1990).

10 I discussed these ideals in chapter 3 in relation to the grid's homogeneity and the possibility for social ascent associated with it. The tensions between free markets in private property and the public interest that were part of the context in which the grid was developed would remain present in later debates about urban planning. These included basic issues of expropriation, but at times were taken to go deeper. Consider these words spoken at the inaugural address of the First Argentine Congress of Urbanism in 1936 by José Rouco Oliva, of the Amigos de la Ciudad (one of the institutions that had invited Le Corbusier, along with other urbanists, to Buenos Aires) and the secretary of the Congress: "No speculation about the venal value of land; no concession to private interests that may damage social interest. Urbanism is a science that is frankly revolutionary. By pursuing the possible happiness of man on earth, it suppresses class differences while reducing economic factors to only the most particular aspects of individual wealth" (cited in Liernur and Pschepiurca 2008, 154).

11 The urbanism of which Corbusier was a key proponent was born amid a set of efforts to improve life in increasingly dense cities that had been upended by industrialization. In her classic work on the history of urbanism, the historian Francoise Choay (1969) describes how cities became thinkable as objects of knowledge and intervention alongside the changes brought about by the industrial revolution and enlightenment ideas about truth, science, and rationality. She describes preindustrial cities as grounded in the polysemantic orderings of clergy, lord, and guild—contexts of meaning that were spatialized through overlapping geographies of churches, palaces, and networks of artisanal production. By the end of the eighteenth century, however, the Industrial Revolution began bringing about radical changes to cities around the globe. Large-scale immigration generated the challenge of mass housing for an industrial labor force, and cities had to be reworked to allow for the transportation of people, raw materials, and goods at new scales and within new networks of production and distribution. As cities

industrialized, the polysemantic ordering of clergy, lord, and guild was superseded by what Choay calls a "monosemantic" urban space organized to meet the exigencies of industrial production.

12 See Picon (2003) and Turnbull (2000). For Buenos Aires, see Aliata (2006).

13 On the rebuilding of San Juan after the earthquake and Perón's rise to power, see Healey (2011).

14 The relationship between Corbusier, angry at not being contracted by the Estudio, and his Argentine colleagues, too, had soured.

15 See Suárez (1995).

16 Making the city autonomous was part of a set of neoliberal restructurings of governance that devolved power, as well as fiscal burdens, to local levels of government.

17 See, for example, an article in the *Los Angeles Times* pondering a consolidation of their urban zoning code, which was originally written in 1946 at 96 pages and which had been modified countless times, swelling to more than 800 pages in 2014 (Logan 2014).

18 Much of this debate was happening in Europe and North America; I deal with its entrance and translation into Argentine contexts later. One useful account with regard to British planning and what he calls the emergent "systems approach" is that of Nigel Taylor (1998). A key text advocating for a systems approach was J. Brian McLoughlin's *Urban and Regional Planning: A Systems Approach* (1969), advocating applying theories of systems and control to the planning of human environments. This wasn't all done in a register of computation, however. In the U.S., for example, Jane Jacobs (1961) criticized the overly ordered separation of functions of modern planning that destroyed or stood in the way of vibrant, organic communities attained through mixed uses of urban space. Similarly, the architect Christopher Alexander (1966) wrote his seminal contribution to architectural theory and urban design, "A City Is Not a Tree," in 1965, in which he argued that the planned modernist city divided the city into independent units, treating it like leaves on a tree while failing to recognize the lattice-like overlaps and interrelations that go beyond unification through the branch.

19 For some, this approach is antithetical to the aims of planning. Rem Koolhaas, for instance, lamented that since 1968 "we have been . . . laughing the professional field of urbanism out of existence . . . , we have ridiculed it to the point where entire university departments are closed, offices bankrupted, bureaucracies fired or privatized. . . . Now we are left with a world without urbanism, only architecture, ever more architecture" (1998, 965–67). When Koolhaas laments the destruction of urban planning and its replacement with "architecture, ever more architecture," he is referring to this rescaling from the city to the fragment. For some observers, this shift amounts to the privileging of private property and commodification in an architectural world that no longer envisions for itself a central public role (see, for example, Neuman 1998).

20 Planners such as Sherry Arnstein, for example, whose "Ladder of Citizen Participation" was published in the *Journal of the American Institute of Planners* in 1969, placed concern for democratic planning front and center, ranking citizen partici-

pation from "manipulation" through "informing," "partnership," and eventually "citizen control."

21 For other work on urban planning during and immediately following the dictatorship of 1976–83, see Jajamovic (2011), Jajamovic and Menazzi (2012), and Menazzi (2013).

22 Curricular change was also a part of the democratic transition, and the Department of Urbanism and Planning was transformed into a postgraduate program, marking a loss of institutional power vis-à-vis architecture. See Jajamovich (2012b).

23 Recall that I introduced *making use of the word* earlier as a literal translation from the Spanish expression used to describe a speaker who has the floor in formal discursive spheres; here I conceptually extend the phrase beyond its typical use in formal discourse.

24 FOT stands for "factor of total occupation"—the technical term in English is *floor area ratio*. It is a coefficient by which the total size of a parcel is multiplied to arrive at the total area that can be built. This area itself is not as straightforward as it may seem, especially if what one is concerned with is the volume of the structure (since area is a two-dimensional measure). FOT interplays with FOS (the factor of surface occupation) and height restrictions to give an idea of the approximate dimensions of a building.

25 The way that neighborhood groups came to understand buildings as enmeshed within a network of relationships that permeated state bureaucratic and legislative structures resonates with the work of scholars who have sought to complicate what they see as an overemphasis on rationality as the primary genre through which the state works. See, for example, Abrams (1988), Aretxaga (2003), Das and Poole (2004), Mitchell (1991b), and Taussig (1997). Gossip about the state feeds off this intrigue in a way similar to jokes (Nelson 1999), infusing bureaucratic structures with the passions that are productive of political engagement. On politics and bureaucracy, see Ferguson (1994). On what she calls a "hermeneutics of suspicion" operative in Argentina more generally, see Muir (2015).

26 Michael Herzfeld's (2009) description of residents' challenging "war of attrition" with real estate developers in Rome is resonant here.

27 I am thinking here with Deleuze and Guattari in the opening pages of *A Thousand Plateaus* (1987), where they speak to the conventionality of naming and the attributions of authorship to individuals, while simultaneously problematizing such conventions and attributions of authorship. Marta makes a similar gesture in different terms.

CHAPTER 5: ARCHITECTURE IS FOR EVERYONE

1 There is no direct equivalent to the cátedra system in U.S. educational institutions. In the FADU, they function within specific subject areas (e.g., design, architectural history, applied physics, construction, structural design), bear the names of the titular professors or collectives who supervise the courses, and generally give an ideological, pedagogic, or theoretical identity to the courses they supervise. Design cátedras in the FADU are "vertical," in that they teach design courses over the five years of student progression through the program (Design 1–4 plus a senior project) and are considered the backbone of architectural education. (In some subjects there

may be only one cátedra, but design is taught by about two dozen.) Molina y Vedia–Sorín is thus a design cátedra offering courses in each of the five years; each course (e.g., Design 1) has a supervisory teacher and several "assistants" who do the bulk of the teaching. Students can move between cátedras over the years, but their identities often become bound up with one, not unlike graduate students and their advisors in U.S. institutions. "What cátedra did you study in?" is one way to track the identities of students and professionals. Cátedras' scale can vary considerably; Molina y Vedia–Sorín is a larger cátedra. At the time of fieldwork I estimate that about fifty professors taught about five hundred students. In the Design 1 workshop in which I conducted fieldwork, there were eleven teachers and about seventy-five students. As one of the UBA professors commented to me, one large FADU cátedra can be the size of Harvard's entire architecture school (but, he added, with only a small fraction of Harvard's economic resources). The scale of the FADU and the number of cátedras are important for understanding the range of pedagogic and political orientations present within the school—a topic I focus on later in the chapter.

2 I reflect further on what this has to say about professional architecture in the epilogue.

3 With regard to this kind of an entrepreneurial ethos, I am thinking in part of Lilly Irani's (2019) work on design, innovation, and entrepreneurialism in India and Peter Redfield's (2012) work on humanitarian design, both of which underscore the ways that market logics flow through design and design education. I am also thinking of Lily Chumley's (2016) work on art education in China, in which she notes the complex ways that creative work and creative self-styling are undertaken in close proximity to the specter of commodification and the art market.

4 The Pastilla de Chiquitolina is a pop-culture reference to a Mexican children's television program from the 1970s, El Chapulín Colorado, that saw wide distribution in Spanish-speaking television markets. Chapulín is a superhero parody, and one of his special skills is becoming smaller by taking a pill: to change his scale and his perspective, much as César was asking his students to do.

5 My description here resonates with recent work on science that aims to situate scientific knowledge production within the entanglements of practitioners and the models and machines they work with. See Helmreich (2009), Masco (2006), Mialet (2012), and Myers (2015). A growing body of work in the social sciences has begun to explore architectural design in this register; see Farías and Wilkie (2016), Keith M. Murphy (2004), and Yaneva (2009a, 2009b).

6 To say that drawings and models are powerful actors in the process of design is to draw into question the notions of subjective intentionality that are often imputed to design and to art in general. This is distinct from modern science, which is often understood as an objective practice that aims to understand phenomena over which the scientist and their practice are figured as having little or no involvement; whereas science is figured as transparently representing an objective reality, the opposite is held for modern conceptions of art, which is taken to be under the near-complete control of the artist as creator. Caroline A. Jones and Peter Galison (1998, 2–3) refer to this bifurcation of science and art as a binary economy in which art and science are yoked together, yet held apart to mark polar positions: "Soft

versus hard, intuitive versus analytical, inductive versus deductive, visual versus logical, random versus systematic. . . . Art, here, occupies the domain of the creative, intervening mind, and the scientific ethos seemed to demand precisely the suppression of such impulses" (see also Daston and Galison 2007). Thus, while much work done in Science and Technology Studies has been focused on complicating the objectivity imputed to modern science, I understand my project here to be a related but inverse questioning of subjective intentionality often imputed to art. Design is not just the result of an imposition of human agency on the environment, but is the outcome of encounters in which drawings are every bit as important as the humans who make them.

7　See Zeynep Ç. Alexander (2017) and Otero-Pailos (2010). I thank Curt Gambetta for pointing out the broader nature of this historical shift.

8　I mean "body" here both figuratively and literally—the figurative body politic, but also literal bodies, including those tortured and disappeared by state terrorism and, as I will describe further, the bodily habitus of the popular classes.

9　There is a rich body of work on Peronism and the built environment. See Aboy (2005, 2007), Ballent (2005), and Healey (2011). Podalsky (2004) describes urban culture with an eye to the relationship between politics and the built environment in the years from 1955 to 1973. Outside Argentina, anthropologists and sociologists who have studied the relationship between politics and design include Borch (2014), Kusno (2000), Keith M. Murphy (2013), and Yaneva and Zaera-Polo (2015).

10　Ismael Viñas, together with his brother David, founded an emblematic journal of the Argentine intellectual left, *Contorno*, in 1953.

11　Juan's particular focus on dispossession, economic and political dependency, and inequality set him apart from other regionalist movements in architecture, like *casablanquismo*, which, through a synthesis between modern and colonial architecture, also sought to produce an architecture regionally appropriate to Argentina.

12　Indeed, there had already been important initiatives that broke with more traditional pedagogical practices hegemonic in Argentina (especially the UBA) at the time. The best known of these is the Escuela de Tucumán, led by Jorge Vivanco (whose writing on scale I cited earlier) at the Universidad Nacional de Tucumán from 1947 to 1952, with the participation of Eduardo Sacriste, Enrico Tedeschi, and others. The Tucumán School was conceived as an alternative to the conservative political and pedagogic stance dominant in Buenos Aires and was part of an effort to bring architecture into closer dialogue with Latin America, and in particular with life in the province of Tucumán. Pedagogic practice was tightly linked to actual construction projects for local state and district governments, including worker housing, civic centers, regional planning, and most notably the campus of the Universidad Nacional de Tucumán. In their work, they paid particular attention to local conditions and to adapting their interventions to them. This drew on an idea of regionalism that was part of the discourse surrounding the diffusion of modernism throughout the world and a position that had been advocated in Argentina a decade earlier by the Grupo Austral. As Liernur (2008) notes, however, since the 1930s, political instability led such experiments to enjoy very short formal institutional lives, instead transmitting their knowledge through personal and extracurricular means. As we will see, Juan's career within the university, twice interrupted by military interventions, speaks to this broader history. On the Escuela de Tucumán, see Liernur (2008, 262–64). On related architectural currents in Argentina and early turns toward bringing architecture into relation with social concerns, see Healey (2011, 91–94).

13 Onganía had taken over the presidency after Arturo Frondizi was deposed by a military coup following his softening of restrictions against Peronism—a party that had been declared illegal following a prior military coup, the Revolucion Libertadora, in 1955. Note that neither of these are the most notorious dictatorship from Argentine history, which would come later in 1976.

14 The activities of TUPAU were part of a broad emergence of Peronist politics in many Argentine universities at the time, beginning soon after Perón's exile but particularly deepening in the 1960s and 1970s in Buenos Aires, marking a transformation of the more acrimonious relationship that had previously characterized the relationship between Peronism and higher education. A variety of student movements were involved in changing this, especially the Cátedras Nacionales in Sociology at the UBA. On the relationship between national politics and university education in this respect, see Barletta (2002), Bonavena, Califa, and Millán (2007), Burgos (2004), Corbacho and Diaz (2014), and Ghilini (2016).

15 The anthology consists of two major sections, the first comprising a myriad of texts from the early years and the second a series of more bureaucratic proposals for the reformulation of the architectural curriculum, which were produced once their project for university reform was taken up by the administration after Campora's election in 1973. This time would be very short-lived, however. The anthology's compilation and publication by the Department of Pedagogy of the School of Architecture at the UBA would have to be carried out underground due to the military intervention of the faculty in September of 1974 by conservative Peronist factions in the lead-up to the dictatorship of 1976 (the ultra-right Argentine Anticommunist Alliance had already begun assassinating leftists by 1974). The anthology has seen enduring circulation, however, and remains an important text for understanding the history and politics of the FADU. The anthology is available in university bookstores and went into a third edition in 2014. It is not continuously paginated; in my citations, I indicate the volume (v) and the sequential number of the document (D).

16 TUPAU criticized, for example, the tendency of *Summa* to valorize, even in its articles on Argentine architecture, work that fit easily into mainstream canons. While often architecture of undisputed quality in the abstract, the authors found such work distant from the problems and realities that confronted most of the country. And even when the journal dealt with relevant problems such as mass housing, it did so with a focus on Europe without making clear under what criteria a parallel could be drawn for Argentina, "as if the problematic of architecture could be expressed in universal terms in a world deeply torn by internal contradictions" (V1D4).

17 I use *provincialize* in the sense developed by Chakrabarty (2000).

18 The former was an armed branch of the Peronist left, the latter of the Partido Revolucionario de los Trabajadores, or Revolutionary Worker's Party, an Argentine Trotskyist party.

19 TUPAU was formally integrated into the national Joventud Universitaria Peronista, or Peronist University Youth, in 1973.

20 Pedagogic experimentation and an attempt to bring architecture into proximity with the needs of the pueblo were also underway in other parts of the country, where they often developed in different ways, within different institutional and regional political contexts, and with different pedagogic approaches. See, for example, Malecki's (2016) analysis of the Taller Total in Córdoba.

21 One of the many books Juan has written is called *Enseñanza sin Dogma* [Teaching without Dogma] (Molina y Vedia 2008).

22 The cátedra is also often categorized as Peronist, which Juan finds discomforting. Recall that Juan does not identify as a Peronist, but as an anti-anti-Peronist, one who shares many of the Peronist left's commitments to National and Popular projects, but denies formal political identification with the party on several grounds. "Remember that I was jailed by Perón!" he told me once, in addition to citing the party's historical connections with militarism and authoritarianism. His words also provide a corrective to any easy identification between contemporary Peronist political affiliation and the kind of everyday architecture he values. Many pro-development architects with values very different from Juan's and Jaime's find homes within Peronism, and I see no simple correspondence between political affiliation and a claim to inheritance from TUPAU and TANAPO, which were, nevertheless, Peronist projects.

23 There are almost mythical stories that dramatize the contrast within the FADU: an architect I know who trained in the 1990s was told, prior to his third-year juries (in which students are evaluated by professors from three cátedras), of a student who was given a perfect score by his own (professionalist) cátedra for his design of an opulent public plaza. At his jury, however, he received a failing grade from a more political cátedra because his project hadn't taken into account the political and economic context of the plaza in a Third World country like Argentina. In Europe it might have been considered good architecture, but the plaza was in Argentina, and in that political-economic setting, it was not good architecture. In practice, however, such distinctions can be difficult to make. When I asked one of my informants to help me make a list of the political positions of different cátedras, we ended up not with a two-column list, but with a nebulous drawing of a "field of intensities" with a few exemplars at either end, but with most cátedras falling within a blurry, nonlinear middle zone. We both laughed at the outcome. I hadn't read the anthology at the time, but if I had we could have laughed at the difficulty of slotting people clearly into the master categories of architect of the system and architect of the pueblo.

24 This is a nonlinear inheritance that does not observe standard forms of descent: Juan's work was in many ways formative for TANAPO, and both Juan and Jaime were part of that moment in addition to being inheritors of it in the present.

EPILOGUE: ENDURING VALUES

1 Vulture funds purchase defaulted debt at highly discounted prices and then litigate to recover their original face value. Argentina's protracted dispute with these funds over defaulted debt from the crisis ended with a decision in favor of the vulture funds, a decision Kirchner's government had previously made efforts to circumnavigate.

2 Indeed, not long after I wrote these words, Macri announced that the government would again seek loans from the IMF, sending the value of the peso plummeting and abruptly dashing the nascent mortgage market.

3 The zoning allowed for a limited number of square meters of construction with a higher-than-normal height limit. This meant that higher ceilings could be built without sacrificing possible floors of habitable space and opened up possibilities that the standard zoning for high-rise construction did not.

4 Heather Paxson refers to this balance between commercial viability and passion as "surviving with sentiment" (2012, 78–92).

5 The difference is between forms of connection grounded in plurality, in which variety is subsumed by superior unity, and those grounded in multiplicity, or variation that resists totalization (Viveiros de Castro 2010; Viveiros de Castro and Goldman 2012). My words here are inspired in part by what Isabelle Stengers has proposed in her cosmopolitical proposal (2010, 2011). See also de la Cadena (2010, 2015).

WORKS CITED

Abelin, Mireille. 2012. "'Entrenched in the BMW': Argentine Elites and the Terror of Fiscal Obligation." *Public Culture* 24, no. 2: 329–56.

Aboy, Rosa. 2005. *Viviendas Para el Pueblo: Espacio Urbano y Sociabilidad en el Barrio los Perales, 1946–1955*. Buenos Aires: Fondo de Cultura Económica.

Aboy, Rosa. 2007. "'The Right to a Home': Public Housing in Post–World War II Buenos Aires." *Journal of Urban History* 33, no. 3: 493–518.

Abrams, Philip. 1988. "Notes on the Difficulty of Studying the State (1977)." *Journal of Historical Sociology* 1, no. 1: 58–89.

Alexander, Christopher. 1966. "A City Is Not a Tree." *Design* 206.

Alexander, Zeynep Ç. 2017. *Kinaesthetic Knowing: Aesthetics, Epistemology, Modern Design*. Chicago: University of Chicago Press.

Aliata, Fernando. 2006. *La Ciudad Regular: Arquitectura, Programas e Instituciones en el Buenos Aires Posrevolucionario, 1821–1835*. Buenos Aires: Universidad Nacional de Quilmes.

Anand, Nikhil. 2017. *Hydraulic City: Water and the Infrastructures of Citizenship in Mumbai*. Durham, NC: Duke University Press.

Anker, Elizabeth S., and Rita Felski, eds. 2017. *Critique and Postcritique*. Durham, NC: Duke University Press.

Appadurai, Arjun, ed. 1986. *The Social Life of Things: Commodities in Cultural Perspective*. New York: Cambridge University Press.

Archambault, Julie. 2016. "Taking Love Seriously in Human-Plant Relations in Mozambique: Toward an Anthropology of Affective Encounters." *Cultural Anthropology* 31, no. 2: 244–71.

Aretxaga, Begoña. 2003. "Maddening States." *Annual Review of Anthropology* 32, no. 1: 393–410.

Arlt, Roberto. 1993. *Aguafuertes Porteñas: Buenos Aires, Vida Cotidiana*. Buenos Aires: Alianza.

Arnstein, Sherry R. 1969. "A Ladder of Citizen Participation." *Journal of the American Institute of Planners* 35, no. 4: 216–24.

Auyero, Javier. 2001. *Poor People's Politics: Peronist Survival Networks and the Legacy of Evita*. Durham, NC: Duke University Press.

Ballent, Anahi. 2005. *Las Huellas de la Política: Vivienda, Ciudad, Peronismo en Buenos Aires, 1943–1955.* Buenos Aires: Universidad Nacional de Quilmes.

Ballent, Anahi, and Jorge F. Liernur. 2014. *La Casa y la Multitud: Vivienda, Política y Cultura en la Argentina Moderna.* Buenos Aires: Fondo de Cultura Económica.

Ballestero, Andrea. 2012. "Transparency Short-Circuited: Laughter and Numbers in Costa Rican Water Politics." *PoLAR: Political and Legal Anthropology Review* 35, no. 2: 223–41.

Ballestero, Andrea. 2015. "The Ethics of a Formula: Calculating a Financial-Humanitarian Price for Water." *American Ethnologist* 42, no. 2: 262–78.

Barletta, Ana M. 2002. "Una Izquierda Universitaria Peronista: Entre la Demanda Académica y la Demanda Política (1968–1973)." *Prismas: Revista de Historia Intelectual* 6: 275–86.

Becker, Edgardo. 2008. "Hormigón Para Arquitectos: Tecnología, Estructura y Forma." *Clarín* ARQ, April 22.

Ben-Joseph, Eran. 2005. *The Code of the City: Standards and the Hidden Language of Place Making.* Cambridge, MA: MIT Press.

Benmergui, Leandro. 2009. "The Alliance for Progress and Housing Policy in Rio De Janeiro and Buenos Aires in the 1960s." *Urban History* 36, no. 2: 303–24.

Besky, Sarah. 2016. "The Future of Price: Communicative Infrastructures and the Financialization of Indian Tea." *Cultural Anthropology* 31, no. 1: 4–29.

Blanco, Javier. 2016. "Ni Tasa ni Dólar: Sólo los Ladrillos Resistieron los Cambios de Modelo." *La Nación*, August 2.

Blaser, Mario. 2009. "The Threat of the Yrmo: The Political Ontology of a Sustainable Hunting Program." *American Anthropologist* 111, no. 1: 10–20.

Blustein, Paul. 2005. *And the Money Kept Rolling In (and Out): Wall Street, the IMF, and the Bankrupting of Argentina.* New York: PublicAffairs.

Bonavena, Pablo, Juan S. Califa, and Mariano Millán, eds. 2007. *El Movimiento Estudiantil Argentino: Historias con Presente.* Buenos Aires: Ediciones Cooperativas.

Borch, Christian, ed. 2014. *Architectural Atmospheres: On the Experience and Politics of Architecture.* Basel: Birkhäuser.

Bores, Tato. 1990. "Tato en Busqueda de la Vereda del Sol: Monólogo 2000." Accessed February 18, 2019. http://www.youtube.com/watch?v=X1rm8I2UT2Y.

Bourdieu, Pierre. 1977. *Outline of a Theory of Practice.* New York: Cambridge University Press.

Branford, Sue, and Bernardo Kucinski. 1988. *The Debt Squads: The US, the Banks, and Latin America.* Atlantic Highlands, NJ: Zed.

Burgos, Raúl. 2004. *Los Gramscianos Argentinos: Cultura y Política en la Experiencia de Pasado y Presente.* Buenos Aires: Siglo XXI.

Çalışkan, Koray. 2010. *Market Threads: How Cotton Farmers and Traders Create a Global Commodity.* Princeton, NJ: Princeton University Press.

Callon, Michel. 1986. "Some Elements of a Sociology of Translation: Domestication of the Scallops and the Fishermen of St. Brieuc Bay." In *Power, Action and Belief: A New Sociology of Knowledge*, edited by J. Law, 196–233. New York: Routledge.

Callon, Michel, ed. 1998. *The Laws of the Markets.* Oxford: Blackwell.

Candea, Matei, ed. 2010. *The Social after Gabriel Tarde: Debates and Assessments.* New York: Routledge.

Carse, Ashley. 2014. *Beyond the Big Ditch: Politics, Ecology, and Infrastructure at the Panama Canal*. Cambridge, MA: MIT Press.

Castro, Ángeles. 2012. "Buenos Aires, Ciudad Monoambiente." *La Nación*, June 10.

Centner, Ryan. 2012. "Moving Away, Moving Onward: Displacement Pressures and Divergent Neighborhood Politics in Buenos Aires." *Environment and Planning A* 44, no. 11: 2555–73.

Chakrabarty, Dipesh. 2000. *Provincializing Europe: Postcolonial Thought and Historical Difference*. Princeton, NJ: Princeton University Press.

Choay, Françoise. 1969. *The Modern City: Planning in the Nineteenth Century*. New York: George Braziller.

Choi, Vivian. 2015. "Anticipatory States: Tsunami, War, and Insecurity in Sri Lanka." *Cultural Anthropology* 30, no. 2: 286–309.

Choy, Timothy K. 2005. "Articulated Knowledges: Environmental Forms after Universality's Demise." *American Anthropologist* 107, no. 1: 5–18.

Choy, Timothy K. 2011. *Ecologies of Comparison: An Ethnography of Endangerment in Hong Kong*. Durham, NC: Duke University Press.

Chronopoulos, Themis. 2011. "The Neoliberal Political–Economic Collapse of Argentina and the Spatial Fortification of Institutions in Buenos Aires, 1998–2010." *City: Analysis of Urban Trends, Culture, Theory, Policy, Action* 15, no. 5: 509–31.

Chu, Julie Y. 2010. "The Attraction of Numbers: Accounting for Ritual Expenditures in Fuzhou, China." *Anthropological Theory* 10, no. 1–2: 132–42.

Chumley, Lily H. 2016. *Creativity Class: Art School and Culture Work in Postsocialist China*. Princeton, NJ: Princeton University Press.

Ciccolella, P., and L. Baer. 2008. "Buenos Aires Tras la Crisis: Hacia una Metrópolis Más Integradora o Más Excluyente?" *Ciudad y Territorio: Estudios Territoriales* 157: 641–60.

Comisión Especial de la Cámara de Diputados 2001. 2005. *Fuga de Divisas en la Argentina: Informe Final*. Buenos Aires: Siglo XXI Editores Argentina.

Corbacho, Mariano, dir. 2016. *70 y Pico*. Buenos Aires: Colorín Colorado Producciones. DVD.

Corbacho, Mariano, and Juan P. Diaz. 2014. "Arquitectura y Dependencia: Vida y Obra de la TUPAU." Paper presented at V Jornadas de Estudio y Reflexión Sobre el Movimiento Estudiantil Argentino y Latinoamericano, Mar del Plata, Argentina, November. Accessed February 10, 2017. http://conflictosocialiigg.sociales.uba.ar/wp-content/uploads/sites/72/2018/05/5-CorbachoyOtros.pdf.

Corsín Jiménez, Alberto, and Adolfo Estalella. 2013. "The Atmospheric Person: Value, Experiment, and 'Making Neighbors' in Madrid's Popular Assemblies." *Hau: Journal of Ethnographic Theory* 3, no. 2: 119–39.

Cronon, William. 1991. *Nature's Metropolis: Chicago and the Great West*. New York: W. W. Norton.

Cvetkovich, Ann. 2012. *Depression: A Public Feeling*. Durham, NC: Duke University Press.

Das, Veena. 2006. *Life and Words: Violence and the Descent into the Ordinary*. Berkeley: University of California Press.

Das, Veena, and Deborah Poole, eds. 2004. *Anthropology in the Margins of the State*. Santa Fe, NM: School of American Research Press.

Daston, Lorraine, and Peter Galison. 2007. *Objectivity*. New York: Zone.

D'Avella, Nicholas. 2014. "Ecologies of Investment: Crisis Histories and Brick Futures in Argentina." *Cultural Anthropology* 29, no. 1: 173–99.

D'Avella, Nicholas. 2016. "Manifestations of the Market: Public Audiences and the Cosmopolitics of Voice in Buenos Aires." In *Urban Cosmopolitics: Agencements, Assemblies, Atmospheres*, edited by A. Blok and I. Farías, 105–24. London: Routledge.

D'Avella, Nicholas. 2018. "How to Care for a Park with Birds: Birdwatchers' Ecologies in Buenos Aires." In *Living with Animals: Bonds across Species*, edited by N. Porter and I. Gershon, 236–48. Ithaca, NY: Cornell University Press.

de Certeau, Michel. 1984. *The Practice of Everyday Life*. Berkeley: University of California Press.

de la Barra, Ximena, and Richard A. Dello Buono. 2009. *Latin America after the Neoliberal Debacle: Another Region Is Possible*. Lanham, MD: Rowman and Littlefield.

de la Cadena, Marisol. 2010. "Indigenous Cosmopolitics in the Andes: Conceptual Reflections beyond 'Politics.'" *Cultural Anthropology* 25, no. 2: 334–70.

de la Cadena, Marisol. 2015. *Earth Beings: Ecologies of Practice across Andean Worlds*. Durham, NC: Duke University Press.

DeLanda, Manuel. 2002. *Intensive Science and Virtual Philosophy*. New York: Continuum.

Deleuze, Gilles, and Félix Guattari. 1987. *A Thousand Plateaus: Capitalism and Schizophrenia*. Translated by Brian Massumi. Minneapolis: University of Minnesota Press.

Departamento Pedagógico, Facultad de Arquitectura y Urbanismo, Universidad Nacional de Buenos Aires. 1974. *Antología Pedagógica: Cuatro Años de Producción Político-Pedagógica del Peronismo en la Facultad de Arquitectura de Buenos Aires Volcados en Quince Meses de Gobierno Popular de la Universidad*.

Diez, Fernando E. 1996. *Buenos Aires y Algunas Constantes en las Transformaciones Urbanas*. Buenos Aires: Fundación Editorial de Belgrano.

Dodero, Marta. 2006. "Memoria y Balance de la Desaparición de la Carrera de Planificación Urbana y Regional." Accessed July 23, 2014. http://documentosapevu .blogspot.com/2007/03/objetivos-del-trabajo-documentar-un.html.

Dodero, Marta. 2007. "Informe Crítico al Plan Urbano Ambiental." Accessed July 24, 2014. http://documentosapevu.blogspot.com/2007/03/informe-crtico-al-pua-07 -marta-dodero.html.

DuBois, Lindsay. 2005. *The Politics of the Past in an Argentine Working-Class Neighborhood*. Toronto: University of Toronto Press.

Duménil, Gérard, and Dominique Lévy. 2011. *The Crisis of Neoliberalism*. Cambridge, MA: Harvard University Press.

Dumit, Joseph. 2004. *Picturing Personhood: Brain Scans and Biomedical Identity*. Princeton, NJ: Princeton University Press.

Durand, Daniel. 2004. *El cielo de Boedo*. Buenos Aires: Ediciones Gog y Magog.

Elena, Eduardo. 2011. *Dignifying Argentina*. Pittsburgh: University of Pittsburgh Press.

Elinoff, Eli. 2016. "A House Is More Than a House: Aesthetic Politics in a Northeastern Thai Railway Settlement." *Journal of the Royal Anthropological Institute* 22, no. 3: 610–32.

Elyachar, Julia. 2012. "Before (and after) Neoliberalism: Tacit Knowledge, Secrets of the Trade, and the Public Sector in Egypt." *Cultural Anthropology* 27, no. 1: 76–96.

Espeland, Wendy N., and Mitchell L. Stevens. 1998. "Commensuration as a Social Process." *Annual Review of Sociology* 24: 313–43.

Estalella, Adolfo, and Alberto Corsín Jiménez. 2014. "Assembling Neighbors: The City as Hardware, Method, and 'A Very Messy Kind of Archive.'" *Common Knowledge* 20, no. 1: 150–71.

Farías, Ignacio, and Alex Wilkie, eds. 2016. *Studio Studies: Operations, Topologies and Displacements*. London: Routledge.

Faulk, Karen A. 2012. *In the Wake of Neoliberalism: Citizenship and Human Rights in Argentina*. Stanford, CA: Stanford University Press.

Fennell, Catherine. 2015. *Last Project Standing: Civics and Sympathy in Post-Welfare Chicago*. Minneapolis: University of Minnesota Press.

Ferguson, James. 1994. *The Anti-Politics Machine: "Development," Depoliticization, and Bureaucratic Power in Lesotho*. Minneapolis: University of Minnesota Press.

Fridman, Daniel. 2010. "A New Mentality for a New Economy: Performing the Homo Economicus in Argentina (1976–83)." *Economy and Society* 39, no. 2: 271–302.

Fridman, Daniel. 2016. *Freedom from Work: Embracing Financial Self-Help in the United States and Argentina*. Stanford, CA: Stanford University Press.

Gaggero, Alejandro, and Pablo Nemiña. 2013. "El Origen de la Dolarización Inmobiliaria en la Argentina." In *Cultura Social del Dólar*, edited by A. Kaufman, 47–58. Buenos Aires: Departamento de Publicaciones, Facultad de Derecho y Ciencias Sociales.

Gambetta, Curt. 2013. "Material Movement: Cement and the Globalization of Material Technologies." *Scapegoat* 2: 26–28.

Gazzoli, Ruben. 2006. "Submercado De Viviendas en Alquiler." *Medio Ambiente y Urbanización* 65, no. 1: 49–62.

Ghannam, Farha. 2002. *Remaking the Modern: Space, Relocation, and the Politics of Identity in a Global Cairo*. Berkeley: University of California Press.

Ghilini, Anabela. 2016. "La Sociología Argentina en los Años Sesenta: Las Cátedras Nacionales, Proyección Editorial y Circulación de Ideas." *Trabajo y Sociedad* 28: 1–16.

Giambartolomei, Mauricio. 2015. "Viviendas: Sin Acceso al Crédito, Una de Cada Tres Familias Alquila." *La Nación*, December 20.

Gibson-Graham, J. K. 1996. *The End of Capitalism (As We Knew It): A Feminist Critique of Political Economy*. Minneapolis: University of Minnesota Press.

Gibson-Graham, J. K. 2006. *A Postcapitalist Politics*. Minneapolis: University of Minnesota Press.

Gordillo, Gastón R. 2004. *Landscapes of Devils: Tensions of Place and Memory in the Argentinean Chaco*. Durham, NC: Duke University Press.

Gordillo, Gastón R. 2014. *Rubble: The Afterlife of Destruction*. Durham, NC: Duke University Press.

Gorelik, Adrián. 2001. *La Grilla y el Parque: Espacio Público y Cultura Urbana en Buenos Aires, 1887–1936*. Buenos Aires: Universidad Nacional de Quilmes.

Graeber, David. 2001. *Toward an Anthropological Theory of Value: The False Coin of Our Own Dreams*. New York: Palgrave.

Graeter, Stefanie. 2017. "To Revive an Abundant Life: Catholic Science and Neoextractivist Politics in Peru's Mantaro Valley." *Cultural Anthropology* 32, no. 1: 117–48.

Grant, Bruce. 2014. "The Edifice Complex: Architecture and the Political Life of Surplus in the New Baku." *Public Culture* 26, no. 3: 501–28.

Grau, Cristina. 1989. *Borges y la Arquitectura*. Madrid: Cátedra.

Grimson, Alejandro. 2008. "The Making of New Urban Borders: Neoliberalism and Protest in Buenos Aires." *Antipode* 40, no. 4: 504–12.

Guano, Emanuela. 2002. "Spectacles of Modernity: Transnational Imagination and Local Hegemonies in Neoliberal Buenos Aires." *Cultural Anthropology* 17, no. 2: 181–209.

Guariano, Julián. 2009. "Dólar y Colchonismo, el Imbatible Combo de Ahorro Argentino del que Keynes Renegaba." *Cronista*, September 17.

Gutiérrez, Ramón. 2014. "La Arquitectura en la Argentina (1965–2000)—Parte 2." *Arquitextos* 15, no. 169: 1–25.

Gutman, Margarita, and Michael Cohen, eds. 2007. *América Latina en Marcha: La Transición Postneoliberal*. Buenos Aires: Ediciones Infinito.

Guyer, Jane I. 2004. *Marginal Gains: Monetary Transactions in Atlantic Africa*. Chicago: University of Chicago Press.

Guyer, Jane I., Naveeda Khan, Juan Obarrio, Caroline Bledsoe, Julie Chu, Souleymane Bachir Diagne, Keith Hart, Paul Kockelman, Jean Lave, Caroline McLoughlin, Bill Maurer, Federico Neiburg, Diane Nelson, Charles Stafford, and Helen Verran. 2010. "Introduction: Number as Inventive Frontier." *Anthropological Theory* 10, no. 1–2: 36–61.

Hacking, Ian. 1983. *Representing and Intervening: Introductory Topics in the Philosophy of Natural Science*. New York: Cambridge University Press.

Han, Clara. 2011. "Symptoms of Another Life: Time, Possibility, and Domestic Relations in Chile's Credit Economy." *Cultural Anthropology* 26, no. 1: 7–32.

Haraway, Donna. 1988. "Situated Knowledges: The Science Question in Feminism and the Privilege of Partial Perspective." *Feminist Studies* 14, no. 3: 575–99.

Haraway, Donna. 1991. *Simians, Cyborgs, and Women: The Reinvention of Nature*. New York: Routledge.

Haraway, Donna. 2003. *The Companion Species Manifesto: Dogs, People, and Significant Otherness*. Chicago: Prickly Paradigm Press.

Hardt, Michael, and Antonio Negri. 2000. *Empire*. Cambridge, MA: Harvard University Press.

Hardt, Michael, and Antonio Negri. 2004. *Multitude: War and Democracy in the Age of Empire*. New York: Penguin.

Harvey, David. 2005. *A Brief History of Neoliberalism*. New York: Oxford University Press.

Harvey, Penelope. 2010. "Cementing Relations: The Materiality of Roads and Public Spaces in Provincial Peru." *Social Analysis* 54, no. 2: 28–46.

Hayden, Cori. 2003. *When Nature Goes Public: The Making and Unmaking of Bioprospecting in Mexico*. Princeton, NJ: Princeton University Press.

Healey, Mark A. 2011. *The Ruins of the New Argentina: Peronism and the Remaking of San Juan after the 1944 Earthquake*. Durham, NC: Duke University Press.

Helmreich, Stefan. 2009. "Intimate Sensing." In *Simulation and Its Discontents*, edited by S. Turkle, 129–50. Cambridge, MA: MIT Press.

Herzfeld, Michael. 2009. *Evicted from Eternity: The Restructuring of Modern Rome*. Chicago: University of Chicago Press.

Hetherington, Kregg. 2011. *Guerrilla Auditors: The Politics of Transparency in Neoliberal Paraguay*. Durham, NC: Duke University Press.

Hinchliffe, Steve, and Sarah Whatmore. 2006. "Living Cities: Towards a Politics of Conviviality." *Science as Culture* 15, no. 2: 123–38.

Ho, Karen. 2005. "Situating Global Capitalisms: A View from Wall Street Investment Banks." *Cultural Anthropology* 20, no. 1: 68–96.

Ho, Karen. 2009. *Liquidated: An Ethnography of Wall Street*. Durham, NC: Duke University Press.

Holston, James. 1989. *The Modernist City: An Anthropological Critique of Brasília*. Chicago: University of Chicago Press.

Hull, Matthew S. 2012. *Government of Paper: The Materiality of Bureaucracy in Urban Pakistan*. Berkeley: University of California Press.

Irani, Lilly. 2019. *Chasing Innovation: Making Entrepreneurial Citizens in Modern India*. Princeton, NJ: Princeton University Press.

Jacobs, Jane. 1961. *The Death and Life of Great American Cities*. New York: Random House.

Jajamovich, Guillermo. 2011. "Arquitectos Proyectistas y Transición Democrática: El Concurso de las '20 Ideas Para Buenos Aires.'" *Anales del IAA* 41: 203–12.

Jajamovich, Guillermo. 2012a. "Intercambios Internacionales, Estrategias Urbanísticas y Aspectos Políticos: España, Buenos Aires, y Rosario (1979–1993)." *Revista Iberoamericana de Urbanismo* 7: 19–30.

Jajamovich, Guillermo. 2012b. "Universidad y Transición Democrática: Reformas Curriculares y Reconfiguraciones en la Facultad de Arquitectura y Urbanismo de la Universidad de Buenos Aires (1984–1987)." *Cuestiones de Sociología* 8: 1–19.

Jajamovich, Guillermo, and Luján Menazzi. 2012. "Políticas Urbanas en un Contexto de Dictadura Militar: Algunos Interrogantes a Partir de Buenos Aires (1976–1983)." *Bitácora* 1: 11–20.

James, Daniel. 1994. *Resistance and Integration: Peronism and the Argentine Working Class, 1946–1976*. New York: Cambridge University Press.

James, William. 1996. *Essays in Radical Empiricism*. Lincoln: University of Nebraska Press.

Jensen, Casper B. 2015. "Experimenting with Political Materials: Environmental Infrastructures and Ontological Transformations." *Distinktion: Scandinavian Journal of Social Theory* 16, no. 1: 17–30.

Jones, Caroline A., and Peter Galison, eds. 1998. *Picturing Science, Producing Art*. New York: Routledge.

Judson, Ruth. 2012. "Crisis and Calm: Demand for U.S. Currency at Home and Abroad from the Fall of the Berlin Wall to 2011." *Board of Governors of the Federal Reserve System International Finance Discussion Papers* 1058: 1–47.

Kaiser, David. 2005. *Drawing Theories Apart: The Dispersion of Feynman Diagrams in Postwar Physics*. Chicago: University of Chicago Press.

Kaufman, Alejandro, ed. 2013. *Cultura Social del Dólar*. Buenos Aires: Departamento de Publicaciones, Facultad de Derecho y Ciencias Sociales.

Klein, Naomi. 2007. *The Shock Doctrine: The Rise of Disaster Capitalism*. New York: Metropolitan.

Klima, Alan. 2002. *The Funeral Casino: Meditation, Massacre, and Exchange with the Dead in Thailand*. Princeton, NJ: Princeton University Press.

Knorr Cetina, Karin, and Urs Bruegger. 2002. "Global Microstructures: The Virtual Societies of Financial Markets." *American Journal of Sociology* 107, no. 4: 905–50.

Kockelman, Paul. 2016. *The Chicken and the Quetzal: Incommensurate Ontologies and Portable Values in Guatemala's Cloud Forest*. Durham, NC: Duke Univeristy Press.

Koolhaas, Rem, and Bruce Mau. 1998. *S, M, L, XL*. New York: Monacelli.

Kovensky, Martín. 2002. *Limbo: Argentina 2002, Un Relato en Imágenes*. Mexico City: Fondo de Cultura Económica.

Kusno, Abidin. 2000. *Behind the Postcolonial: Architecture, Urban Space, and Political Cultures in Indonesia*. New York: Routledge.

Kwak, Nancy. 2015. *A World of Homeowners: American Power and the Politics of Housing Aid*. Chicago: University of Chicago Press.

Langer, Sergio, and Rubén Mira. 2006. *La Nelly: Argentinísima!!* Buenos Aires: Del Nuevo Extremo.

Larkin, Brian. 2008. *Signal and Noise: Media, Infrastructure, and Urban Culture in Nigeria*. Durham, NC: Duke University Press.

Latour, Bruno. 1988. *Science in Action: How to Follow Scientists and Engineers through Society*. Cambridge, MA: Harvard University Press.

Latour, Bruno. 2004. "Why Has Critique Run Out of Steam? From Matters of Fact to Matters of Concern." *Critical Inquiry* 30, no. 2: 225–48.

Latour, Bruno. 2005. *Reassembling the Social: An Introduction to Actor-Network Theory*. New York: Oxford University Press.

Latour, Bruno, and Vincent A. Lépinay. 2009. *The Science of Passionate Interests: An Introduction to Gabriel Tarde's Economic Anthropology*. Chicago: Prickly Paradigm.

Latour, Bruno, and Albena Yaneva. 2008. "'Give Me a Gun and I Will Make All Buildings Move': An ANT's View of Architecture." In *Explorations in Architecture: Teaching, Design, Research*, edited by R. Geiser, 80–89. Basel: Birkhäuser.

Law, John. 2002. *Aircraft Stories: Decentering the Object in Technoscience*. Durham, NC: Duke University Press.

Law, John, and John Hassard. 1999. *Actor Network Theory and After*. Malden, MA: Blackwell.

Lendoiro, Florencia. 2014. "Un Alquiler en Bs.As. Rinde Igual que un Bono de EE.UU." *Ámbito Financiero*, March 3.

Lépinay, Vincent A. 2011. *Codes of Finance: Engineering Derivatives in a Global Bank*. Princeton, NJ: Princeton University Press.

Levitsky, Steven, and Kenneth M. Roberts, eds. 2011. *The Resurgence of the Latin American Left*. Baltimore: Johns Hopkins University Press.

Lewis, Avi, dir., and Naomi Klein. 2004. *The Take*. Toronto: Barna-Alper Productions. DVD.

Liernur, Jorge F. 2008. *Arquitectura en la Argentina del Siglo XX: La Construcción de la Modernidad*. Buenos Aires: Fondo Nacional de las Artes.

Liernur, Jorge F., and Pablo Pschepiurca. 2008. *La Red Austral: Obras y Proyectos de Le Corbusier y Sus Discipulos en la Argentina (1924–1965)*. Bernal: Universidad Nacional de Quilmes.

Logan, Tim. 2014. "L.A. Is Working on Major Zoning Code Revamp." *Los Angeles Times*, July 30.

Luzzi, Mariana. 2010. "Las Monedas de la Crisis: Pluralidad Monetaria en la Argentina de 2001." *Revista de Ciencias Sociales* 2: 205–21.

Luzzi, Mariana, and Ariel Wilkis. 2018. "Soybean, Bricks, Dollars, and the Reality of Money: Multiple Monies during Currency Exchange Restrictions in Argentina (2011–15)." *Hau: Journal of Ethnographic Theory* 8, no. 1: 252–64.

Lyons, Kristina. 2016. "Decomposition as Life Politics: Soils, Selva, and Small Farmers Under the Gun of the U.S.–Colombia War on Drugs." *Cultural Anthropology* 31, no. 1: 56–81.

MacKenzie, Donald, Fabian Muniesa, and Lucia Siu, eds. 2007. *Do Economists Make Markets? On the Performativity of Economics*. Princeton, NJ: Princeton University Press.

Malecki, J. Sebastián. 2016. "Crisis, Radicalización y Política en el Taller Total de Córdoba, 1970–1975." *Prohistoria* 19, no. 25: 79–103.

Manning, Erin. 2016. *The Minor Gesture*. Durham, NC: Duke University Press.

Manzoni, Carlos. 2016. "La Paradoja de los Alquileres: Precios Altos y Rentabilidad Baja." *La Nación*, December 18.

Marcuse, Peter. 1987. "The Grid as City Plan: New York City and Laissez-Faire Planning in the Nineteenth Century." *Planning Perspectives* 2, no. 3: 287–310.

Marshall, Wesley C. 2008. "Foreign Banks and Political Sovereignty: The Case of Argentina." *Review of Political Economy* 20, no. 3: 349–66.

Martínez, Tomás E. 1997. *Santa Evita*. New York: Vintage.

Marx, Karl. 1990. *Capital, Vol. 1: A Critique of Political Economy*. New York: Penguin.

Masco, Joseph. 2006. *Nuclear Borderlands: The Manhattan Project in Post–Cold War New Mexico*. Princeton, NJ: Princeton University Press.

Masiello, Francine. 2001. *The Art of Transition: Latin American Culture and Neoliberal Crisis*. Durham, NC: Duke University Press.

Massumi, Brian. 2002. *Parables for the Virtual: Movement, Affect, Sensation*. Durham, NC: Duke University Press.

Maurer, Bill. 2000. "A Fish Story: Rethinking Globalization on Virgin Gorda, British Virgin Islands." *American Ethnologist* 27, no. 3: 670–701.

Maurer, Bill. 2005. *Mutual Life, Limited: Islamic Banking, Alternative Currencies, Lateral Reason*. Princeton, NJ: Princeton University Press.

Maurer, Bill. 2006. "The Anthropology of Money." *Annual Review of Anthropology* 35, no. 1: 15–36.

Mauss, Marcel. 1966. *The Gift: Forms and Functions of Exchange in Archaic Societies*. London: Cohen and West.

McLean, Stuart. 2009. "Stories and Cosmogonies: Imagining Creativity Beyond 'Nature' and 'Culture.'" *Cultural Anthropology* 24, no. 2: 213–45.

McLoughlin, J. Brian. 1969. *Urban and Regional Planning: A Systems Approach*. London: Faber and Faber.

Menazzi, Luján. 2013. "Ciudad en Dictadura: Procesos Urbanos en la Ciudad de Buenos Aires Durante la Última Dictadura Militar (1976–1983)." *Scripta Nova* 17, no. 429: 1–34.

Mendoza, Marcos. 2016. "Educational Policing: Park Rangers and the Politics of the Green (E)State in Patagonia." *Journal of Latin American and Caribbean Anthropology* 21, no. 1: 173–92.

Mercé, Cayetana. 2007. "Emprender Construyendo: La Propiedad Horizontal en la Práctica Profesional de la Arquitectura." *Summa+* 87: 50–55.

Mialet, Hélène. 2012. *Hawking Incorporated: Stephen Hawking and the Anthropology of the Knowing Subject*. Chicago: University of Chicago Press.

Miller, Marilyn G., ed. 2014. *Tango Lessons: Movement, Sound, Image, and Text in Contemporary Practice*. Durham, NC: Duke University Press.

Mitchell, Timothy. 1991a. *Colonising Egypt*. Berkeley: University of California Press.

Mitchell, Timothy. 1991b. "The Limits of the State: Beyond Statist Approaches and Their Critics." *American Political Science Review* 85, no. 1: 77–96.

Mitchell, Timothy. 2002. *Rule of Experts: Egypt, Techno-Politics, Modernity*. Berkeley: University of California Press.

Miyazaki, Hirokazu. 2013. *Arbitraging Japan: Dreams of Capitalism at the End of Finance*. Berkeley: University of California Press.

Mol, Annemarie. 2002. *The Body Multiple: Ontology in Medical Practice*. Durham, NC: Duke University Press.

Molina y Vedia, Juan. 2008. *Enseñanza sin Dogma*. Buenos Aires: Nobuko.

Monti, Marina. 1997. "La Enseñanza del Diseño Arquitectónico Frente a los Requerimientos del 3er Milenio. Arquitectura: La Crisis de un Proyecto." Paper presented at 2nd Encuentro Nacional: La Universidad Como Objeto de Investigación, Buenos Aires, Argentina. Accessed March 3, 2012. http://www.naya.org.ar/congresos/contenido/cea_1/2/36.htm.

Mouffe, Chantal. 2005. *On the Political*. New York: Routledge.

Muehlmann, Shaylih. 2012. "Rhizomes and Other Uncountables: The Malaise of Enumeration in Mexico's Colorado River Delta." *American Ethnologist* 39, no. 2: 339–53.

Muir, Sarah. 2015. "The Currency of Failure: Money and Middle-Class Critique in Post-Crisis Buenos Aires." *Cultural Anthropology* 30, no. 2: 310–35.

Mumford, Lewis. 1961. *The City in History: Its Origins, Its Transformations, and Its Prospects*. New York: Harcourt Brace Jovanovich.

Munn, Nancy D. 1993. *The Fame of Gawa: A Symbolic Study of Value Transformation in a Massim Society*. Durham, NC: Duke University Press.

Muñoz, José E. 2009. *Cruising Utopia: The Then and There of Queer Futurity*. New York: New York University Press.

Murphy, Keith M. 2004. "Imagination as Joint Activity: The Case of Architectural Interaction." *Mind, Culture, and Activity* 11, no. 4: 267–78.

Murphy, Keith M. 2013. "A Cultural Geometry: Designing Political Things in Sweden." *American Ethnologist* 40, no. 1: 118–31.

Murphy, Michelle. 2006. *Sick Building Syndrome and the Problem of Uncertainty: Environmental Politics, Technoscience, and Women Workers*. Durham, NC: Duke University Press.

Musaraj, Smoki. 2011. "Tales from Albarado: The Materiality of Pyramid Schemes in Postsocialist Albania." *Cultural Anthropology* 26, no. 1: 84–110.

Myers, Natasha. 2015. *Rendering Life Molecular*. Durham, NC: Duke University Press.

Nading, Alex M. 2012. "Dengue Mosquitoes Are Single Mothers: Biopolitics Meets Ecological Aesthetics in Nicaraguan Community Health Work." *Cultural Anthropology* 27, no. 4: 572–96.

Neiburg, Federico. 2006. "Inflation: Economists and Economic Cultures in Brazil and Argentina." *Comparative Studies in Society and History* 48, no. 3: 604–33.

Neiburg, Federico. 2010. "Sick Currencies and Public Numbers." *Anthropological Theory* 10, no. 1–2: 96–102.

Nelson, Diane M. 1999. *A Finger in the Wound: Body Politics in Quincentennial Guatemala*. Berkeley: University of California Press.

Neuman, Michael. 1998. "Does Planning Need the Plan?" *Journal of the American Planning Association* 64, no. 2: 208–20.

Nudler, Julio. 2002. "Maldita Casa, Maldito Auto." *Página/12*, February 20.

Otero-Pailos, Jorge. 2010. *Architecture's Historical Turn: Phenomenology and the Rise of the Postmodern*. Minneapolis: University of Minnesota Press.

Ovalle, Lalo. 2014. *Estudio Molina y Vedia + Batlle*. Accessed May 10, 2016. https://www.youtube.com/watch? v=WYXwIiLJ71k.

Page, Joanna. 2009. *Crisis and Capitalism in Contemporary Argentine Cinema*. Durham, NC: Duke University Press.

Pandolfo, Stefania. 1997. *Impasse of the Angels: Scenes from a Moroccan Space of Memory*. Chicago: University of Chicago Press.

Pauls, Alan. 2015. *A History of Money: A Novel*. Brooklyn: Melville House.

Paxson, Heather. 2012. *The Life of Cheese: Creating Food and Value in America*. Berkeley: University of California Press.

Pickering, Andrew. 1995. *The Mangle of Practice*. Chicago: University of Chicago Press.

Picon, Antoine. 2003. "Nineteenth-Century Urban Cartography and the Scientific Ideal: The Case of Paris." *Osiris* 18: 135–49.

Pignarre, Philippe, and Isabelle Stengers. 2011. *Capitalist Sorcery: Breaking the Spell*. Basingstoke, UK: Palgrave Macmillan.

Podalsky, Laura. 2004. *Specular City: Transforming Culture, Consumption, and Space in Buenos Aires, 1955–1973*. Philadelphia: Temple University Press.

Poe, Melissa R., Joyce LeCompte, Rebecca McLain, and Patrick Hurley. 2014. "Urban Foraging and the Relational Ecologies of Belonging." *Social and Cultural Geography* 15, no. 8: 901–19.

Poovey, Mary. 1998. *A History of the Modern Fact: Problems of Knowledge in the Sciences of Wealth and Society*. Chicago: University of Chicago Press.

Porter, Natalie. 2013. "Bird Flu Biopower: Strategies for Multispecies Coexistence in Việt Nam." *American Ethnologist* 40, no. 1: 132–48.

Povinelli, Elizabeth A. 2011. *Economies of Abandonment: Social Belonging and Endurance in Late Liberalism*. Durham, NC: Duke University Press.

Praspaliauskiene, Rima. 2016. "Enveloped Lives: Practicing Health and Care in Lithuania." *Medical Anthropology Quarterly* 30, no. 4: 582–98.

Procupez, Valeria. 2016. "The Perfect Storm: Heat Waves and Power Outages in Buenos Aires." *Public Culture* 28, no. 2: 351–57.

"Protestas de Palermo Despierta." 2008. *Palermo online,* June 1. https://palermonline.com.ar/noticias_2008/nota255_palermo_despierta.htm.

Puig de la Bellacasa, Maria. 2011. "Matters of Care in Technoscience: Assembling Neglected Things." *Social Studies of Science* 41, no. 1: 85–106.

Raffles, Hugh. 2010. *Insectopedia.* New York: Pantheon.

Rancière, Jacques. 1999. *Disagreement: Politics and Philosophy.* Minneapolis: University of Minnesota Press.

Rancière, Jacques. 2004. *The Politics of Aesthetics: The Distribution of the Sensible.* New York: Continuum.

Rancière, Jacques. 2010. *Dissensus: On Politics and Aesthetics.* New York: Continuum.

Redfield, Peter. 2012. "Bioexpectations: Life Technologies as Humanitarian Goods." *Public Culture* 24, no. 1: 157–84.

Reese, Eduardo, Florencia Almanci, Julia del Valle, and Andrés Juan. 2014. "Políticas Habitacionales y la Regulación del Alquiler en Argentina." In *Busco Casa en Arriendo: Promover el Alquiler Tiene Sentido,* edited by Andrés Blanco, Vicente Fretes Cibils, and Andrés Muños, 93–132. Washington, DC: Interamerican Development Bank.

Rheinberger, Hans-Jörg. 2010. *An Epistemology of the Concrete: Twentieth-Century Histories of Life.* Durham, NC: Duke University Press.

Riles, Annelise. 2000. *The Network Inside Out.* Ann Arbor: University of Michigan Press.

Riles, Annelise. 2011. *Collateral Knowledge: Legal Reasoning in the Global Financial Markets.* Chicago: University of Chicago Press.

Ring, Laura. 2006. *Zenana: Everyday Peace in a Karachi Apartment Building.* Chicago: University of Chicago Press.

Rock, David. 2002. "Racking Argentina." *New Left Review* 17: 54–86.

Roddick, Jacqueline. 1988. *The Dance of the Millions: Latin America and the Debt Crisis.* London: Latin America Bureau.

Roitman, Janet. 2005. *Fiscal Disobedience: An Anthropology of Economic Regulation in Central Africa.* Princeton, NJ: Princeton University Press.

Roitman, Janet. 2013. *Anti-Crisis.* Durham, NC: Duke University Press.

Sargent, Charles. 1974. *The Spatial Evolution of Greater Buenos Aires, Argentina, 1870–1930.* Tempe: University of Arizona Press.

Sarlo, Beatriz. 1988. *Una Modernidad Periférica: Buenos Aires 1920 y 1930.* Buenos Aires: Neuva Visión.

Scobie, James. 1974. *Buenos Aires: Plaza to Suburb, 1870–1910.* New York: Oxford University Press.

Scott, James C. 1998. *Seeing Like a State: How Certain Schemes to Improve the Human Condition Have Failed.* New Haven, CT: Yale University Press.

Searle, Llerena G. 2013. "Conflict and Commensuration: Contested Market Making in India's Private Real Estate Development Sector." *International Journal of Urban and Regional Research* 38, no. 1: 60–78.

Sennett, Richard. 1990. *The Conscience of the Eye: The Design and Social Life of Cities*. New York: Alfred Knopf.

Shapiro, Nicholas. 2015. "Attuning to the Chemosphere: Domestic Formaldehyde, Bodily Reasoning, and the Chemical Sublime." *Cultural Anthropology* 30, no. 3: 368–93.

Shaviro, Steven. 2009. *Without Criteria: Kant, Whitehead, Deleuze, and Aesthetics*. Cambridge, MA: MIT Press.

Shever, Elana. 2012. *Resources for Reform: Oil and Neoliberalism in Argentina*. Stanford, CA: Stanford University Press.

Simmel, Georg. 1990. *The Philosophy of Money*. London: Routledge.

Simone, AbdouMaliq. 2004. "People as Infrastructure: Intersecting Fragments in Johannesburg." *Public Culture* 16, no. 3: 407–29.

Solanas, Fernando E., dir. 2004. *Memoria del Saqueo*. Paris: ADR. DVD.

Soriano, Osvaldo. 1989. "Vivir con la Inflación." *Nueva Sociedad* 100: 38–43.

Sorín, Jaime, and Juan Molina y Vedia. 2005. "Yo Alumno, yo Arquitecto: Juan Molina y Vedia Entrevista a Jaime Sorín." *Dirección de Archivos de Arquitectura y Diseño Argentinos*. Accessed May 20, 2016. http://archivosdarentrevistas.blogspot.com/2013/01/arquitecto-jaime-sorin.html.

Srinivas, Smriti. 2001. *Landscapes of Urban Memory: The Sacred and the Civic in India's High-Tech City*. Minneapolis: University of Minnesota Press.

Stengers, Isabelle. 2005a. "Introductory Notes on an Ecology of Practices." *Cultural Studies Review* 11, no. 1: 183–96.

Stengers, Isabelle. 2005b. "The Cosmopolitical Proposal." In *Making Things Public: Atmospheres of Democracy*, edited by B. Latour and P. Weibel, 994–1003. Cambridge, MA: MIT Press.

Stengers, Isabelle. 2010. *Cosmopolitics I*. Minneapolis: University of Minnesota Press.

Stengers, Isabelle. 2011. *Cosmopolitics II*. Minneapolis: University of Minnesota Press.

Stewart, Kathleen. 2007. *Ordinary Affects*. Durham, NC: Duke University Press.

Stewart, Kathleen. 2011. "Atmospheric Attunements." *Environment and Planning D: Society and Space* 29, no. 3: 445–53.

Sticco, Daniel. 2011. "Los Argentinos Acumulan US$ 189.000 Millones en los Colchones." *Infobae*, December 8.

Stoetzer, Bettina. 2018. "Ruderal Ecologies: Rethinking Nature, Migration, and the Urban Landscape in Berlin." *Cultural Anthropology* 33, no. 2: 295–323.

Stout, Noelle. 2016. "Petitioning a Giant: Debt, Reciprocity, and Mortgage Modification in the Sacramento Valley." *American Ethnologist* 43, no. 1: 158–71.

Strathern, Marilyn. 1988. *The Gender of the Gift: Problems with Women and Problems with Society in Melanesia*. Berkeley: University of California Press.

Strathern, Marilyn. 2004. *Partial Connections*. Walnut Creek, CA: AltaMira.

Strathern, Marilyn. 2012. "Eating (and Feeding)." *Cambridge Anthropology* 30, no. 2: 1–14.

Suárez, Odilia E. 1995. *Planes y Códigos Para Buenos Aires, 1925–1985*. Buenos Aires: Secretaría de Extensión Universitaria de la Facultad de Arquitectura y Urbanismo de la Universidad de Buenos Aires.

Svampa, Maristella. 2001. *Los Que Ganaron: La Vida en los Countries y los Barrios Privados*. Buenos Aires: Biblos.

Taussig, Michael T. 1997. *The Magic of the State*. New York: Routledge.

Taussig, Michael T. 2011. *I Swear I Saw This: Drawings in Fieldwork Notebooks, Namely My Own*. Chicago: University of Chicago Press.

Taylor, Diana. 2003. *The Archive and the Repertoire: Performing Cultural Memory in the Americas*. Durham, NC: Duke University Press.

Taylor, Julie M. 1998. *Paper Tangos*. Durham, NC: Duke University Press.

Taylor, Nigel. 1998. *Urban Planning Theory Since 1945*. London: SAGE.

Terranova, Juan, ed. 2007. *Buenos Aires/Escala 1:1: Los Barrios por Sus Escritores*. Buenos Aires: Entropía.

This American Life. 2008. "Episode 355: The Giant Pool of Money." Produced by Alex Blumberg and Adam Davidson. Original air date: May 9. Radio program.

Trouillot, Michel-Rolph. 1995. *Silencing the Past: Power and the Production of History*. Boston: Beacon.

Tsing, Anna L. 2005. *Friction: An Ethnography of Global Connection*. Princeton, NJ: Princeton University Press.

Tsing, Anna L. 2015. *The Mushroom at the End of the World: On the Possibility of Life in Capitalist Ruins*. Princeton, NJ: Princeton University Press.

Turnbull, David. 2000. *Masons, Tricksters and Cartographers*. Amsterdam: Overseas Publishers Association.

Varas, Alberto. 2006. *Buenos Aires: Una Trilogía Metropolitana*. Buenos Aires: Nobuko.

Vargas, Eduardo V. 2010. "Tarde on Drugs, or Measures against *Suicide*." In *The Social after Gabriel Tarde: Debates and Assessments*, edited by M. Candea, 208–29. New York: Routledge.

Verbitsky, Horacio. 1985. *Ezeiza*. Buenos Aires: Contrapunto.

Verran, Helen. 2001. *Science and an African Logic*. Chicago: University of Chicago Press.

Verran, Helen. 2012. "Number." In *Inventive Methods: The Happening of the Social*, edited by C. Lury and N. Wakeford, 110–24. London: Routledge.

Verran, Helen, and Michael Christie. 2011. "Doing Difference Together: Towards a Dialogue with Aboriginal Knowledge Authorities through an Australian Comparative Empirical Philosophical Inquiry." *Culture and Dialogue* 1, no. 2: 21–36.

Vertesi, Janet. 2012. "Seeing Like a Rover: Visualization, Embodiment, and Interaction on the Mars Exploration Rover Mission." *Social Studies of Science* 42, no. 3: 393–414.

Visacovsky, Sergio E. 2010. "'Hasta la Próxima Crisis': Historia Cíclica, Virtudes Genealógicas y la Identidad de Clase Media entre los Afectados por la Debacle Financiera en la Argentina (2001–2002)." *CIDE Documentos de Trabajo*: 1–28.

Vivanco, Jorge. 1988. "Las Escalas." *Trama: Revista de Arquitectura* 22: 54–62.

Viveiros de Castro, Eduardo. 2003. "And." *Manchester Papers in Social Anthropology* 7.

Viveiros de Castro, Eduardo. 2010. "Intensive Filiation and Demonic Alliance." In *Deleuzian Intersections: Science, Technology, and Anthropology*, edited by C. B. Jensen and K. Rødje, 219–53. New York: Berghahn.

Viveiros de Castro, Eduardo, and Marcio Goldman. 2012. "Introduction to Post-Social Anthropology: Networks, Multiplicities, and Symmetrizations." Translated by Ashley Lebner. *Hau: Journal of Ethnographic Theory* 2, no. 1: 421–33.

von Schnitzler, Antina. 2016. *Democracy's Infrastructure: Techno-Politics and Protest after Apartheid*. Princeton, NJ: Princeton University Press.

Weiner, Annette B. 1992. *Inalienable Possessions: The Paradox of Keeping-While-Giving.* Berkeley: University of California Press.

Weiss, Brad. 2016. *Real Pigs: Shifting Values in the Field of Local Pork.* Durham, NC: Duke University Press.

Whitington, Jerome. 2016. "Modernist Infrastructure and the Vital Systems Security of Water: Singapore's Pluripotent Climate Futures." *Public Culture* 28, no. 2: 415–41.

Yaneva, Albena. 2009a. *Made by the Office for Metropolitan Architecture: An Ethnography of Design.* Rotterdam: 010 Publishers.

Yaneva, Albena. 2009b. *The Making of a Building: A Pragmatist Approach to Architecture.* Bern: Peter Lang.

Yaneva, Albena, and Alejandro Zaera-Polo, eds. 2015. *What Is Cosmopolitical Design? Design, Nature, and the Built Environment.* London: Ashgate.

Yujnovsky, Oscar. 1984. *Claves Políticas del Problema Habitacional Argentino, 1955–1981.* Buenos Aires: Grupo Editor Latinoamericano.

Zaiat, Alfredo. 2012. "Por Qué, Cuántos y Quiénes Compraron." *Página/12,* November 4.

Zaloom, Caitlin. 2003. "Ambiguous Numbers: Trading Technologies and Interpretation in Financial Markets." *American Ethnologist* 30, no. 2: 1–15.

Zaloom, Caitlin. 2006. *Out of the Pits: Traders and Technology from Chicago to London.* Chicago: University of Chicago Press.

Zaloom, Caitlin. 2009. "How to Read the Future: The Yield Curve, Affect, and Financial Prediction." *Public Culture* 21, no. 2: 245–68.

Zee, Jerry. 2017. "Holding Patterns: Sand and Political Time at China's Desert Shores." *Cultural Anthropology* 32, no. 2: 215–41.

Zeiderman, Austin. 2016. *Endangered City: The Politics of Security and Risk in Bogotá.* Durham, NC: Duke University Press.

Zelizer, Viviana A. 1994. *The Social Meaning of Money.* New York: Basic Books.

INDEX

....

Page numbers followed by *f* indicate illustrations.

architecture education and students, 18, 20, 28–30; Argentina and, 253n23; attention and, 184–85, 190–91, 192f; bodies and, 181, 211–12, 217; China and, 250n3; curriculum reform and, 252n15; daily life and, 182, 194, 215–17; democracy and, 249n22; elite architecture and, 197, 202, 217–18; ideologies and, 211–18; mass education and, 213–14; materialities and, 186, 193, 194; neoliberalism and, 218–19; participatory democracy and, 249n22; particularity (specificity) of, 186, 187; political history and, 180, 181–82, 194–211, 212, 251n12; popular classes and, 199–200, 217, 228; possibilities and, 218–23, 225; professional practice and, 214; reality and, 218–19; values and, 179–80, 194. *See also* Bárbara; *cátedras*; Design I class; disappearances; drawings; models, architectural; University of Buenos Aires

architecture for everyone, 215, 216, 218, 219

architecture for the majority, 214

architecture of the *pueblo* (of the people) and of the system (*del regimen*), 180–83, 202–4, 206–8, 207f, 210, 211, 217–18, 219, 233, 253n23

the *argentinazo*, 10, 11, 19, 23, 24, 240n19

Argentine Anticommunist Alliance, 252n15

Argentine Central Bank (BCRA), 241n27

Arlt, Roberto, 108, 112, 121

Arnstein, Sherry, 248n20

Arquitectos que no fueron ("Architects That Weren't") (National University of Córdoba's architecture school), 196f

La Arquitectura de Hoy (journal), 150, 151f

arquitectura del regimen. See architecture of the *pueblo*

art, 7, 20, 240n9, 250n6

articulation, 123–24, 126–31, 138, 153, 158–59

art nouveau, 112

"arts of noticing," 96. *See also* attention, noticing and sensitivity

asamblea (popular assembly), 104

athletic clubs, 100–101, 102

ATM example, 24, 25

attention, noticing and sensitivity, 27, 96–97; Amigos del Lago and, 99–101, 103; architecture education and, 184–85, 190–91, 192f; *barrios* and, 94–97; capitalism and, 225; daily life practices and, 103, 107–8, 184–85; eventful presence and, 123; politicization and, 139; to space, 187–88; speculation and,

128–31. *See also* perceptions; perspectives (points of view)

austral (currency), 44, 45, 240n14

automobile traffic, 150, 151f, 152

avant-gardes, 199, 203, 204

Avellaneda blockade, 122, 125

Avenida Directorio, 245n19

Avenida Pedro Goyena, 245n19

Avenida Salvador María del Carril (del Carril), 142, 144–45

balconies, 2, 104, 107, 108f, 113, 141

bancarización (bankization), 52

Banco Hipotecario Nacional (National Mortgage Bank), 55

banking: bricks vs., 54–63; cash vs., 48–51; *la crisis* and, 10–11, 12f, 24, 39, 47–51; histories of, 40, 41, 42–51; Mariela's story and, 1, 32–33, 36–37; practices and, 5, 23, 25; protests and, 48, 49f, 50–51, 51f; storytelling and, 37. *See also corralito*; finance; money; mortgages; savings; Wall Street

banner (FADU), 2, 182, 194–96, 195f, 208, 209

banners, 50, 50f, 104, 122, 125, 139

Bárbara (architecture student), 1–2, 3–4, 5, 9, 15, 23, 29, 183

Baring's Bank, 198, 247n7

Barracas neighborhood, 217

barrios (neighborhoods), 26, 108–9, 138–39, 243n7; architecture education and, 217; attention, noticing and sensitivity and, 94–97; buildings and, 21, 27, 106f, 108–16, 110f, 114f, 115f, 116f, 126; bureaucracies and, 137; city and nature and, 94–96; construction boom and, 26–27; *cordial* (polite), 118, 120–21; critique and, 19–20; culture and, 139; dreams, concrete, and, 119–20; history and, 97, 117–18, 121, 128, 138, 139, 247n8; participatory democracy and, 226; particularity (specificity) of, 109, 117–18; *pintoresco*, 119, 120–21; politics and culture and, 11, 13, 26–27, 104–5, 116–21, 127, 128, 139; practices and, 27; *reo* (rough), 119; scale and, 229–30; values and, 9, 26–27, 134–35, 138, 139. *See also* codes; daily (quotidian) life; particularity (specificity); SOS Caballito; *vecino* groups; *vecinos; and individual neighborhoods*

barrios (neighborhoods), specific: Abasto, 243n7; Barracas, 217; Belgrano, 26, 246n25; Flores, 112; Liniers, 217; La Matanza, 217; Palermo, 26, 120, 127, 186, 187f; Parque

Patricios, 217; Saavedra, 122; San Telmo, 243n7; Villa Urquiza, 26, 163, 243n7

barter economies, 47

"Basics for a Political-Technical Project of Mass Construction with Popular Participation" ("Little Red Book of Architecture") (Estrella Gutiérrez), 206, 207f

BCRA (Argentine Central Bank), 241n27

being, metaphysics of, 38, 41

"being-in-society" vs. "thing-in-itself," 203

Belgrano neighborhood, 26, 246n25

Benedetti, Mario, 233

big corral. See corralito

birds, 97, 103, 108, 112, 243n6

black market (dólar blue), 224

blockades, 10, 48, 122, 125, 138, 174, 223

Blustein, Paul, 240n18

BODEN bonds, 49, 50

bodies: architecture and architects and, 29, 221; architecture education and, 181, 211, 217; disappearances and, 251n8; market-based possibilities and, 220; mind and, 235n2; protests and, 10. See also drawings (planos): en carne propia; models, architectural

bonds, 35, 45, 49–50, 58, 224, 240n20

Bonex bonds, 45

Bores, Tato, 44

Borges, Jorge Luis, 120, 121, 199, 244n15; Jorge Guillermo Borges (father), 198

Bosques de Palermo. See Parque 3 de Febrero

Bouvard, Joseph-Antoine, 150

Brazil, 15, 51, 224

bribes and corruption, 28, 161–62, 170, 171, 172, 174–76, 177, 224. See also city government; codes: authorship of; development and developers

bricks (ladrillos) (investments): banks vs., 54–63; cash and, 57–58, 59, 241n27; constitutive relationality and, 38; la crisis and after, 222; graphs and, 80–88, 82f, 84f, 85f, 87f; history of investment and, 54–58; knowledge and reality and, 62; liquid assets vs., 90, 91; pesos/U.S. dollars and, 63f, 83, 84f, 226; possibilities and, 34; U.S. dollars and, 61–62, 63f, 80–81. See also banking; cash; construction boom; homes; Mariela's story; pequeños ahorristas; real estate investment; savings; stability; values

bubbles (economic), 35, 89

Buenos Aires, 10, 149–50. See also barrios (neighborhoods); buildings; history; planning, urban; politics; porteños (residents of Buenos Aires)

Buenos Aires: Una Trilogia Metropolitana (Varas), 158–59

Buenos Aires y Algunas Constantes en las Transformaciones Urbanas (Diez), 109, 111f, 111–12

"Building, Dwelling, Thinking" (Heidegger), 199

building and loan companies, 247n8

buildings: appearances of, 28; architecture student values and, 181; barrios and, 21, 27, 106f, 108–16, 110f, 114f, 115f, 116f, 126; as center of analysis, 9, 236n5; charts and graphs and, 92; disagreement and, 9; ecology of practice and, 21; la crisis and, 23; materialities and, 6, 186; partial connections and, 66; practices and, 236n5; quantification and, 91; relationality and, 213; singularity vs. multiplicity and, 236n5; storytelling and, 41–42; value of, 26–27. See also codes; construction boom; historic preservation; low-rise buildings; planning, urban; tall buildings

bureaucracy: barrios and, 137; citizen participation vs., 159; codes and, 145, 146, 154–55; corruption and, 171; documents and, 235n2; dreams and regulation and, 152–53; economic interests and, 146; experts and, 164; Mariela's story and, 36; planning and codes and, 28–29, 146, 175; power and, 172–73; Salvemos al Barrio and, 174–75; transparency and, 171–73. See also city government; codes; General Directorate Registry of Construction and Cadastre (DGROC)

business schools, 76, 77, 88, 90, 92

búsqueda (a searching), 204, 229, 232

Caballito neighborhood. See SOS Caballito and Caballito neighborhood

Cabrera, Quintín, 135

Caiga Quien Caiga (Fall Who May) (CQC), 175

Çalışkan, Koray, 242n3

call and response rituals, 209

Cámpora, Héctor, 205, 252n15

capitalism: architecture and, 197; la crisis and, 10–11; critique and, 20–21; domesticity and, 245n20; eventful presence of, 225; Gibson-Graham on, 238n19; global

la crisis (2001) and after, 9–13, 12f, 23–24,
63–65, 83, 84f; architects and, 228–30;
Argentine cinema and, 240n9; artwork
and, 12f, 240n9; banks and, 10–11, 12f, 24,
39, 47–51; *corredor verde* and, 122; developers and, 59, 237n13; digital vs. print media
and, 64; dreams and hopes and, 180; free
market development and, 130; history
and, 16–17; major-key histories and, 13, 16;
minor key and, 20, 23–30; mortgages and,
28–29, 59–60, 241n28; neoliberalism and, 8,
10, 17; possibilities and, 13, 19, 128, 228–33;
prices and, 241n25; privatization and, 128;
real estate market and, 229; *Reporte Inmobiliario* and, 77–78; savings and, 51–54;
used housing prices, 82f; values and, 23,
27, 222–28; Wall Street and, 240n18; water
services and, 127. *See also* bricks; devaluations of peso; Kirchner, Nestor; Macri,
Mauricio; Mariela's story
critique, 19–20, 238n15, 240n9
Croce, Benedetto, 199
Cronon, William, 242n7
cross-sections, 188–89, 189f, 190–91, 193
Cruces, Juan José, 241n27
C3II, 141, 142, 144–45, 171, 173, 177, 246n2
Cuba, 200
cultural center example, 1–2
cultural heritage, 127
cultural relativism, 232
culture, 104–5, 116–21, 127, 139, 212–13, 236n5,
251n9. *See also* daily (quotidian) life; poetry,
literature, and music; tango
currencies, national, 41–51, 224, 240n14,
241n24. *See also* pesos/U.S. dollars
currency reserves (after 2008), 223–24
Cvetkovich, Ann, 245n20

daily (quotidian) life: *Aguafuertes Porteñas*
and, 112; architecture and, 212–14; architecture education and, 182, 194, 215–17;
barrios and, 96; construction boom and,
105–6; drawing and, 183–84, 210, 213–14;
the exceptional and, 96; inflation and, 43;
Lago de Regatas and, 103; models and, 221;
planning and codes and, 5; poetry and, 138;
popular classes and, 218; public arena and,
245n20; talk about money and, 240n9;
value and, 5; Yupanqui and, 30. *See also*
collective life and collective well-being;
gardens, patios, and terraces; good life

(quality of life); inflation; intimate social
spaces; minor and major keys; particularity
(specificity); Patricia *and other individuals*;
storytelling
Daniel (real estate investment expert), 52,
59, 70
The Death and Life of Great American Cities
(Jacobs), 159
debt, foreign, 33, 46, 224, 240n20, 241n25.
See also defaults; International Monetary
Fund
Deby (FADU professor), 182–83, 186, 220
decada ganada (decade gained), 8
de Certeau, Michel, 153
decks, 116, 116f
defaults, 10, 35, 37, 40, 47, 48–49, 222–23,
240n18, 253n1
de la Cadena, Marisol, 21
del Carril (Avenida Salvador María del Carril), 142, 144–45
Deleuze, Gilles, 18, 238n14, 238n20, 249n27
democracy, 208. *See also* participatory
democracy
densification, 112
Department of Pedagogy of the School of
Architecture, 202, 252n15, 253n23
depression (public feeling), 245n20
derivatives, 242n3
Design I class, 179, 183, 211, 214–18, 219, 249n1.
See also drawings; models, architectural;
Molina y Vedia–Sorín (*cátedra*)
devaluations of peso: "betting on dollar"
and, 61; bricks vs., 59; *la crisis* and after,
25, 42–43, 43f, 86, 87f; history and, 25, 34;
inflation of 1970s and, 42–43, 43f; Mariela
and, 33, 37; 1970s, 240n12; 1980s, 241n25;
relationality among people and, 39; trade
and, 46. *See also* inflation
development and developers: architects and,
29, 59, 219, 229, 231, 253n22; barrios and,
243n7; Caballito and, 138; city government and, 122–23, 128; corruption and,
170; credit and, 247n8; *la crisis* and after,
59, 237n13; green space and, 136f; outdoor
ecologies and, 107; political activism and,
28, 221; properties vs. multi-unit buildings
and, 244n16; protests and, 135, 137; public
audience and, 168; railroad lands and,
122–23; war of attrition and, 249n26. *See
also* codes; construction boom; *La Nelly*;
private property; speculation

dictatorships. *See* military governments/
dictatorships
Diego (small business manager), 52–53, 64
Dieguez, Tristán, 229
Diez, Fernando, 109, 111f, 111–12, 113, 246n25
difference, 75, 91, 237n5. *See also* divergence;
emergence; minor and major keys; particularity (specificity); situating/situated
digital vs. print media, 50, 64. *See also* cash
Directorate of Archives of Argentine Architecture and Design (DAR), 201
disagreement, 9
disappearances, 17, 209; architecture education
and students and, 30, 194–96, 195f, 196f, 208;
banner and, 2; bodies and, 251n8; FADU
banner and, 2, 182, 194–96, 195f, 208, 209;
held present, 209, 219; Kirchner recalls, 13;
I. Perón and, 208; TANAPO and, 197
The Distribution of the Sensible (Rancière), 7
divergence: architecture and, 212; buildings
and, 236n5; characterized, 21; of cultural
production, 236n5; currencies and, 46;
materialities and, 64; media of investment and, 64; practices and, 5, 21, 22, 30,
31, 236n5; real estate market analysis and,
69–70; small investors and, 92; songs
and, 30; values and, 3, 9, 21, 23–30, 31,
181, 231, 234, 238n19. *See also* difference;
emergence
documents, 235n2
"doing difference together," 31, 232
"doing relations," 69
dólar blue (black markets), 224
dollarization, 241n29
"do memory" (*hacer memoria*), 41
domesticity, 126, 245n20
dónde están parados ("where they are standing"), 213
Dosplaza complex, 134–35, 136f
drainpipe, 100–101, 102
drawings: *aquí y ahora* (here and now),
214–18, 219; bodies and, 181, 182–94;
bureaucracy and, 235n2; caring for the
possible and, 220–21; concrete dreams and,
220–21; daily life and, 183–84, 210, 213–14;
dreams and, 7; *en carne propia*, 182–84,
188–90, 193–94, 210, 211–12, 214–15, 217,
219–20; guiding plans and, 152–53; history
of planning and, 145, 147, 148f, 150–52, 151f;
knowledge and, 235n2; planos, 157, 181, 210;
plans and codes and, 154, 157, 159; politics

and, 29, 153, 211–12, 213; postmodern epistemology and, 158; realities and, 219; science
compared, 250n6; student projects, 215–17;
values and, 181
dreams, concrete, 6–8; ceiling on, 130, 132f;
la crisis and after, 180; of democratic
planning, 178; drawing and modeling and,
220; histories and ethnographies and, 31;
Japanese traders and, 65; Kirchner's, 13,
16; materiality and, 7, 31, 66, 93; minor
keys and, 31, 139; Sergio and Adrián and,
225; singing and, 234; *vecinos* and, 226–27.
See also charts (spreadsheets); codes;
drawings; graphs; models, architectural;
planning, urban; possibilities; protests;
storytelling; values
Durand, Daniel, 94–96, 107, 116, 121, 138

ecological collapse, 130, 132f
ecological concerns, 117
ecological reserves, 162, 233. *See also* Parque 3
de Febrero
ecologies, 184, 213, 239n21. *See also* practices
ecology of investments, 37–41; BODEN and, 49;
bricks and, 40–41, 54–62, 64; *colchonismo*
(mattressism) and, 51–54; *la crisis* and after,
222; global economy and, 39–40; Mariela's
story and, 32–33; mortgages vs. cash and,
35–37; objects and, 38; savings after 2001
and, 51–54; storytelling and, 41, 42–51,
62–66; values and, 65. *See also* bricks; history; particularity (specificity); practices;
relationality and connection; savings
ecology vs. environment, 238n18
economic epochs/events, 87f, 92. *See also la crisis* (2001) and after; history; neoliberalism
economic life, 242n30
economic policy, 8, 10. *See also* neoliberalism
economic/political interests, 146, 147, 161,
162–63, 177. *See also* corporations; corruption and bribes; speculation
economic theory, 91, 241n30. *See also* numbers
and calculation; supply-and-demand
thinking
Economist, 43
education, 163, 164, 228. *See also* architecture
education and students; business schools
egalitarianism, 117, 118, 150, 160
eighteenth century, 247n11
Ejercito Revolucionario del Pueblo, 204,
252n18

27; real estate marketing and, 134–35; real estate prices and, 164; rooftop of new building and, 116f; rural histories and, 109–10; tall buildings and, 104, 134; Vivienda en Hilera and, 111f. *See also* air; green spaces; light and sun; Pablo (*casa chorizo*); pampas; plants and animals; Sergio and Adrián

gated communities, 128–30

Gawans, 235n1

general and particular, 18

General Directorate of Fiscalization and Control of Construction (DGFYCO), 175, 177

General Directorate Registry of Construction and Cadastre (DGROC), 172–73, 174–75, 177

gentrification, 243n7

geography, 6, 34, 36, 199, 211, 242n3, 242n7. See also *aquí y ahora*; pampas

gesture, minor, 238n15

getting on together, 31, 234

Ghana, 40, 64

"The Giant Pool of Money" (podcast), 237n12

Gibson-Graham, J. K., 20–21, 238n19

gift exchange, 39

global contexts: architecture education and, 212; *cátedras* and, 210; ecology of investments and, 39–40; elite, abstract nonplaces and, 216; investments and, 49; materialities and, 64; modernism and, 198; particular real estate markets vs., 18, 22, 75, 88–91; recession of 2008 and, 22–23; "SWOT analysis" and, 243n11; the system and, 238n16. *See also* capitalism; colonialism; imperialism; trade

global crisis of 2007–8, 85, 85f

globalization, 15, 19, 22

"god's eye view," 153

golf course, 101

González Castillo, José, 119

good life (quality of life): barrio values and, 139, 140; Caballito and, 138; daily life and, 107–8; modernist urban planning and, 159, 160; poetry and, 138; real estate marketing and, 134–35; speculation vs., 134. *See also* collective life and collective well-being; daily (quotidian) life; domesticity; gardens, patios, and terraces; infrastructure and services; intimate social spaces; relationality and connection

Gorelik, Adrián, 117–18, 119, 120, 150, 244n14

gossip, 28, 170–71, 175

government. *See* city government; national government

Graeber, David, 235n1

Gramscian concept of hegemony, 166

graphs, 25–26, 67–70, 91–92; attention to bodies vs., 181; concrete dreams and, 7; cotton market and, 242n3; historical data and, 80–88, 82f, 84f, 85f, 87f; international finance and, 235n2; knowledge and, 76, 235n2; material realities, as, 7, 68–69; narrative and, 83–88, 84f, 87f, 92; realities and, 68–69; relationality and, 91–92; specific real estate markets and, 91; storytelling and, 66. *See also* appraisals; charts (spreadsheets); experts; real estate market analysts

graspings (Haraway), 21

green spaces, 27, 122–23, 127, 134–35, 136f, 160, 220–21, 227. *See also* APEVU (Permanent Assembly for Green Urban Spaces); ecological reserves; environmental impact statements; gardens, patios, and terraces; open space; parks; yards

grids, 117–18, 121, 149–50

gross domestic product from construction, 86, 87f

Grupo Austral, 251n12

Guattari, Félix, 237n6, 238n14, 238n20, 249n27

Guevara, Che, 204

guiding plans, 152–53, 154. See also *Plan Director para Buenos Aires*; planning, urban

Guyer, Jane, 242n5

hacer memoria ("do memory"), 41, 177

Hadid, Zaha, 216, 217

Han, Clara, 65

Haraway, Donna, 6, 21, 153, 232, 236n4

Hardt, Michael, 15

Harvey, Penelope, 31

heat islands (*islas de calor*), 127

hegemonic measure of values, 22

hegemony, 166

Heidegger, Martin, 199

height restrictions. *See* maximum height

"Los Hermanos" (folksong), xiii

"hermeneutics of suspicion," 249n25

Herzfeld, Michael, 249n26

hierarchically organized cities, 117

high ceilings, 190–91

high rises. *See* tall buildings

La Híper (period of hyperinflation in the 1980s), 43–46

historical data. *See* graphs; prices

historical events/moments/epochs, 8–9, 86, 87*f*. See also *la crisis* (2001) and after; disappearances; politics

historic preservation, 126–27

history: architecture and, 29, 111–12, 199, 202, 205, 211, 212; architecture education and, 180, 181–82, 194–211, 212; banking and money and, 40, 41–51; barrios and, 97, 117–18, 121, 128, 138, 139, 247n8; bricks and dollars and, 62; capitalism and, 149–50; of codes, 147–78; drawings and planning and, 145, 147, 148*f*, 150–52, 151*f*; of investment, 54–58; leftists and, 209; margins of, 219; planning and, 28, 145, 147–55, 148*f*, 150–52, 151*f*, 157–62, 164, 246nn2–3; politics and education and, 220, 251n12; possibilities and, 221; real estate investment and, 5, 41–51, 54–58, 131, 132*f*–33*f*, 134; rural, 109; values and, 221. *See also* holding present; inheritances; narrative; 1990s *and other decades*; politics; situating/situated; storytelling

A History of Money (Pauls), 56–57, 241n25

holding present, 209, 210, 219, 225, 226, 237n5, 245n18. See also *aquí y ahora*

Holston, James, 145

home (*oikos*), 239n21

homeownership, 20, 55, 57–58, 241n23, 247n8. *See also* bricks

homes (*casas*), 21

homogenization, 71–74, 72*f*, 118, 242n1

hope, 30, 180, 234

hotels, 101, 103

hot tubs, 116, 116*f*

housing project drawings, 216

Huarpes (currency), 46

hug of the lake (*abrazo al lago*), 99–101, 100*f*, 103, 120–21, 138

Hull, Matthew, 246n4

humanitarian design, 250n3

hyperinflation (*La Híper*) (1980s), 42, 43–46, 86, 87*f*. See also inflation

identity, 38, 118, 121, 158–59, 226, 250n1

ideological orientations, 211–14, 215

images and news media: *abrazo al lago* and, 101; barrio resistance and, 92–93; Caballito protest and, 123, 124*f*, 128, 131, 132*f*–33*f*; construction audits and, 175; Le Corbusier and, 153; dollars and bricks and, 62, 63*f*; inflation and, 43*f*; Lago de Regatas and, 101; plan-

ning and, 145–46, 147; protests and, 122; romanticism and, 134–35. See also *La Nelly*

imaging technologies, 235n2

immigration, urban, 16, 118, 149, 247n11

imperialism, 16–17, 22, 23, 203

inclusion, 117–18

income capitalization model, 74

INDEC (National Institute of Statistics and Census), 240n13

India, 250n3

industrialization, 145, 247n11

inequality, 128, 236n4. *See also* elites and upper classes; popular classes

inflation, 42–51, 43*f*, 56, 61, 223, 226, 240n13. *See also* devaluations of peso

informal exchanges, 46

infrastructure and services, 118–19, 121, 127–28, 149, 163, 164, 244n11, 247n8

inheritances, 30, 121, 194, 195, 209–11, 233, 253n22, 253n24. *See also* history

el innombrable (Méndez), 17. *See also* Menem, Carlos

installment purchases, 149. *See also* mortgages

intentionality, 250n6

International Monetary Fund (IMF), 15, 46, 47, 224, 254n2

intimate social spaces, 107, 113, 116, 117, 125, 126, 140, 183, 244n10. *See also* communal spaces; gardens, patios, and terraces

intuition, 77

investments. *See* ecology of investments; finance; real estate investment

Irani, Lilly, 250n3

IRSA (corporation), 122, 131–38

Islamabad, 246n4

Jacobs, Jane, 159, 248n18

Jajamovich, Guillermo, 160

James, William, 7

Japanese traders' dreams (*yume*), 65

jogging, 97, 98, 99, 103, 139

Jones, Caroline A., 250n6

Jorge (FADU professor), 186–88, 187*f*, 216

Jorge (Salvemos al Barrio), 107, 140, 173

Joventud Universitaria Peronista (Peronist University Youth), 205–6, 207*f*, 253n19

Juan's story (entertainment planner), 52, 59

Kesselman, Pedro (lawyer), 168, 227

Kirchner, Cristina. *See* Fernández de Kirchner, Cristina

neighborhood residents. See *vecinos*

neighborhoods. *See* barrios

neoclassical education, 200

neoliberalism, 11–13, 12*f*, 17; architecture education and, 218–19; Brazil and, 224; city government and, 248n16; *la crisis* and after, 8, 10, 17; democratic participation and, 159–60; dictatorship and, 17; dreams and, 225; economic theory and, 91; inflation of 1970s and, 42; 1990s and, 63; price stabilization and, 45–46; privatization and, 168; professional conferences and, 76–77; UBA and, 218–19. *See also* analytical frames; Macri, Mauricio

news media. *See* images and news media

19th century: Casa Chorizo and, 111; defaults and, 40, 198, 247n7; economic instability and, 34; grids and parks and, 117, 118; immigration and, 149; Juan's grandfather and, 197–98; mapping and, 152; national currency and, 241n24; romanticized barrios and, 135; suburbs and, 109

1904, 149

1904 to 1919, 247n8; 1907, 150; 1915, 112

1920s, 118, 147, 150

1930s, 198, 247n8

1940s, 55, 112, 244n16, 251n12. *See also* Perón, Juan, and Peronism

1950s, 55, 81, 198, 251n9, 251n12, 252n13

1960s: codes and, 161; culture and, 251n9; dictatorships and, 30; homeownership and, 55; leftist movements and, 182, 195, 197; low-rise buildings and, 140; Peronism and, 252n14; planning and, 157–58, 159, 248nn18–19; public audiences and, 164. *See also* Onganía dictatorship; phenomenology; TUPAU

1970s: brick investments and, 61–62; codes and, 154; construction boom and, 81; culture and, 30, 251n9; curriculum reform and, 252n15; elections and, 205; homeownership and, 55; inflation and, 42; investment stories and, 56–57; leftist architectural movements and, 182, 197; low-rise buildings and, 140; macroeconomic stability and, 34; military dictatorship and, 182; modernist planning and, 160; mortgages and inflation and, 56; national currency of, 44; Peronism and, 208, 252n14; planning and, 157–58, 159; *plata dulce* and, 86, 87*f*; price per square meter and, 87*f*; price/salaries and, 83, 84*f*; rents and, 55; student movement and,

204–5. *See also* disappearances; military governments/dictatorships

1980s: Argentine debt and, 237n13; Circular 1050 and, 56; democratic ethos and, 160; dictatorship and, 13, 30; homeownership and, 55; hyperinflation and, 86, 87*f*; inflation and, 43–44; investment stories and, 56–57; national currencies of, 44; planning and, 158–59, 160; poetry and, 233; price/salaries and, 83, 84*f*; prices and, 82*f*, 83, 241n25; professional conferences and, 76; used housing prices, 82*f*. *See also* disappearances

1990s: architecture education and, 218–19; *bancarización* and, 52; capital flows and, 25; city constitution and, 155–56; convertibility and, 59, 240n17; environmentalism and, 155; FADU and, 218–19, 253n23; mortgage loans and, 241n28; national currency and, 44; pesos/U.S. dollars and, 33, 63–64; prices/salaries and, 82*f*, 83, 84*f*; privatization and, 27, 103, 128, 130; professional conferences and, 76–77; used housing prices, 82*f*. *See also* neoliberalism

NML Capital (hedge fund), 40

noche de los bastones largos (night of the long clubs), 201

Noel, Carlos, 150

noise vs. speech, 166, 171

nomos, 37

nonhumans, 243n6

normas (regulations), 154

norteño sector, 113

noticing. *See* attention, noticing and sensitivity

nuevo cancionero singers, 30

numbers and calculation, 26, 34, 67–69, 83, 242n3, 242n5. *See also* appraisals; charts (spreadsheets); graphs

objectivity, 163. *See also* realities

objects, 21, 38, 236n5, 237n5

obligations and requirements, 4, 18, 22, 181, 209, 220, 232, 236n3, 236n5

oikos, 37, 239n21

one to one (*uno a uno*), 45–46

Onganía dictatorship, 197, 201, 252n13

opacity, 171–73, 246n2

OPEC oil crisis, 237n13

open space, 111*f*, 112–13. *See also* green spaces

Oscar (FADU student), 215

Osvaldo (Amigos del Lago), 98–104, 225, 233, 246n1
otherness, 119, 232
outdoors, 109. *See also* air; gardens, patios, and terraces; green spaces; light and sun
overconstruction, 107

Pablo (*casa* chorizo), 113
Pablo (plant-filled balcony), 113, 115*f*
Page, Joanna, 240n9
Página/12 (newspaper), 50
Palermo neighborhood, 26, 120, 127, 186, 187*f*. *See also* Amigos del Lago de Palermo
Palermo Viejo, 134
Palermo Woods. *See* Parque 3 de Febrero
pampas, 117, 120, 121, 148*f*
parks: Caballito and, 125; as communal, 121; gardens, patios, and terraces and, 27, 96, 107–8; political mobilization and, 27, 121; real estate marketing and, 134–35; real estate prices and, 164; tall buildings and, 134. See also *corredor verde*; ecological reserves; gardens, patios, and terraces; green spaces; Lago de Regatas ; light and sun; pampas; Parque 3 de Febrero; Parque España (Rosario); plants and animals
par le milieux, 18, 239n21. *See also* milieu
Parque España (Rosario), 160
Parque Patricios neighborhood, 217
Parque 3 de Febrero (Bosques de Palermo) (Palermo Woods), 97–104, 137
parrilla (charcoal grill), 104
participatory democracy: architecture education and, 249n22; barrio identity and history and, 226; *la crisis* and after, 11–12; dreams of, 178; from manipulation to citizen control, 248n20; modernist urban planning and, 159–60; placards and, 171; plans and codes and, 28–29, 145–47, 153, 154–57, 160–61, 163, 165, 176–77, 225, 227, 248n20; power and, 166; PUA and, 155–57. *See also* political activism/advocacy; public audiences; transparency, bureaucratic; voice
particularity (specificity): architecture education and, 186, 187; barrios and, 109, 117–18, 217; charts and graphs and, 91; codes and, 145–46, 147; concrete and, 6; history and geography and, 199; of language and speech, 21, 235n2; major-key materialisms vs., 6; market analysis and, 88–91; planning

and, 153, 158–59; real estate brokers and, 77; "regimes of perceptibility" and, 235n2; resistance and, 22; Tucumán School and, 251; zoning and, 144–45. See also *aquí y ahora*; difference; minor and major keys; situating/situated
Partido Obrero (Workers Party), 162–63
Partido Revolucionario de los Trabajadores (Revolutionary Worker's Party), 252n18
Pasaje Güemes, 112
passion, 254n4
Pastilla de Chiquitolina (the "Tiny Person Pill"), 182, 220, 250n4
Patacones (currency), 46, 47*f*
patios. *See* gardens, patios, and terraces
Patricia (light and airy apartment and terrace), 26–27, 113; attention and, 96–97; daily life of, 2–3, 4, 5; history and, 9, 27; minor forms of value and, 15, 23; particularity (specificity) of, 6; poetry and, 107; privatization of 1990s and, 27; tall buildings and, 107, 108*f*, 140, 141–42; value and, 9
Pauls, Alan, 56–57
Paxson, Heather, 254n4
the people (the *pueblo*), 201–8
pequeños ahorristas (small savers), 25, 33, 34, 54, 66; architects and, 29; banks and, 40–41, 54; bricks and, 54, 58; capitalism and, 231; *la crisis* and after, 225–26; long-term real estate market values and, 225; real estate market values and, 58, 89, 93; value of bricks and, 62. *See also* bricks; Mariela's story *and other stories*; savings
perceptions, 235n2, 237n5. *See also* attention, noticing and sensitivity; perspectives (points of view)
performative public acts, 138
performativity, 241n30
Permanent Assembly for Green Urban Spaces (APEVU), 155, 233
permits, 81, 82*f*, 127–28, 173
Perón, Evita, 14, 237n11
Perón, Isabel, 14, 208
Perón, Juan, and Peronism, 16, 54–55; election (1945) and, 241n21; election (1973) and, 205; factions and, 239nn1–2; Frondizi and, 252n13; Molina y Vedia and, 198–99; Molina y Vedia–Sorín (*cátedra*) and, 253n22; Peronist left and, 208; planning and, 154; politics/built environment and, 251n9; rent control and, 81; TUPAU and, 252n14; UBA and, 199

Peronist party, 205
Peronist University Youth (Joventud Universitaria Peronista,), 205–6, 207f, 253n19
personhood, Melanesian, 6
perspectives (points of view), 200, 204, 206, 250n4. See also *aquí y ahora*; attention, noticing and sensitivity; perceptions
pesificar ("pesify"), 223
Peso Argentino, 44
Peso Ley, 44
Peso Moneda Nacional, 44, 241n24
pesos/U.S. dollars: bricks and, 226; constitutive relationality and, 38; conversions, 237n13; *corralón* and, 49; *la crisis* and after, 51, 54, 64, 89, 223, 225–26, 237n12; graphs and, 67–68, 83; IMF loans and, 254n2; instabilities of, 50; investment and, 34; Mariela's cash and, 36–37; materiality and, 34; 1990s and, 63–64; pegging of (1990s), 86, 87f; prices and, 90; price stability and, 45; salaries compared, 83, 84f; unpegging of, 48. See also *convertibilidad* (convertibility); *corralito*; devaluations of peso
petitions, 91, 101, 125, 138, 141, 177
petroleum prices, 85f
phantom corporation (*corporación fantasma*), 131
phenomenology, 194, 199, 211–12
pieces of real estate (*inmuebles*), 21
Pignarre, Philippe, 209
piqueteros, 10, 48
placard. See *cartel de obra*
Plan Director para Buenos Aires, 150, 151f, 152, 154
planning, urban: architects and, 159, 246n1; bureaucracy and, 175; codes and, 27–28, 141, 145–61, 162, 175; drawings and, 147, 148f, 151f, 154, 157, 159; free markets/public interest and, 247n10; history and, 28, 145, 147–55, 148f, 150–52, 151f, 157–62, 246nn2–3; market logics and, 168; modernism and after, 157–61; power and knowledge and, 146–47; public audiences and, 164, 165, 226–27; Salvemos al Barrio and, 141, 142; systems approach and, 248n18; technical, 158. See also codes; Le Corbusier; modernism; participatory democracy
plano limite. See maximum height
planos. See drawings
plants and animals, 16, 103, 107–8, 112–13, 115f, 116, 243n6. See also birds; gardens, patios, and terraces; Pablo (plant-filled balcony)

Plan Urbano Ambiental (PUA), 155–57, 162
plata dulce (1970s), 86, 87f
plurality/singularity, 236n5, 254n5
Podalsky, Laura, 251n9
poetry, literature, and music, 94–97, 109, 118–20, 121, 128, 138, 139, 216, 233, 244n9. *See also* Kovensky, Martín *and other artists*; singing; tango
Polanyi, Karl, 76
"policing," 166
political activism/advocacy: animals and, 243n6; articulation and, 123; barrios and, 121; buildings and, 27; divergence/emergence and, 232; drawing and, 181; Kirchnerismo and, 223; modern urbanism and, 159; possibilities and, 221; twentieth century and, 247n8; *vecinos'* interests and, 125. *See also* blockades; leftist politics; "making use of the word"; "manifestaciones en la sala"; participatory democracy; petitions; protests; resistance; student movements; voice
political space, 139
politics: architects and, 200, 251n9; architecture education and students and, 180, 181–82, 194–211, 212, 251n12; Argentina and, 8; articulation and, 123–24; Bárbara and, 2, 5; barrio culture and, 11, 13, 104–5, 116–21, 127, 128, 139; casualties, 48; *cátedras* and, 253n23; concrete dreams and, 7; culture and, 104–5, 116–21; drawings and models and, 29, 153, 211–12, 213; environmental, 103, 132; gardens, patios, and terraces and, 27, 103; gossip and, 175; knowledge and, 153, 211, 251n12; majority and, 214; minor keys and, 20, 30; modern urbanism and, 157; Molina y Vedia–Sorín and, 210; money and, 138; neighborhoods and, 11, 13; *La Nelly* and, 246n21; nineteenth-century default and, 247n7; planning and codes and, 156; poetry, literature, and music and, 97; privatization of parkland and, 103; Salvemos al Barrio and, 174–76; saying and, 235n2; shadows of, 146, 163, 166, 167, 168, 169; TANAPO and, 206; transmission of knowledge and, 251n12; university education and, 252n14; University of Buenos Aires and, 30; values and, 7, 8, 9, 16–17, 18–20, 27, 30, 126; *vecinos* and, 97, 243n4. *See also* city government; disappearances; economic/political interests; history; ideo-

logical orientations; inheritances; political activism/advocacy

politics of care, 29–30, 181

pools, 116, 116f

popular classes: architecture education and, 199–200, 217, 228; beauty and, 214; bodily habitus of, 251n8; capitalism and, 202; daily life of, 218; education and, 228; history and, 10, 247n8; modernism and, 198; movements and, 204; Peronism and, 55; political actions and, 10; professional practice and, 213; property ownership and, 54. *See also* architecture for everyone; architecture of the *pueblo*; barrios; *pequeños ahorristas*; TANAPO; TUPAU

Popular University Movement of Architecture and Urbanism. *See* TUPAU

population, 247n8

"Por qué cantamos" ("Why We Sing"), 233–34

porteños (residents of Buenos Aires), 33, 34–35, 96, 109, 212, 220, 243n2. *See also* barrios; social classes

possibilities, 31; analytical frames/critique and, 19, 20; architecture and, 194, 195–96; architecture education and, 218–23, 225; bricks and, 34; caring for, 218–23, 229–30; charts and graphs and, 92; construction and, 64; Corbusier and, 152; *la crisis* and after, 13, 19, 128, 228–33; democratic process and, 178; emergent, 65–66; forecasts and, 70; "getting on together" and, 31; graphs and, 68; history and, 221; inheritances and, 209, 210; Lago de Regatas and, 103; Mariela's story and, 226; *pequeños ahorristas* and, 66; political activism and, 221; practices and, 7; real estate market analysis and, 74; storytelling and, 65–66; TUPAU and, 204. *See also* architecture for everyone; *búsqueda*; dreams, concrete; prediction

posters, 123, 124f

postmodernism, 158

power relations: *aquí y ahora* and, 200; bureaucracy and, 172–73; codes and, 28, 142, 145–47, 176–77; critique and, 20; histories of, 166; inheritances and, 209; knowledge and, 28, 236n4; liberal democracies and, 166; planning and codes and, 156; practices and, 3; technical knowledge and, 173–74. *See also* economic/political interests; hegemonic measure of values; participatory democracy

"practice of memory," 212. *See also* history practices, 3, 4, 9; analytical frames and, 19; buildings and, 236n5, 237n5; concrete compared, 22; concrete dreams and, 7; divergent, 5, 21, 22, 30, 31, 236n5; ecologies of, 21, 22, 69; emergent, 232; ethnography and, 236n5; future/past relationality and, 66; history and, 3, 9–10; knowledge and, 3, 232, 235n2; materiality and, 6; neighborhoods and, 27; numbers and, 69; possibilities and, 7; regimes of perceptibility and, 235n3; situating, 3, 236n4; thinking *par le milieux* and, 18; values and, 4–5, 6, 9, 16–17, 18–23, 235n1; worlds and, 3–4. *See also* architectural design and architects; ecologies; particularity (specificity); real estate market analysis; storytelling

precious metals, 34

prediction, 77–78, 159

the present, 195–96, 234. *See also* copresence; holding present

prices: cost of living and, 57; historical data and, 82f, 83–92, 84f, 85f, 87f; homogenized, 71–74, 72f; infrastructure and services and, 164; mortgages and, 83, 85; 1970 to 2016, 58; per square meter, 26, 72f; *plata dulce* (1980s) and, 241n25; prejudice against finance and, 241n27; salaried workers and, 83, 225; stabilized, 45–46, 57–58; sticky, 90, 91; supply-and-demand thinking and, 90–91; used housing 1980–2008, 82f, 84f; wages and, 58; zoning and, 163. *See also* appraisals; charts (spreadsheets); graphs; inflation

private life of public culture, 245n20

private property: advocacy groups and, 19–20; arts of noticing and, 101; defense of, 125; historical echoes and, 120–21; history and, 120–21; intimate social spaces compared, 126; parks vs., 121; privileging of, 248n19; urbanism and, 247n10. *See also* development and developers; gated communities; privatization; real estate investment

private spaces, 126

privatization: green space and, 135; history of, 168–69; Lago de Regatas and, 101–2, 103–4; 1990s and, 103, 128, 130, 168–69; noticing and, 102–3. *See also* neoliberalism; private property; real estate investment

PRO (Propuesta Republicana), 245n17

Proceso dictatorship, 197, 208

processual forms of engagement, 189, 190, 193

professionalization, 76–78, 92, 152, 159

professional organizations, 162

professional practice, architectural, 179–80, 203, 212, 213, 214, 218–19

profit: architects and, 230–31; architecture education and, 219; Caballito and, 134; investors and, 89; power and, 174; progress and, 128; scales and, 229; stability vs., 58; subprime mortgage crisis and, 90. *See also* capitalism; commodity culture

progresismo, 119

progress, 128, 164

project dossiers, 171

property auctions (*loteos*), 54, 149

property ownership. *See* homeownership; private property

Propuesta Republicana (PRO), 245n17

protests: banks and, 48, 49*f*, 50–51, 51*f*; Caballito, 122, 130–32, 132*f*–33*f*, 138, 174; *la crisis* and after, 10; development and, 135, 137; *La Nelly* and, 131, 132*f*–33*f*; railroad lands and, 122–25, 124*f*. *See also* political activism/advocacy

provincialize, 252n17

proyectos (projects of design), 21

Pschepiurca, Pablo, 246n5

psychological factors, 42, 240n12

PUA (Plan Urbano Ambiental), 155–57, 162

pubic interest, 248n19

public audiences, 163–69, 226–27. *See also* "making use of the word"; participatory democracy

Public Feelings (research program), 245n20

public interest, 247n10

public life of private culture, 245n20

public opinion, 153

public spheres, 118, 121, 126, 245n20

the *pueblo* (the people), 201–8. *See also* architecture of the *pueblo*

Puerto Madero, 162–63, 237n13, 243n7

Puig de la Bellacasa, María, 220

pyramid schemes, 240n6

quantification, 68, 91. *See also* charts (spreadsheets); graphs; numbers and calculation; spreadsheets

quasi-monedas, 46, 47*f*

Quebrachos (currency), 46

queremos buenos aires ("we want good airs") (umbrella group), 98, 155, 163, 233

railroad lands, 122–25, 124*f*, 131, 134, 138, 220–21, 227, 245n16

rail transit corporations, 149

Rancière, Jacques, 7, 9, 166

rationality, 249n25

real estate brokers, 123

Real Estate Chamber of Commerce of Rosario study (2011), 241n26

real estate investment, 25, 32–34; architecture student values and, 180; built environment and, 66; cash and, 89; constitutive relationality and, 38–39; enduring values and, 232; geographies and, 5, 34; history and, 5, 41–51, 54–58, 131, 132*f*–33*f*, 134; materiality and, 24, 64; middle-class, 25; opacity and, 171; *pequeños ahorristas* and, 33, 34; politics of value and, 9, 16–17, 18–20, 27; prejudice against finance and, 241n27; price and, 83–85, 84*f*; small investors and, 92; storytelling and, 34–35, 41–42, 63–66; 2011 study results, 241n26; U.S. dollars and, 89. *See also* banking; bricks; construction boom; development and developers; ecology of investments; finance; geography; history; money; real estate markets; speculation; storytelling; Wall Street

real estate market analysts, 25–26, 68, 70–71, 78–79, 80–81, 91, 92, 93, 225. *See also* business schools; charts (spreadsheets); experts; graphs

real estate marketing, 134–35, 136*f*, 246n25

real estate markets, 67–70; architectural professional practice and, 218; architecture education and, 180; codes and, 161–63, 164; constitutive relationality and, 41–42; *la crisis* and after, 224; design and design education and, 250n3; financial sector and, 89; historical contexts and, 26, 41–42, 81–88, 82*f*, 149; planning and, 168; U.S. dollars and, 89, 241n29; use of the word and, 177. *See also* appraisals; charts (spreadsheets); construction boom; development and developers; dreams, concrete; graphs; particularity (specificity); prices; real estate market analysts

real estate market values, 8, 23, 29, 180, 181, 197, 212. *See also* prices; real estate markets

real estate seminars, 232

realities, 62, 68–69, 218–20, 250n6. *See also* constitutive relationality; possibilities; worlds

the really real, 7
recessions, 22–23, 222, 240n17
Recoleta neighborhood, 26
Redfield, Peter, 250n3
redistribution of wealth, 223
Regatta Lake. *See* Lago de Regatas
"regimes of perceptibility," 235n3
regionalism, 251, 253n20
regulations (*normas*), 154
relationality and connection: abstraction and,
91; "arts of noticing" and, 96; barrios and,
109; bricks and dollars and, 62; buildings
and, 213, 249n25; built environment and,
245n18; constitutive, 38–39, 117; emergent,
38–39; graphs and, 91–92; Lago de Regatas
and, 103; lived, 220; market-based possibilities and, 220; materialities and, 39; numbers
and, 69; partial, 65, 66; plants, animals, and
elements and, 112; possible futures and, 66;
the private vs. public space and, 126; real
estate market analysis and, 69–70; storytelling and, 64, 86; tacit knowledge and, 79–80.
See also ecologies; systems
remainders, 23
rentals, 54, 55, 58, 73, 81, 241n21, 241n27
reos del barrio (neighborhood delinquents),
198
replacement cost, 74
Reporte Inmobiliario (Real Estate Report)
(publication), 70, 76, 77–78, 80. *See also*
Rozados, José
report of UBA (1997), 218–19
representations, 193, 194
requirements and obligations, 4, 18, 22, 236n3,
236n5
Research Institute, 205–6, 207f
resistance: analytical frames and, 19; articulation and, 123–24; barrios and, 104–7,
116–21; codes and, 27; to construction
boom, 26–28, 105–6, 125, 129–30; dreams
of, 232; films and, 23–24; images and news
media and, 92–93; Marx and, 15; particularity (specificity) of, 22. *See also* Amigos del
Lago de Palermo *and other groups*; political
activism/advocacy
retentions, 223
Revolución Libertadora, 252n13
the Rodrigazo, 240n12
romanticism, 118–20, 121, 128, 135
Rome, 249n26
Rosario, 60, 160

Rouco Oliva, José, 247n10
rough barrio (*barrio reo*), 119
Rousseff, Dilma, 224
Rozados, José, 76–77, 88, 226
R2bI and R2bII, 141–42, 143–44, 177
rural areas, 109, 149, 200, 247n8

Saavedra neighborhood, 122
Sabrina (saver), 52
Sacriste, Eduardo, 251n12
safe deposit box, 52
salary levels, 67–68, 83–85, 84f, 225–26.
See also wages
Salvemos al Barrio (Save the Barrio) (Villa
Pueyrredón and Agronomía), 104–5, 140;
achievements of, 177; architects and, 233;
audit of new construction and, 172, 175,
233; *Código Urbanístico* and, 227; green
space and, 125; "muy barrio" and, 244n8;
participatory forums and, 163, 167, 226–27;
placards and, 171–72; planning and codes
and, 140–45, 152, 154–55, 169–70, 173, 175,
177, 246n1; political actions and, 138; political history and, 117, 121, 142; political
tactics and, 173–76; social classes and,
243n7; survey of new construction and,
171; unsympathetic voices and, 128. *See also*
Abel and Nelly
San Isidro (suburb), 215
San Juan, 46, 48n13, 154
Santa Evita (Martinez), 237n11
San Telmo neighborhood, 243n7
Santiago (FADU professor), 179
Santiago del Estero, 199
Save the Barrio. *See* Salvemos al Barrio (Save
the Barrio)
savings, 25, 36, 58, 89. *See also* banking; cash;
colchonismo (mattressism); liquidity;
money; *pequeños ahorristas*
savings and loan programs, 241n23
the sayable, 7, 166
saying, 9, 21, 235n2. *See also* voice
scale, 188–90, 192f, 193, 194, 229–30, 250n4,
251n12
science, 235n2, 236n4, 247n11, 250nn5–6
Science and Technology Studies, 235n2, 251n6
Scott, James, 145, 153
Seeing Like a State (Scott), 153
Sennett, Richard, 149
sensitivity. *See* attention, noticing and
sensitivity

worlds: analytical frames and, 19; building stability and, 236n5; concrete dreams and, 31; construction boom and, 26; divergent, 231–32; of models, 220–21; multiplicities and, 23; practices and, 3–4; values and, 22, 65, 66